汤姆·索耶历险记

The Adventures of Tom Sauyer

编写	杜瑞清	
校译	方华文	
主审	王巍	
副主改		
主编译		
审翻		

陕 西 出 版 集 团
陕西人民出版社

（陕）新登字001号

图书在版编目（CIP）数据

汤姆·索耶历险记/〔美〕马克·吐温（Twain,M.）著；
王巍改写.—西安：陕西人民出版社，2002

ISBN 978-7-224-06068-3

Ⅰ.汤… Ⅱ.①马…②王… Ⅲ.英语－语言读物，
小说 Ⅳ.H319.4：I

中国版本图书馆CIP数据核字（2001）第076675号

书　　名：汤姆·索耶历险记
作　　者：原著〔美〕Mark Twain
　　　　　改写
　　　　　翻译　　王　巍
出版发行：陕西出版集团
　　　　　陕西人民出版社（西安北大街147号　邮编：710003）
印　　刷：安康天宝实业有限公司
开　　本：787mm×1092mm　42开　10.375印张　2插页
字　　数：179千字
版　　次：2002年10月第1版　2013年1月第4次印刷
书　　号：ISBN 978-7-224-06068-3/H·226
定　　价：18.00元

序

　　提高文化素质的最佳途径是读书，不少成名作家都是在读书中成长起来的。我喜欢文学，幼时特别爱读长篇小说。开始是在父亲单位的图书室借，像《西游记》、《三国演义》、《水浒传》等，我在十一岁时就统统读过。后来图书室的书不够看了，恰好新华书店开展租书业务，我便把不多的零用钱换了书来读，我看过全部的《沫若文集》、《巴金文集》、《茅盾文集》等，虽然是囫囵吞枣，但总觉得兴味无穷。这期间，我读的主要是中国的各种名著。

　　考上西安外国语学院以后，我更多地接触了外国名著。记得我看的第一部小说是《沉船》，泰戈尔那诗一般的语言，他描述的那田园诗一般的生活，深深地打动了我，使我受到了心灵的震撼，我初次感到了外国文学的巨大力量。恰好碰上了"文化大革命"，我就有更多的时间徜徉在外国图书的海洋中了。曾经给我国一代年轻人深刻教育的《牛虹》、《古丽雅的道路》、《卓娅和舒拉的故事》、《钢铁是怎样炼成的》等作品，便是在这时期读过的。此外，我还系统地阅读了狄更斯、巴尔扎克、雨果、莫泊桑、托尔斯泰、德莱赛、大仲马、陀思妥耶夫斯基、高尔基、果戈理等外国大师的著名作品，从此我与世界名著结下了不解之缘，而这些名著带给我的不仅是一种享受，更多的是一生受用不尽的精神财富。

世上新人换旧人，但世界文学名著却为一代代人青睐，你可以随之轻轻松松地走进异国他乡，去享受大师们驾驭语言的神奇魅力。而且，随着我国进一步的改革开放，只读译著已经不够，有条件的，还需要去涉猎原汁原味的外国文学，以回避译文中可能发生的种种不足。涉猎要一步步的来，原著，对于一般的外语学习者而言，是太难了，它会让人望而生畏，甚至丧失学习的信心和兴味。怎么办呢？思来想去，还是先搞一些英汉对照的改写本吧。让有一定外语基础的青少年读者，既了解了名著，又学习了语言，两全其美，何乐而不为呢？

本着这个初衷，我社约请著名学者、西安外国语学院英语学科带头人杜瑞清博士和著名翻译家方文华先生主编了这套丛书，第一辑十册：《飘》、《鲁宾逊漂流记》、《简·爱》、《雾都孤儿》、《蝴蝶梦》、《少年维特之烦恼》、《莎士比亚戏剧故事集》、《巴黎圣母院》、《汤姆·索耶历险记》和《金银岛》。"年年岁岁花相似"，愿经典名著这不败的鲜花，伴随着我们年轻的朋友成长。

这套丛书如果能受到广大青少年读者的喜欢，且对他们在名著与语言的学习上有一定的裨益，我们将陆续推出第二辑、第三辑……读者的需要就是我们的使命。值此出版前夕，抚今追昔，不由一笔在手，感慨系之。

但愿书长久，人间日月圆。

周鹏飞
二零零二年九月写于西安逍遥斋

THE ADVENTURES OF TOM SAWYER

汤姆·索耶历险记

目 录
CONTENTS

Chapter 1
Tom Plays, Fights, and Hides

"Tom!"

No answer.

"Tom!"

No answer.

"What is that boy doing, I wonder? You, TOM!"

No answer.

The old lady pulled her glasses down and looked over them about the room; then she put them up and looked out under them. She looked puzzled for a moment, and then said, not angrily, but still loud enough for the furniture to hear:

"Well, if I can get hold of you I'll—"

She did not finish, for by this time she was bending down and searching under the bed with the broom, resting now and then for breath. She awakened nothing but the cat.

第一章　汤姆玩耍、打架、藏猫猫

"汤姆!"

没有回答。

"汤姆!"

还是没有回答。

"这小子到底在干吗呢? 汤姆, 你给我出来!"

仍没有动静。

老太太将眼镜向下挪了挪, 从眼镜上方环视了一下整个屋子, 然后又把眼镜推了上去, 从眼镜下面又四处扫视了一遍, 一时间她有些迷惑, 随后嚷嚷起来, 语气虽然不很凶, 声音却大得足以让屋里的每件家具都听得到:

"哼, 如果让我抓着你了, 我可……"

话还没说完, 她已经弯下腰, 拿着把扫帚在床底下找去了, 不时还得停下来歇歇, 喘口气。可她除了捅醒了那只猫外, 什么也没有找到。

"I never did see where that boy was going!"

She went to the open door and stood in it and looked out among the garden. No Tom. She lifted up her voice, and shouted:

"Y – o – u – u, Tom!"

There was a little noise behind her and she turned just in time to see a small boy and seize him in flight.

"There! I might have thought of that closet. What have you been doing there?"

"Nothing."

"Nothing! Look at your hands. And look at your mouth. What is that truck?"

"I don't know, aunt."

"Well, I know. It's jam. I've said to you for many times that if you didn't let that jam alone, I'd skin you. Hand me that stick."

The stick was flying dangerously in the air over his aunt's head.

"My! Look behind you, aunt!"

The old lady turned around, and seized her skirts out of danger. The boy fled, at that moment, climbed onto the high fence and disappeared over it.

His aunt Polly stood surprised for a moment, and then broke into s gentle laugh.

"Damn the boy, he never plays the same tricks two

"可我的确没看到那小子跑哪儿去了。"

门开着，她走到门口，向花园望去，没见汤姆，她提高了嗓门拖长了声音喊道："你——给我出来，汤姆！"

听到身后发出的轻微的声音，她忙转过身去，眼前晃过一个小男孩的身影，她一把抓住他：

"在这儿呢！我早该想到那个柜子了，你钻到那里干啥呢？"

"啥也没干。"

"啥也没干！看看你的手，再看看你的嘴，那小推车是怎么回事呀？"

"我不知道，姨妈。"

"哼，我可知道，你又偷吃果酱了，我跟你说过多少次，如果你再打果酱的主意，小心我剥了你的皮。把那棍子递给我。"

姨妈已经高高地举起棍子，形势紧急。

"姨妈，小心你背后！"

老太太真以为有什么危险，忙转过身去，把裙子扯到了一边，而此时，那小子早已跃过高高的篱笆墙，溜走了。

波莉姨妈吃惊地站在那儿，突然轻轻地笑了起来。

"这该死的小子，一天换着招数捉弄我，我简

days, and how is a body to know what's coming? He's my own dead sister's boy, poor thing. I haven't got the heart to beat him for his tricks, but I'm afraid of spoiling him. He'll play truant this evening, I'll be obliged to make him work tomorrow to punish him. It's very hard to make him work Saturdays, when all the boys are having holiday, but he hates work more than he hates anything else, and I've got to do some of my duty by him, or I'll ruin the child."

Tom did play truant, and he had a very good time. He got back home hardly in time to help Jim, the small colored boy, but he was at least there in time to tell his adventures to Jim while Jim did three-fourths of the work. Tom's younger brother(or rather, half brother), Sid, was already through with his part of the work, for he was a quiet boy and had no adventurous, troublesome ways.

While Tom was eating his supper, and stealing sugar when it was possible, Aunt Polly asked him questions that were full of tricks in order to trap him to tell the truth. Like many other simple-hearted people, she would like to believe that she was a talented speaker.

"Tom, it was a little warm in school, wasn't it?"

"Yes."

"Very warm, wasn't it?"

直不知道怎么对付他。唉，这可怜的孩子是我那死去的妹妹的儿子。他搞这些鬼把戏，我真不忍心揍他，可又怕宠坏了他。他今天下午说不准又要逃学，我得惩罚惩罚他，让他明天干活。明天是星期六，别的孩子都在度周末，让他干活可真够难的。他最最讨厌的就是干活，可我得尽尽我的责任，不能手软，否则我非毁了这孩子不可。"

汤姆的确逃学了，玩得可快活了。他很晚才回家，都差一点儿没帮不上吉姆——那个黑人小男孩什么忙，可汤姆却能及时地把他一天的探险经历讲给吉姆听，从而让吉姆边听边干完了四分之三的活。汤姆的弟弟（或者说表弟）已经把他的活做了，他属于那种安静的男孩，既不爱冒险，也不去惹麻烦。

晚饭桌上，汤姆一有机会就偷吃糖，波莉姨妈问了他好几个布满陷阱的问题，想从他嘴里套出实话。像许多心地单纯的人一样，她总觉得自己讲话很有技巧。

"汤姆！学校今天有点热，是吧？"

"嗯。"

"特别热吧？"

"Yes."

"Didn't you want to go swimming, Tom?"

A bit of a fear shot through Tom—a bit of uncomfortable doubt. He searched Aunt Polly's face, but it told him nothing. So he said:

"No—well, not very much."

The old lady reached out her hand and felt Tom's shirt and said:

"But you are not too warm now, though."

Tom knew what she meant, now. So he said immediately to prevent Aunt from saying anything against him:

"Some of us watered on our heads—mine's damp yet. See?"

Aunt Polly was annoyed to think she could not prove Tom had swum by the damp clothes. Then she had a new idea:

"Tom, you didn't have to undo your shirt collar where I sewed it, to water your head, did you? Unbutton your jacket!"

The trouble disappeared out of Tom's face. He opened his jacket. His shirt collar was firmly sewed.

"Bother! I've made sure you'd played truant and been swimming. But I forgive you, Tom, this time."

She was half sorry that her wise trick had failed and half glad that Tom had been obedient for once.

"对。"

"汤姆，你没想去游泳？"

一丝恐惧闪过汤姆全身——他有点怀疑波莉姨妈是不是知道了什么，这令他感到不舒服。他试图从她的脸上找到答案，可却什么也看不出。因此他说：

"没——嗯，没太想。"

老太太伸手摸了摸汤姆的衬衣，说：

"不过这会儿你可不会觉得暖和。"

汤姆现在明白了她的意思，为了阻止她再说任何不利于他的话，汤姆马上辩解道：

"噢，那是我们互相往头上浇水来着——我身上还湿着呢。明白了？"

波莉姨妈想自己的确不能因为汤姆的衣服湿了就确定他去游泳了，心里觉得挺烦恼的。这时，她脑子里又闪过一个新的念头。

"汤姆，浇头可不必把我昨天给你缝的衬衣领子拆开吧？把你夹克衫扣子打开！"

不安从汤姆脸上消失了，他打开了夹克衫，衣领很结实地缝着。

"得了！我肯定你逃课去游泳了，汤姆，这次我原谅你。"

波莉姨妈心中悲喜参半，悲的是她的妙计没能奏效，喜的是汤姆居然还能有一次这么听话。

But Sid said:

"Well, now, I think you sewed his collar with white thread, but it's black."

"Why, I did sew it with white! Tom!"

But Tom did not wait for the rest. As he went out at the door he said: "Sid, I'll beat you for that."

In a safe place Tom examined two large needles which were pushed into the collars of his jacket, and had thread bound about them—one needle carried white thread and the other black. He said:

"She would have never noticed if it hadn't been for Sid. Damn it! Sometimes she sews it with white, and sometimes she sews it with black. I wish she would stick to one or the other—I can not follow it. But I bet you I'll beat Sid for that. I'll teach him a lesson!"

He was not the Model Boy of the village. He knew the model boy very well though—and disliked him very much.

Within two minutes, or even less, he had forgotten all his troubles. Not because his troubles were not serious to him, but because a new and powerful interest was coming to him and drove all the troubles out of his mind—just as men's bad luck is forgotten in the excitement of new plans. This new interest was a valued new way in whistling, which he had just learned from a

可赛德说：

"嗯，我记得你当时给他缝领子时用的是白线，可现在却成黑线了。"

"是啊，我的确是用白线缝的！汤姆！"

可汤姆没等他们再说什么就已经溜走了。到门口时他说："赛德，等着我揍你吧！"

汤姆找到一处安全的地方，察看了别在夹克衫领上的两根大针，一根针穿的是白线，另一根穿的是黑线。

"要不是那个赛德，她永远也发现不了。有的时候姨妈用白线缝衣服，有的时候又用黑线缝。我希望她始终只用白的或只用黑的。我简直摸不透。不过我肯定要揍赛德这小子一顿的，我得给他个教训！"

他不是村子里的模范男孩，可他非常了解那个模范男孩，特别不喜欢他。

过了两分钟后，甚至还不到两分钟，他就把所有烦恼都抛到脑后了。并不是他的事不够烦心，而是他找到了一个新的、更大的乐趣，从而驱走了他所有的烦恼。——这就好比面对令人激动的新计划的到来，人们可以忘记那些倒霉事一样。汤姆找到的乐趣就是从一个黑人那儿学到的吹口

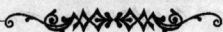

Negro. Hard work and attention soon made him skillful in whistling, and he walked down the street with his mouth full of happiness. He felt much as an astronomer feels who has discovered a new planet.

The summer evenings were long. It was not dark, yet. Presently Tom stopped his whistle. A stranger was before him—a boy stronger than him. A new comer of any age or either sex would make people feel impressive and curious in the poor little village of St. Petersburg. This boy was well dressed, even on a weekday. The more Tom stared at him, the higher he turned up nose at his fine clothes and the shabbier his own clothes seemed to be. Neither boy spoke. If one moved, the other moved—but only towards the other side, in a circle; they kept face to face and eye to eye all the time. Finally Tom said:

"I can beat you!"

"I'd like to see you try it."

"Well, I can do it."

"No, you can't."

"I can."

"You can't."

"Can!"

"Can't!"

An uncomfortable pause. Then Tom said:

哨的新方法——这在他看来十分珍贵。全神贯注、努力苦练很快就使他精于此道。他沿着街道走着，嘴里吹的满都是欢快的曲子。他此时的感觉就像宇航员发现了新行星一样。

夏天的傍晚总是很长的，现在天还没黑。不一会儿汤姆的口哨声停下来了，他面前站了一个陌生人，一个比他壮实的男孩。在圣彼兹堡这个穷困的小村子，任何陌生人的出现，无论他是男还是女，老或是幼，都足以勾起人们的好奇心，给他们留下深刻的印象。这男孩衣着讲究，尽管今天并非周末，汤姆越盯着新的男孩看就越瞧不上人家考究的衣服，可又越觉得自己的这身衣裳有些寒酸。两个男孩谁也不说话，如果一个人动了一下，另一个也会动一下，只不过是朝相反的方向，就像绕圈一样。两个人一直是脸对脸、眼对眼地瞪着。最后汤姆终于开口了。

"我能揍你一顿！"

"我倒是想看看你怎么揍我。"

"哼，我能揍。"

"你不能。"

"我能。"

"你不能。"

"能。"

"不能。"

一阵令人不舒服的停顿之后，汤姆问：

"What's your name?"

"This isn't any of your business."

"Well, I'll make it my business."

"Well, why don't you?"

"If you say much, I will."

"Much – much – much. There now."

"Oh, you think you're very smart, don't you? I could beat you with one hand tied behind me, if I wanted to."

"If you show me much more of your rudeness, I'll throw a rock on your head."

"Well, why don't you do it then? It's because you're afraid."

"I'm not afraid."

"You are."

Another pause. Presently they were shoulder to shoulder. Tom said:

"Get away from here!"

"Go away yourself!"

"I won't."

"I won't either."

So they stood firmly, and both pushing each other with all the strength, and looking at each other angrily. But neither could get an advantage. After struggling till both were hot and red-faced, each was relaxed a little

"你叫什么?"

"关你什么事。"

"哼,我就要把它变成我的事。"

"哼,怎么不变呢?"

"你再多说,我就开始了。"

"说了,说了,说了,来吧。"

"哦!你以为你挺聪明的,是吗?如果我愿意的话,可以一只手绑在身后就把你揍了。"

"如果你跟我动粗的话,小心我拿石头砸你的脑袋。"

"好哇,怎么不砸呢?你怕了,对吧?"

"我不怕。"

"你怕。"

又是一阵停顿。现在他俩已经是肩顶肩了,汤姆说:

"给我从这儿滚开!"

"你滚开!"

"我不!"

"我也不!"

两人都站在原地,互相瞪视着,企图用尽浑身的力量推走对方,可谁也占不了上风。两人就这么对峙着,直到浑身燥热,面红耳赤,才稍稍

but still watchful, and Tom said:

"You're a coward. I'll tell my big brother to teach you a lesson, and he can hit you with his little finger."

"What do I care for your big brother? I've got a brother that's bigger than he is—and what's more, he can jump over that fence." (Both brothers were imaginary.)

"That's a lie."

"Yours too."

Tom drew a line in the dust with his big toe, and said:

"If you dare to step over that, I'll beat you till you can't stand up."

The new boy stepped over quickly, and said:

"Well, you said you'd do it—why don't you do it?"

"For two cents I'll do it."

The new boy took two broad coppers out of his pocket and held them out with mockery. Tom struck them to the ground. In an instant both boys were rolling in the dirt, tearing and beating each other. Through the dirt of the battle Tom appeared, seated on the new boy and beating him with fists.

"Say 'nuff'!" said he.

The boy only struggled to free himself. He was cry-

有些放松，但仍保持着警惕。汤姆说：

"你是个胆小鬼，我要我哥教训你，他可是身材高大，一个小拇指就能把你揍了。"

"我还怕你哥？我哥比你哥魁实。而且他能把你哥扔过那个篱笆。"（两个哥哥都是瞎编的）

"你撒谎。"

"你也撒谎。"

汤姆用他那大脚在灰土路上划了一条线，说：

"你要是敢越过这条线，我非把你打得让你站不起来。"

新来的那个男孩马上越过了那条线，说：

"哼，你不是说揍我吗？——怎么不揍呢？"

"你给我两分钱我就揍你。"

新来的男孩从兜里掏出两个铜币，满脸嘲弄地递到汤姆面前，汤姆一手把铜币打到地上。立刻两个男孩扭成一团，滚打在灰土中，透过战争的尘土，只见汤姆正坐在那个新来的男孩身上拳头一阵猛捶。

"说'饶命'！"汤姆命令道。

男孩只是挣扎着要挣脱自己，哭着——主要

ing—mainly from anger.

"Say 'nuff'!"—and the beating went on.

At last the stranger got out a "Nuff!" out of breath and Tom let him up and said:

"Now that'll teach you. Better look out who you're fooling with next time."

The new boy went off brushing the dust from his clothes, sobbing, snuffling, and occasionally looking back and shaking his head and threatening what he would do to Tom the next time he "caught him out." To this Tom responded with jeers, and as soon as his back was turned the new boy picked up a stone, threw it and hit him between the shoulders and ran away rapidly. Tom chased the boy home and thus found out where he lived. He then stood at the gate, asking the enemy if he's daring enough to go out, but the enemy only made faces at him through the window and refused. At last the enemy's mother appeared, and called Tom a bad boy and ordered him away. So he went away, but said something threateningly to that boy.

He got home quite late that night. When his aunt saw what his clothes were like, she determined firmly she must turn his Saturday holiday into a hard labor for punishment.

是出于愤怒。

"说'饶命'!"——汤姆继续打着。

最终这个新来的男孩上气不接下气地吐出"饶命"两字,汤姆让他站起来,说:"你最好牢记住这次教训,下次再想愚弄人时先看清了是谁。"

男孩走开了,边走边拍着身上的土,哭啼啼的,还不时抽着鼻子,偶尔回过头来望望,摇摇头,嘴里还嘟囔着,扬言再见到汤姆他会"如何如何"。对此汤姆只有讥笑他了。可当他刚一转身,那男孩就捡起一块石头,朝汤姆砸去,正好砸到汤姆的背上,之后就飞快地跑掉了。汤姆猛追,一直追到那男孩家,从而知道了他住在哪儿。汤姆站在门口,问他的敌人敢不敢出来,可敌人却只是透过玻璃冲他做鬼脸,就是不出来。最后敌人的妈妈出现了,称汤姆是个坏小子,命令他马上离开。汤姆只好走掉了,可却不忘向那男孩嚷嚷几句威胁他的话。

他回家时已经很晚了。姨妈看到他一身脏样儿,就下定决心要让汤姆星期六干上一天苦工,惩罚惩罚他。

Chapter 2
The Glorious Whitewasher

Saturday morning came, and all the summer world was bright and fresh, and filled with life. There was a song in every heart. There was cheer in every face and a spring in every step. The village was sweet with flowers and green with plants.

Tom appeared on the sidewalk with a bucket of whitewash and a long-handled brush. He examined the fence, and all gladness left him and a deep sadness settled down upon his spirit. Thirty yards of board fence nine feet high. Life seemed to him empty and a burden. Sighing he dipped his brush and painted along the fence, repeated the action, did it again; compared the narrow whitewashed part with the broad land of unwhitewashed fence, and sat down on a tree-box discouraged. Jim came skipping out at the gate with a tin pail, and singing "Buffalo Gals". Bringing water from the town pump had always been hateful work in Tom's eyes before, but now it was no longer hateful. He remembered that there were many boys and girls at the pump, resting, exchanging playthings, quarreling, fighting and playing. Tom said:

"Jim, I'll fetch the water if you'll whitewash

第二章　光荣的粉刷匠

星期六的早晨到来了,夏天的世界到处阳光灿烂,空气清新,生机盎然。每个人心中都充满了欢歌,每张脸上都洋溢着欢乐,每个脚步都富有弹性。整个村庄都弥漫着甜甜的花香,郁郁葱葱。

汤姆出现在人行道上,一手拎着一桶石灰,一手握着一把长柄刷。他仔细打量了一下篱笆墙,顿时所有的欢乐都烟消云散,整个人都被笼罩在了深深的痛苦中。这篱笆墙可是三十码长、九英尺高呀。汤姆觉得生活是那么的空虚,简直成了负担。边叹着气,他边把刷子浸到石灰水里,再沿着篱笆墙刷起来。浸刷子,刷墙;浸刷子,刷墙。汤姆看了看自己刷过的那一窄溜儿,再看一看那一大片儿没刷的辽阔区域,他垂头丧气地坐在了一个树墩上。这时,吉姆拎着个铁桶蹦蹦跳跳地从门里出来,嘴里还哼着"布法罗的姑娘们"。要在以前汤姆的眼里,去镇上那口泵井打水可是够烦人的活儿了,但现在汤姆可不这么认为。他记得那儿总是围着可多的姑娘小子,休息的休息,交换玩物的交换玩物,吵吵打打的吵吵打打,玩耍的玩耍,于是汤姆说:

"吉姆,你要是能给我刷会儿墙的话,我去给

some."

Jim shook his head and said:

"I can't, Master Tom. Old Madam told me I had to go and get water and not stop fooling around with anybody. She said that Master Tom might ask me to whitewash, and I should go along and do my own business."

"Oh, never mind what she said, Jim. That's the way she always talks. Give me the bucket—I'll be back only in a minute. She won't ever know."

"Oh, I dare not, Master Tom. Old Madam said she would take the head off me if I whitewash for you."

"She! She never beats anybody—except beat people over the head with her thimble—and who cares for that, I'd like to know. She talks terribly, but talk doesn't hurt. Jim, I'll give you a wonderful thing. I'll give you a white alloy!"

Jim began to hesitate.

"White alloy, Jim!"

"My! That's quite a wonderful thing, I tell you! But Master Tom, I'm quite afraid of old Madam—"

Jim put down his pail, took the white alloy. In another moment, he was flying down the street with his pail while Tom was left to whitewash.

Soon Tom began to think of the fun he had planned for this day, and his sadness increased. The boys would

你打水。"

吉姆摇摇头，说：

"这可不行，汤姆少爷，夫人吩咐过我一定要自己去打水，不许和任何人胡混。她还说汤姆少爷可能会叫我刷墙，她让我别理你。"

"噢，吉姆，别管她说什么。她总是那一套，把桶给我——我只一分钟就回来了。她永远不会知道的。"

"噢，汤姆少爷，我可不敢。夫人说了，如果我替你刷墙的话，她会把我脑袋拧掉的。"

"她！她会打谁呀，用她那顶针在你脑袋上敲一敲——我倒想知道谁在乎呀！她总是说得挺可怕，可说话又弄不疼你。吉姆，我会给你一个特别棒的玩意儿，一只白色弹球！"

吉姆开始犹豫了。

"白色弹球，吉姆！"

"哎呀，那可太好了。可是汤姆少爷，我还是怕夫人……"

吉姆放下了水桶，拿着那个白色弹球看了看。可一转眼，他还是拎着桶跑走了，留下汤姆独自刷墙。

汤姆想起他打算今天干的那些趣事，悲伤油然而生。不一会儿，那帮小子们就要去玩了，他

come here on their way to play and make fun of him for having to work. The idea burned him like fire. He got out his wealth and examined it—bits of toys, stones, and trash. Not enough. So he gave up the idea of trying to buy the boys. At this dark and hopeless moment, a splendid idea hit him.

He took up his brush and went quietly to work. Ben Rogers was coming. He was eating an apple. He was playing happily by making himself like a steamboat.

Tom went on whitewashing—paid no attention to the "steamboat." Ben stared a moment and then said:

"Hi! You're on a tree-box, aren't you!"

No answer. Tom examined his last touch with the eye of an artist. His mouth watered for the apple, but he stuck to his work. Ben said:

"Hello, old fellow, you got to work, hey?"

Tom turned suddenly and said:

"Why, it's you, Ben! I wasn't noticing."

"I'm going swimming, I am. Don't you wish you could?"

Tom looked at the boy a bit, and said:

"What do you call work?"

"Why, isn't that work?"

Tom continued his whitewashing, and answered carelessly:

们肯定会路过这儿，肯定要笑话他还要干苦工的。想到这儿，他心里火烧火燎地难受。他把他的宝物都取了出来，浏览一遍，一一检查——各种各样的玩具，石子，还有其他乱七八糟的小零碎。这些不够，他只好放弃了用他的宝物收买那帮小子给他干活的想法。就在这毫无希望的黑暗时刻，他突然想到了一个绝妙的主意。

他拿起刷子，静静地开始干活。本·罗杰斯过来了，他正吃着苹果，快乐地把自己扮成了一艘行驶中的汽船。

汤姆继续刷他的墙，没注意这艘驶来的汽船。本瞪着眼看了一会儿，说：

"喂，你坐树墩上了，是吗？"

没有回答。汤姆只以一个艺术家的眼神审视着自己的点睛之笔。那苹果勾引得他满嘴口水，可他仍坚守着自己的岗位。本又说：

"喂，老伙计，你干活呢？"

汤姆猛地转了过来，说：

"哇，是你啊，本！我都没注意。"

"我要去游泳，游泳，你不想来吗？"

汤姆盯了一会儿本说：

"你说我在干活？"

"对呀！难道这不是干活？"

汤姆又继续刷着他的墙，不经意地回答道：

"Well, maybe it is, and maybe it isn't. All I know is, it suits Tom Sawyer."

"Oh, you don't mean that you like it?"

The brush continued to move.

"Like it? Well, I don't see why I oughtn't to like it. Does a boy get a chance to whitewash a fence every day?"

That changed the thing. Ben stopped eating his apple. Tom swept his brush carefully back and forth—Ben watching every move and getting more and more interested, more and more absorbed. Presently he said:

"Tom, let me whitewash a little."

Tom considered, was about to agree; but he changed his mind:

"No – no – I think it wouldn't be easy. You see, Aunt Polly's very particular about this fence. I think there isn't one boy in a thousand, maybe two thousand that can do it the way it has been done."

"Oh, come,—let me just try. Only a little. I'd let you, if I were you."

"Ben, I'd like to, but Aunt Polly—well, Jim wanted to do it, but she wouldn't let him; Sid wanted to do it, and she wouldn't let Sid."

"Oh, I'll be just as careful. I'll give you the core of my apple."

"嗯，或许是，或许不是。我只知道，这很适合汤姆·索耶。"

"噢，你不是说你喜欢刷墙吧？"

刷子继续在挥舞着。

"喜欢？我没看出我为什么不喜欢，你觉得每一个男孩都会有机会刷篱笆墙吗？"

这句话可扭转了整个局面，本不再吃他的苹果了。汤姆上上下下仔细地挥动着刷子——本盯着他的每个动作，兴趣越来越浓厚，注意力越来越集中，不一会儿他说：

"汤姆，让我刷会儿吧。"

汤姆想了想，正准备同意呢，可又改变想法了：

"不——不——我想这可不是件简单的事。你知道，波莉姨妈对刷墙这事儿可挑剔了。我觉得一千个男孩，或许两千个男孩中都未必能找出一个男孩，干得像我这样。"

"噢，来吧，——就让我试试，我只刷一点儿。如果我是你的话，我就让你刷了。"

"本，我是想让你刷的，可波莉姨妈——你瞧，吉姆想刷她不让，赛德要刷，她还是不允许。"

"噢，我一定小心的，我把苹果核给你。"

"Well, here—No, Ben, now don't. I'm afraid—"

"I'll give you all of it!"

Tom gave up the brush with unwillingness in his face, but satisfaction in heart. Boys appeared here every little while. They came to laugh but waited to whitewash. One after one, hour after hour. When the middle of the afternoon came, from a poor boy in the morning, Tom was rolling in wealth. He had twelve stones, a blue glass, six firecrackers, a kitten with only one eye, the handle of a knife, etc.

He had had a nice, good, idle time all the while—plenty of boys around him—and the fence had been whitewashed three times! If he hadn't run out of whitewash, he would have made every boy in the village lose their properties.

Tom had discovered a great law of human action, without knowing it—that is, in order to make a man or a boy want to possess a thing, it is only necessary to make the thing difficult to get. If he had been a great and wise thinker, like the writer of this book, he would now have understood that work is whatever a person is forced to do and play is whatever a person is not forced to do. The boy thought for a while over the great change which had taken place here, and then went toward headquarters to

"嗯，这——不行，本，现在不行，我担心——"

"我把剩下的苹果都给你。"

汤姆把刷子给了本，脸上露出很不情愿的样子，可心里别提多高兴了。男孩子们不时地路过这儿，刚开始都是笑话干活的，后来全都开始排队等着刷篱笆。一个又一个小时过去了。下午三四点时，汤姆从大清早的穷小子，摇身一变成了大富翁了。他现在一共有十二块石头弹子、一块蓝玻璃、六个小鞭炮、一只独眼猫、一个刀柄等等。

他这一天可过得够美好、够休闲了——一大堆的男孩围着他——篱笆一共刷了三遍！如果不是他的石灰水用完了，他非得让镇上的每个男孩都倾家荡产不可。

汤姆不知不觉中发现了人类行为的一个规律——那就是，你要想让一个大人或一个男孩想得到什么，你只要把一件东西弄得难以到手就行了。如果汤姆是一个伟大而又睿智的思想家，就像本书的作者一样，他现在就应该明白，凡是一个人迫不得已要去做的事就要称为干活或是工作，而凡是没有出于逼迫而为之事，那就可算为玩耍了。男孩想了一会儿发生在这儿的巨大变化，之后就前往总部汇报工作去了。

report.

Chapter 3
Busy at War and Love

Tom appeared before Aunt Polly, who was sitting by an open window in a pleasant apartment and nodding over her sleeping cat—for she had no other partners. He said: "May I go and play now, aunt?"

"What, already? How much have you done?"

"It's all done, aunt."

"Tom, don't lie to me—I can't bear it."

"I'm not, aunt; it is all done."

Aunt trusted little. She went out to see for herself; and she would have been satisfied to find twenty percent of Tom's statement true. When she found the whole fence whitewashed, and not only whitewashed but finally painted and repainted, and even a part added to the ground, her astonishment was almost unspeakable. She said:

"Well, I never! You can work when you make up your mind to." And then she weakened the praised by adding, "But you seldom made up your mind to, I'm certain to say. Well, go along and play."

She was so happy with his splendid achievement

第三章　忙于战争和爱情

汤姆出现在波莉姨妈面前，此时，她正在舒适的房间里靠窗坐着打盹呢。窗户开着，她的膝盖上还卧着一只猫，也正睡觉呢——那可是她惟一的伴儿。汤姆说："我现在可以去玩了吗，姨妈？"

"什么，已经干完了？你刷了多少？"

"全刷完了，姨妈。"

"汤姆，可别跟我撒谎——我受不了。"

"姨妈，我没撒谎，确实刷完了。"

姨妈觉得这几乎不可信，她要亲自出去看看，哪怕是只刷了百分之二十，她都心满意足了。可当她发现，整个篱笆都刷完了，而且不仅是刷完了，还刷了一遍又一遍，甚至连墙脚边都刷了，她的那种惊讶几乎难以形容。她说：

"我简直不敢相信！汤姆，只要你决心去做一件事，你是能做好的。"接着她又淡化了自己对汤姆的表扬，"可是，我可以肯定地说，你很少下决心去做什么事。好啦，去玩吧。"

波莉姨妈为自己的辉煌成就感到无比的兴奋，

that she took him into the closet and selected a fine apple and gave it to him. While she was teaching him the value of wok, he "hooked" a doughnut.

Then he jumped out, and saw Sid just standing outside. He caught some lumps of earth and threw them to Sid in a second. Before Aunt could react to this out of surprise and save Sid, six or seven lumps had struck him, and Tom was over the fence and gone. There was a gate and usually Tom was in too great a hurry to make use of it. His soul was at peace, now that he had settled with Sid for calling attention to his black thread and getting him into trouble.

Tom walked along the block, and came round into a muddy alley. He presently escaped Aunt's capture and punishment and got safe. He hurried toward the public square of the village to lead a war against another team, which they had already planned. Tom's army won a great victory, after a long and hard battle. Then the dead were counted, prisoners exchanged, the terms of the next disagreement agreed upon, and the day for the necessary battle arranged. After the armies marched away, Tom turned homeward alone.

As he was passing by the house where Jeff Thatcher lived, he saw a new lovely girl in the garden. The fresh – crowned hero fell without firing a shot. A girl named

她把汤姆带到了储藏室，挑了一个好苹果给他。正当她向汤姆谆谆教导劳动的价值时他又"钓"走了一个炸圈饼。

汤姆蹦蹦跳跳出了门，看到赛德正在外边站着。他立刻抓起了几块土坷垃，朝赛德砸去。姨妈满脸惊吓，还没等她反应上来去救赛德，赛德已经被六七块土坷垃砸上了，而汤姆早已翻过篱笆溜了。其实篱笆中间是有门的，可汤姆每次离家时都是匆匆忙忙，很少用得上那门，就是因为赛德，姨妈才注意到他衣领上的黑线，给他惹了一身麻烦，现在可是把事情摆平了，汤姆因而觉得自己心里舒坦多了。

汤姆经过一排排房子，拐进了一条泥泞小道，他终于摆脱了姨妈的追捕和惩罚，获得了安全。他急急忙忙朝小镇的公共广场走去。两拨男孩已经计划好在这儿开战，汤姆将做一队的统率。经过长时间艰巨的战斗，汤姆的部队获得了巨大的胜利。双方清点了死亡人数，交换了战俘，就下一次争端因何而起达成了一致，安排了下一次必要的开战时间。随后，双方部队浩浩荡荡地离开了，汤姆独自朝家走去。

就在他路过杰夫·撒切尔家时，他在花园里看到了一个新来的可爱的姑娘，刚刚加冕的英雄还没中一枪一弹就倒下了。那个名叫艾米·劳伦斯的

Amy Lawrence disappeared out of his heart whom he had been months winning and he had been the happiest and proudest boy in the world for only seven days when she accepted his love hardly a week ago.

He worshiped this new angel secretly till he saw that she had discovered him; then he pretended he did not know she was present, and began to "show off" in all sorts of funny boyish ways, in order to win her admiration. But by and by, when he was doing some dangerous action, he glanced aside and saw that the little girl was leaving for the house. Tom came up to the fence and leaned on it, feeling sad that she could not stay here a little longer. Yet his face lit up when he saw she threw a flower over the fence a moment before she disappeared. He used tricks to pick the flower up for fear of being discovered.

He returned, now, and hung about the fence till nightfall, "showing off," as before; but the girl never showed herself again, though Tom comforted himself a little with the hope that she had been near some window. Finally he went home unwillingly, with his poor head full of imaginations.

All through supper his spirits were so high that his aunt wondered "what had got into the child." He was scolded for throwing lumps of earth at Sid, but seemed

姑娘也从他心中消失了。可就是那个姑娘，他曾追求了好几个月，就在不到一个星期前，当姑娘接受了他的爱情时，汤姆还觉得自己是世界上最快乐、最自豪的男孩，可这种感觉才持续了七天。

汤姆暗自倾慕着这个新到的天使。当他发现天使看到他时，他马上假装着自己没注意有别人在这儿，却又使尽男孩子那些可笑招数卖弄自己，渴望赢得她的芳心。然而不久，就在他挑战一高难度动作时，他向旁边瞥了一下，发现那姑娘正在走回房间。汤姆走到篱笆前，靠在上边，为这个姑娘不多呆一会儿而难过。可当看到这个女孩走上前把一枝花扔在了篱笆上，他的脸上立刻闪烁出熠熠光彩。他又用了点儿伎俩把那枝花摘了过来，惟恐被别人看见。

直到黄昏，他还一如既往地在篱笆前"卖弄着自己"，那女孩却再也没出现，可汤姆安慰自己说那女孩保不准正在哪个窗户前看他呢。最终他只得极不情愿地回家了，可怜的小脑袋瓜里浮想联翩。

整个晚饭汤姆都显得非常兴奋，使得她姨妈琢磨"这孩子脑子装着什么呢"。他因为朝赛德砸土坷垃受到了批评，却显得毫不在意。他试图在

not to mind it at all. He tried to steal sugar under his aunt's very nose, and got his finger knocked for it. He said:

"Aunt, you don't beat Sid when he takes it."

"Well, Sid doesn't hurt a person the way you do. You'd be always into that sugar if I wasn't watching you."

Presently she stepped into the kitchen, and Sid, happy for being protected, reached for the sugar bowl—a sort of pride over Tom which was unbearable. But Sid's fingers slipped and the bowl dropped and broke. Tom was in great joy. In such great joy that he even controlled his tongue and was silent. He said to himself that he would not speak a word, even when his aunt came in, but sit perfectly quiet till she asked who did this; and then he would tell, and there would be nothing so good in the world as to see that pet model being caught. When Aunt came in, she raised her hand to strike Tom again when Tom cried out:

"Hold on, now, what are you beating me for? — Sid broke it."

Aunt Polly paused, puzzled, and Tom looked for healing pity. But when she got her tongue again, she only said:

"Umf! Well, you didn't get beating wrong, I

姨妈鼻子底下偷糖吃，却让姨妈把他手指头敲了一下。汤姆说：

"姨妈，赛德拿糖吃，你怎么不打他呀！"

"那是因为赛德可不像你那样害人。况且只要我不盯着你，你那手就老往糖碗里塞。"

一会儿，姨妈进了厨房。赛德因为受到保护高兴地把手伸向糖碗——那种自豪哇，汤姆可受不了。就在这时，赛德手指头滑了，碗掉到地上摔碎了。汤姆兴奋无比。可即便如此激动，他还是紧闭嘴巴，保持沉默。他告诫自己一句话都不要说，即便姨妈进来，他也要静静地坐着，等姨妈问这一切都是谁干的，那会儿他再张口。世界上再没有比看到这个受宠的小模范被当场捉住更美妙的事了。不料姨妈一进来就扬手打了汤姆，汤姆喊道：

"停，停，你打我干吗？——是赛德打碎的。"

波莉姨妈刹住手，困惑不解，汤姆在一旁指望着姨妈说句安慰的话，以抚平他受到的伤害。然而姨妈张口却说：

"哼！打你也没白打，我进厨房那会儿，你一

think. You must have been into some other mischief when I wasn't around."

Then she scolded herself in her heart, and she longed to say something kind and loving, but she judged that this would suggest she had been in the wrong. So she kept silent, and went about her affairs with a troubled heart.

Tom stayed in a corner silently and sadly. He could not bear to have any cheeriness or delight. So, presently, when his cousin Mary danced in, all alive with the joy of seeing home again after an age-long visit of one week to the country, he got up and moved in clouds and darkness out at one door as she brought song and sunshine in at the other.

He wandered far from the familiar places where boys always played, and looked for empty places that fit his spirit. A boat in the river invited him, and he seated himself on its outer edge and gazed at the boring broadness of the stream, wishing, the while, that he could only be drowned, all at once and unconsciously, without suffering from the uncomfortable routine made by nature. Then he thought of his flower. He got it out, wilted, it greatly increased his sadness. He wondered if she would pity him if she knew? Would she cry, and wish that she had a right to put her arms around his neck and comfort

准又干什么其他坏事了。"

说完她心里开始自责，希望自己能够向汤姆说些亲切慈爱的话，可又觉得这么一来，不就说明自己做错了吗？因而她一句话也没说，就干自己的事去了，心里很是不安。

汤姆一声不吭地在一个角落里呆着，心里充满了悲伤。这会儿他无法忍受任何人的喜悦或者快乐。因此，当他表姐玛丽，在乡下呆了如一年之久的七天，蹦蹦跳跳，满心欢喜地回家时，当她将歌声与阳光从一个门口带进来时，汤姆站了起来，在阴云和黑暗中移步走出另一道门。

他漫无目的地在镇上走着，远远地避开平时男孩子们总在一起玩耍的地方，去寻找那适合他此时心境的荒凉地带。河里的一条小船吸引了他。他坐在船沿上，盯着那宽阔却了无生气的河水，希望自己要是能不知不觉地一下子淹死就好了，这样就可以摆脱大自然安排的痛苦了，就可以不再受罪了。随后他想到了那枝花。他取了出来，花已经凋了，这更增加了他的悲伤。他在想，如果她知道了这一切，会不会同情他，会不会为他掉眼泪，会不会希望自己也有权搂着他的脖子安

him? Or would she turn coldly away like all the hollow world? At last he rose up sighing and left the boat in the darkness.

About half past nine or ten o'clock he came along the empty street to where the lovely unknown girl lives; he paused a moment; no sound fell upon his listening ear. A candle was burning within the window. He climbed the fence, went secretly through the plants, till he stood under that window; he looked up at it long, and with emotion; then he laid him down on the ground under it, with his hands holding his poor wilted flower on the chest. And thus he would die—out in the cold world, with no shelter over his homeless head, no friendly hand to wipe the death damps from his brow, no loving face to bend pityingly over him when the great pain came. And thus she would see him when she looked out upon the glad morning, and oh! would she drop one little tear upon his poor, lifeless body, would she make one little sigh to see a bright young life so rudely withered, so untimely cut down?

The window opened, a servant's harsh voice disrespectfully broke the holy calm, and a flood of water drenched the lying hero's dying body!

The dying hero sprang up with a relieving snort and scudded away in the dark with the murmur of a curse.

慰他？还是会像周围这虚假的世界一样也冷冰冰地走开？最后他站了起来，叹着气，在漆黑的夜里离开了那条小船。

大约九点或十点的时候，他沿着空无一人的街道走着，来到了那个可爱的却不知名的女孩的住处。他停了下来，竖起耳朵，却什么也没听到，窗内一支蜡烛在点着。他爬过篱笆，悄悄地穿过树木花草，站在那扇窗下，满怀深情地抬头仰望着，很长时间。随后躺在了窗下那块地上，胸前握着那支可怜的凋谢的花儿。他会这样死去——在外面这冰冷的世界。没有什么可以遮盖他那无家可归的身体，没有一只友爱的手可以拂去他眉上死神带来的湿气，没有一张慈爱和怜悯的脸庞可以在那巨大的痛苦降临时俯向他。她会在快乐的早晨推窗望去时看到他的样子。噢！她会不会将她的哪怕是一小滴眼泪掉在他可怜的已毫无生命的身体上？她会不会在看到一个聪明、年轻的生命就这样残酷地凋谢了，就这样过早地夭折了而发出哪怕是一小声叹息？

窗户推开了，一个侍从那刺耳的声音玷污了神圣的宁静，一盆水哗的倾泻而下，浇湿了躺在地上的那位即将死去的英雄的身体！

这位即将死去的英雄一下子跳了起来，如释重负般地打了个喷嚏，迅速地消失在黑暗中，嘴里还嘟嘟囔囔地骂着。

Not long after, as Tom, all undressed for bed, was looking at his wet clothes by the light of a candle, Sid woke up and was going to say something, but decided not to do it, for there was danger in Tom's eye.

Tom turned in without the added trouble of prayers, and Sid made mental note of the omission.

Chapter 4
Showing off in Sunday School

The sun rose upon a peaceful world, and shone down upon the peaceful village like a blessing. Breakfast over, Aunt Polly had family worship.

Tom prepared for his action and chose the shortest part of the Bible to recite. At the end of half an hour Tom had a vague general idea of his lesson, but no more, for his mind was wandering wildly and his hands were busy with playthings. Mary took his book to hear him recite, and he tried his way through the fog, but failed.

"Oh, Tom, you poor stupid thing. You must learn it again. Don't you be discouraged, Tom, you'll manage it—and if you do, I'll give you something ever so nice."

"All right! What is it, Mary? Tell me what it is."

没过多久，汤姆已经脱掉衣服准备睡觉了。正当他借着烛光看着他的一身湿衣裳时，赛德醒来了，正准备说些什么，却把话又吞了回去，因为他在汤姆眼中看到了凶光。

汤姆省去了做祷告的麻烦，上床就睡了，赛德可把这一笔又记上了。

第四章　主日学校里大出风头

太阳在这安谧的世界中升起，照耀着这宁静的小镇，像在祝福它。早饭过后，波莉姨妈开始了家庭祷告。

汤姆选了《圣经》中最短的一部分开始背诵。半个小时过后他对这一部分有了一个模模糊糊的大体了解，但也仅此而已，因为他的心思早已不知神游到哪儿去了，两只手也忙着摆弄着这个玩的，那个玩的。玛丽拿过他的书，听他背。可汤姆的感觉真有如在迷雾中寻路，怎么找也找不着。

"噢！汤姆，你这可怜的小笨蛋，你还得再背，可别灰心啊。汤姆！你一定能行——如果你背过的话，我还会送你一样特别好的东西！"

"那好哇！什么东西？玛丽！告诉我是什么呀？"

"Never you mind, Tom. You know if I say it is nice, then it is nice."

"You bet you that's so, Mary. All right, I'll deal with it again."

And he did "deal with it again"—under the double pressure of curiosity and the coming gain, he did it with such spirit that he made a shining success. Mary gave him a knife worth twelve and a half cents; and the excitement and delight swept him all over.

Mary gave him a basin of water and a piece of soap, and he went outside the door and set the basin on a little bench there; then he dipped the soap in the water and laid it down; turned up his sleeves; poured the water on the ground, gently, and then entered the kitchen and began to wipe his face carefully on the towel behind the door. But Mary removed the towel and said:

"Now aren't you ashamed, Tom! You mustn't be so lazy. Water won't hurt you." Tom was a little embarrassed. The basin was refilled, and this time he stood over it a little while, gathering bravery; took in a big breath and began. With the help of Mary, he was a man, and his wet hair was neatly brushed. Then Mary got out a suit of clothing that had been used only on Sundays during two years and helped him well-dressed. Then he was crowned with his straw hat. He now looked

"别费神了，汤姆！你知道我如果说是好东西的话，那就是好东西。"

"你保证那是好东西，玛丽，好吧。我重新开始对付它。"

他的确"重新对付那一部分"了——在好奇心和即将到来的收获的双重压力之下，他的劲头那么大，因而取得了辉煌的成功。玛丽给他了一个价值十二分半的小刀，汤姆激动坏了，浑身充满着幸福。

玛丽给他端来了一盆水，一块肥皂，汤姆走出门，把脸盆放在一个小凳子上，然后把肥皂放在水里浸了浸，又放回了原处；卷起袖子；把水泼到地上，轻轻地进了厨房。躲在门后拿起毛巾认真地擦着脸。可玛丽一把扯住了毛巾，说：

"你不害臊吗？汤姆！你可不能这么懒，水又伤不了你。"汤姆感到有点儿尴尬。脸盆又接满了水放在那儿，他站在跟前，鼓足勇气，深吸了一口气，又开始洗脸。在玛丽的帮助下，他可变成了一个男人，头发也打湿梳整齐了。玛丽取出了一套他在过去的两年中只有星期天才穿的衣服，帮汤姆穿好，又给他戴了顶草帽，汤姆现在看起

quite improved and uncomfortable. He was as uncomfortable as he looked, for there was a control about whole clothes and cleanness that annoyed him. He hoped that Mary would forget his shoes, but the hope faded; she brought them out. He lost his temper and said he was always being made to do everything he didn't want to do. But Mary said persuasively:

"Please Tom—that's a good boy."

So he got into his shoes, showing his teeth and shouting angrily. Mary was soon ready, and the three children set out for Sunday school—a place that Tom hated with his whole heart; but Sid and Mary were fond of it.

Sunday-school hours were from nine to half past ten; and then church service. At one door, Tom traded his treasures for tickets of various colors with the boys. Then he entered the church and went to his seat, and started a quarrel with the boy near him. The teacher, a serious elderly man, interfered, and then turned his back a moment; Tom pulled a boy's hair in the next bench, and was absorbed in his book when the boy turned around; stuck a pin in another boy, presently, in order to hear him say "Ouch!" and got a new scolding from his teacher. Tom's whole class was of a pattern—restless, noisy, and troublesome. When they came to recite their

来可是好多了，可也看着特别别扭，他的确也觉得不自在。因为那身衣服，那种干净整齐太约束人了，让他很烦。她希望玛丽会忘了拿那双鞋，可他的希望很快就破灭了，她把它们取出来了。他大发脾气，嚷嚷着自己总被摆弄着做所有他不喜欢的事情，可玛丽的话却很有说服力：

"别这样，汤姆——做个好男孩。"

因而他穿上了那双鞋，却又龇牙咧嘴，生气地喊叫着，玛丽很快就准备好了，三个孩子一起出发去主日学校——那可是汤姆满心憎恨，却又为玛丽和赛德喜欢的地方。

主日学校上课时间是早九点到十点半，之后就是教堂做礼拜了，汤姆站在教堂的一个门口用他的那些宝物和男孩子们换了各种颜色的小票，之后他走进教堂，坐在他的位置上，就开始和旁边的一个男孩吵开了。老师是一位严肃的老头，走过来制止了他们。可他身子一转过去，汤姆又去拽旁边凳子上那个男孩的头发。男孩扭过头，他马上装着在聚精会神地读书。接着他又去用大头针扎另一个男孩，只为了听他喊"哎哟"。因此，他又让老师臭骂了一顿。汤姆这个班的孩子全都是一个模子浇出来的，全都不安宁，吵吵闹

lessons, not one of them knew his part perfectly, but had to be hinted all along. However, each got his reward—in small blue tickets; each blue ticket was a pay for two verses of the recitation. Ten blue tickets equaled a red one, and could be exchanged for it; ten red tickets equaled a yellow one; for ten yellow tickets the teacher gave a very plainly bound Bible (worth forty cents in those easy times) to the pupil. It's so hard to remember two thousand verses of a Bible. And yet Mary had got two Bibles in this way—it was the patient work of two years—and a German boy had won four or five. He once recited three thousand verses without stopping; but the tension upon his mind was too great, and he was little better than an idiot from that day on—a sad bad luck for the school, for on great occasions, before crowd, the teacher had always made this boy come out and show himself.

When the Sunday-school teacher, Mr. Walters almost ended his customary little speech, visitors appeared at the entrance and aroused a good part of the whispering among boys and girls. They were: Lawyer Thatcher; a fine middle-aged gentleman with iron-gray hair; and a dignified lady who was doubtless the latter's wife. The lady was leading a child. When Tom saw this small newcomer his soul was all burning with happiness in a mo-

闹，惹是生非。他们没人背得过课文，都得一边背，一边要人提示。尽管这样，每个孩子还是会得到自己的奖励——蓝色的小票。背过两节就可以获得一张蓝票。十张蓝票等于一张红票，可以换来一张红票；十张红票等于一张黄票；如果谁拿到了十张黄票，老师就会奖励他一本平装《圣经》（在那个物价平稳的年代里相当于四十美分）。要记住《圣经》中的两千节可太难了。然而玛丽因此已经得到了两本《圣经》——那可是花了她两年时间耐心背下来的——还有一个德国男孩得到了四本还是五本。有一次他一口气把《圣经》的三千节都背下来了；可能是脑子里的那根弦绷得太紧了，自此他就变得比白痴好不到哪儿去了——这对学校来说简直是天大的不幸，因为以前在重大场合，众人面前，老师总是让这个男孩站出来，展示他对《圣经》有多么熟悉。

就在主日学校校长——沃尔特先生马上结束他那惯常的简短讲话时，门口出现了几位来访者，引起了孩子们的一阵低语，这些来访者是：撒切尔律师，一位相貌堂堂、头发铁灰的中年绅士，一位高贵的妇人，无疑是那位绅士的妻子，这位妇人还领着一个孩子。当汤姆认清这位小来访者

ment. The next moment he was "showing off" with all his power—blowing boys, pulling hair, making faces—in a word, using every art that seemed likely to fascinate a girl and win her applause.

The visitors were given the highest seat of honor, and as soon as Mr. Walter's speech was finished, he introduced them to the school. The middle-aged man was a great respectable person—the great Judge Thatcher, brother of their own lawyer. Jeff Thatcher immediately went forward, to be familiar with the great man and be envied by the school.

Mr. Walters fell to "showing off," with all sorts of official activities, giving orders, delivering judgments, giving directions here, there, everywhere that he could find a target. The librarian "showed off"—running here and there with his arms full of books. The young lady teachers "showed off"—bending sweetly over pupils that were just being boxed, lifting pretty warning fingers at bad little boys, and patting good ones lovingly. The young gentlemen teachers "showed off" with small scolding and other little displays of leadership and fine attention to rules. The little girls and boys also "showed off" in various ways. And above all of it the great man sat with a grand fair smile upon all the house, and warmed himself in the sun of his own magnificence—for

是谁时，他的内心立刻燃起幸福的火焰。他马上开始竭尽全力卖弄自己——打人，拽别人头发，做鬼脸———句话，使尽浑身解数，尽可能地吸引这个女孩的注意力，赢得她的掌声。

　　来宾被邀请坐在了最荣耀的位置上。沃尔特先生一结束自己的讲话，就开始向学校学生介绍来宾。那位中年绅士是个颇受人尊重的大人物——了不起的撒切尔法官，他们镇上律师的兄弟。杰夫·撒切尔立刻走上前去，以显示自己和这位大人物有多么熟悉，好引起师生们的羡慕。

　　沃尔特先生开始在各种接下来的正式活动中展示自己。只要能找到目标，他就会过去发号施令，指指点点。图书管理员也显示着自己——手里捧满了书跑这儿跑那儿。年轻的女教师们展示着自己——她们温和地弯向那些她们刚刚揍过的学生，竖起她们可爱的手指警告那些坏孩子，又充满爱意地拍拍好学生。年轻的男教师则一会儿轻声责备学生，一会儿用其他方式显示自己的威信和对校规的重视。小男孩小女孩们也是各显其能，尤其是那位大人物，坐在那里，带着一种自豪的微笑俯视整个房间，他整个人都沉浸在自己辉煌的光环中，暖洋洋的——因为他也在"显示"

he was "showing off," too.

There was only one thing wanting, to make Mr. Walters's happiness complete, and that was a chance to give a Bible prize and show a talented pupil. Several pupils had a few yellow tickets but none had enough—he had been around among the star pupils asking. He would have given worlds, now, to have that German boy back again with a healthy mind.

And now at this moment, when hope was dead, Tom Sawyer came forward with nine yellow tickets, nine red tickets, and ten blue ones, and demanded a Bible. This was a thunderbolt out of a clear sky. Walters would not be expecting him for the next ten years. Tom was therefore raised to a place with the judge and other best pupils. The boys were all sad with envy—but those who suffered the bitterest pain were those who understood too late that they themselves had lost this splendor by selling tickets to Tom for the wealth he had collected in selling whitewashing rights. These boys despised themselves, as being the fool of a foxy cheat, a cunning snake in the grass.

Tom was introduced to the judge; but his tongue was tied, his breath would hardly come, his heart trembled—partly because of the respectful greatness of the man, but mainly because he was her parent. He would

自己。

现在只需再做一件事就可以为沃尔特先生的快乐划上圆满的句号，这就是展示一个聪明孩子，颁发奖品《圣经》了。有几个孩子已经有几张黄票了，可没有一个人够十张票——沃尔特先生在他的明星学生中走来走去地询问。他觉得如果那个德国男孩此时能神志清醒地回到这些学生当中，他甚至愿意把整个世界都奉献出去。

就在这绝望的时刻，汤姆·索耶走上前去，手里握着九张黄票、九张红票和十张蓝票，请求得到一本《圣经》。这简直有如晴天霹雳。就是再等十年，沃尔特先生也没有指望过汤姆能出现在这种地方。汤姆因而被邀请和法官以及其他最好的学生坐在一起。男孩子们都嫉妒得难过起来了，最难过的当然还属那些把自己的票卖给汤姆的孩子，以换得他在出卖粉刷权时积攒的宝物。现在他们才明白自己失去的是多么大的荣耀，然而知道这一切时却太晚了。这些男孩子们因为自己被那个有如狐狸般狡猾，有如藏在草里的蛇一样狡诈的骗子给捉弄了一把，开始瞧不起自己啦。

汤姆被介绍给了法官；面对这样的场合，他舌头似乎粘住了，气好像也喘不上来了，心怦怦乱跳———部分原因是面前这个人是个大人物，他太威严了，但主要还是因为他是她的爸爸。如

have liked to fall down and worship him, if it were in the dark. The judge put his hand on Tom's head and called him a fine little man, and asked him what his name was. The boy stammered, gasped, and got out:

"Tom."

"Oh, no, not Tom – it is – "

"Thomas."

"Ah, that's it. I thought there was more to it, maybe. That's very well. But you've another one I dare say, and you'll tell it to me, won't you?"

"Tell the gentleman your other name, Thomas," said Walters, "and say sir. You mustn't forget your manners."

"Thomas Sawyer—sir."

"That's it! That's a good boy. Fine boy. Fine, manly little fellow. Two thousand verses is a great many—very, very great many. And you never can be sorry for the trouble you took to learn them; for knowledge is worth more than anything else in the world; it's what makes great men and good men; you'll be a great man and a good man yourself, someday, Thomas, and then you'll look back and say, 'It's all owing to the precious Sunday-school benefits of my boyhood—it's all owing to my dear teachers that taught me to learn—it's all owing to the good teacher, Mr. Walters, who encour-

果这周围漆黑一片的话，他愿意跪下来，朝他顶礼膜拜。法官将手放在汤姆头上，称他是个不错的小大人，还问他叫什么。这孩子结结巴巴，喘着粗气，终于说出：

"汤姆。"

"噢，不，不该是汤姆，是……"

"托马斯。"①

"啊。这就对了，我想你或许还没说完呢，这已经很好了。但我敢说，你还应该有个姓，你会告诉我的，是吗？"

"告诉这位先生你姓什么，托马斯，"沃尔特说，"说话要称先生，你可不能没礼貌。"

"托马斯·索耶——先生。"

"好！好孩子，不错，小男子汉，圣经两千节很多……很多，很多，可你永远不会后悔自己费这么大劲儿去背的，因为世界上再没有什么比知识更宝贵了；知识使人们变得伟大、善良；你将来一定会成为一个伟大而又善良的人的，托马斯。那时你回过头来一想，你会说，'多亏了当年宝贵的主日学校，使童年的我受益匪浅——多亏了那些亲爱的老师，他们教会了我——多亏我的好校

---

① 译注：托马斯是汤姆的正式称法。

aged me, and watched me over, and gave me a beautiful Bible—a splendid nice Bible—to keep and have it all for my own, always—it's all owing to right bringing up!' That is what you will say, Thomas—and you wouldn't take any money for those two thousand verses—no indeed you wouldn't. And you wouldn't mind telling me and this lady some of the things you've learned—no, I know you wouldn't—for we are proud of little boys that learn. Now, no doubt you know the names of all the twelve disciples. Won't you tell us the names of the first two?"

Tom's face turned red now, and his eyes fell. Mr. Walters's heart sank within him. He said to himself, "It is not possible that the boy can answer the simplest question— Why did the judge ask him?" Yet he felt a duty to speak:

"Answer the gentleman, Thomas—don't be afraid."

Tom still hung fire.

"Now I know you'll tell me," said the lady. "The names of the first two disciples were—"

"DAVID AND GOLIATH!"

The answer is certainly wrong. Let us be kind enough to draw the curtain and not see the rest of the scene.

长，沃尔特先生，他鼓励我，监督我，还送我一本好看的《圣经》——一本精美的《圣经》——让我自己一直保留着，——多亏了他们教育有方。'你那时会这么说的，托马斯——就是给你再多的钱也换不回这两千节《圣经》的，你也不会换的，你不介意告诉我和这位夫人你学会的东西吧——我想你不会的——我们为这些爱学习的孩子而感到自豪，好，毫无疑问你知道耶稣十二个门徒的名字，告诉我前两个，好吗？"

汤姆的脸红了，他的眼睛低了下来，沃尔特先生的心也随之沉了下去，他心里嘀咕着："这孩子连最简单的问题也不可能答出来的——为什么法官问他呀？"然而他觉得自己有责任说话：

"回答这位先生，托马斯——别怕。"

汤姆还是没有反应。

"我知道你会告诉我的，"夫人说，"前两个门徒的名字是——"

"大卫和格列尔斯！"

回答肯定是错的，咱们还是发发善心，快把帷幕拉下来，别再往下看了。

Chapter 5
The Pinch Bug and His Prey

About half past ten the old bell of the small church began to ring, and presently the people began to gather for the morning sermon. The Sunday-school children occupied seats with their parents, so as to be under management. Aunt Polly came, and Tom and Sid and Mary sat with her—Tom being placed next to the passage, in order that he might be as far away from the open window and the attractive outside summer scenes as possible. The crowd stood in line in the passage: the old and poor postmaster, who had been better in the past; the mayor and his wife; the justice of the peace; the Widow Douglas, fair, smart and forty, a generous, goodhearted person and wise, her hill building the only palace in the town, and the most hospitable and much the most generous in offering parties that St. Petersburg could have; the bent and respectable Major and Mrs. Ward; Lawyer Riverson; the most beautiful woman of the village, followed by a troop of young heart – breakers; then all the young clerks in town; and last of all came the Model Boy, Willie Mufferson, taking as attentive care of his mother as if she were cut glass. He always brought his

第五章　夹人虫和他的俘虏

大约十点半，小教堂古老的钟声开始响起，人们都聚到教堂开始听早晨的布道。主日学校的孩子们都给爸妈占了座位，和他们坐在一起，也好让他们管着点儿。波莉姨妈来了，汤姆、赛德、玛丽和她坐在一起——汤姆被安排坐在靠过道的座位，为的是让他远离窗口，免得被夏日迷人的风景吸引。还有一大堆人站在过道上，这些人有：年迈而又贫穷的邮局局长，他过去的光景可比现在好多了；镇长和他的太太；治安官；道格拉斯寡妇，她四十岁了，皮肤白皙，衣着时髦，慷慨大方，善良聪慧，她坐落在山上的家可是镇上惟一的宫殿，她举办的聚会是圣彼兹堡镇最热情好客的；德高望重的老人沃德少校和他的太太；瑞吾森律师；村里头号美人，后面跟着一大群令人心醉的年轻姑娘；镇上所有的职员；最后是男孩子们的榜样，威利·马弗森，他对妈妈照顾得无微不至，仿佛她是一块易碎的玻璃，他总是把他的

mother to church, and was the pride of all the middle – aged and old women. The boys all hated him, for he was so good. And besides, he had been made the model to the boys so much. His white handkerchief was hanging out of his pocket behind, as usual on Sundays. Tom had no handkerchief, and he looked upon boys who had as snobs.

The clergyman gave out the hymn, and read it through with great enjoyment, in a strange style which was much admired in that part of the country. His voice began in a medium tune and climbed steadily till it reached a certain point, and then fell down.

After the hymn had been sung, the Rev. Mr. Sprague turned himself into a bulletin board and read off "notices" of meetings and societies and things—a strange custom which is still kept up in America, even in cities, in this age of plenty of newspapers.

And now the clergyman prayed. A good, generous prayer it was, and went into details; it pleaded for the church and the little children of the church; for the other churches of the village; for the village itself; for the country; for the state; for the state officers; for the United Sates; for the churches of the United States; for Congress; for the President; for the officers of the government; for the poor sailors; for the oppressed millions in

妈妈带到教堂来，都成了这儿所有中老年妇女的骄傲了。男孩子们憎恶他，因为他太杰出了，还因为他们总是被教导要向他学习，他的白手帕在星期天总是挂在衣兜外。汤姆没有白手帕，他认为带手帕的男孩子都是势利小人。

牧师开始诵读赞美诗，读得津津有味。他的方法很奇特，却为这块儿的村人所爱慕。他的声调先是中度，然后再慢慢升高，达到一个点，之后再落下来。

赞美诗后，瑞伍·斯伯莱格先生就把自己变成了一个布告牌，向人们发布关于各种集会、社团及其他事情的消息；这个奇特的习俗在今天的美国还保留着，哪怕是城市，尽管这已经是一个报纸充斥的年代了。

现在牧师开始祈祷了，祈祷非常具体，充满了浓浓爱意与慷慨。他为教堂和教堂里的小孩子们祈祷；为村里其他的教堂祈祷；为村子祈祷；为乡镇祈祷；为这个州祈祷；为州里官员祈祷；为美国祈祷；为美国教堂祈祷；为国会祈祷；为总统祈祷；为政府官员祈祷；为可怜的水手祈祷；为全世界受压迫的成百万上千万人祈祷；为盲人

the world; for the blind and the deaf; for the wild people on the far islands of the sea; and closed with a pleading that the words he was about to speak might find grace and favor, and be as seed planted in rich ground, producing in time a grateful harvest of good. Amen.

There was a rustling of dresses, and the standing crowd sat down. Tom did not enjoy the prayer, he only endured it. He was restless all through it.

The clergyman gave out his text that was so boring that many a head by and by began to nod. Tom counted the pages of the sermon; after church he always knew how many pages there had been, but he seldom knew anything else about the content.

Presently he thought of a treasure he had and got it out. It was a large black beetle with terrible jaws—a "pinch bug," he called it. The first thing the beetle did was to take him by the finger. A natural flick followed, the beetle went onto the passage and lay on its back, and the hurt finger went into the boy's mouth. The beetle lay there working its helpless legs, unable to turn over. Tom looked at it and longed for it; but it was safe out of reach. Other people uninterested in the sermon found relief in the beetle, and they looked at it too. Presently a wandering poodle dog came idling along, sad at heart, lazy with the summer softness and the quiet, tired of be-

聋子祈祷，为住在大海上遥远岛屿的野蛮人祈祷；最后，牧师祈祷，他的话能够为人们带来天恩与宠爱，能够像种子一样撒播在富庶的地里，及时给人们带来丰硕的收获，感谢上帝，阿门。

紧接着就是衣服窸窸窣窣的声音，站起来的人们纷纷落座了。汤姆可不喜欢这祷告，他不过一直在忍受着罢了，因而他一刻也不安宁。

牧师开始讲道，听着这无聊的布道，很多人的脑袋都开始不由自主地向下点着。汤姆数了数道文的页数；每次离开教堂后，他总是能记住道文有多少页，即便对其内容一无所知。

这会儿他想到了他还有一个宝物，便取了出来。这是一个大大的黑甲壳虫，长着一对可怕的钳子——他把它叫做"夹人虫"，甲壳虫一放出来的第一件事就是夹住了汤姆的手指头。出于本能，汤姆捧了一下，甲壳虫掉到了过道上，仰面朝天。汤姆忙把弄痛的指头塞进了嘴里。甲壳虫躺在那儿，腿脚乱蹬，可是没用，它还是翻不过身，汤姆看着它，想抓它，却又觉得还是别碰它为妙。其他对布道毫无兴趣的人从这只甲壳虫身上找到了解脱，他们也盯着看，这时一只四处游逛的鬈毛小狗晃悠过来了，它看起来情绪低落，在夏日的柔和与宁静中显得有些慵懒。它腻味透了各种

ing controlled, sighing for change. He watched the beetle; the hanging tail lifted and shaken. He examined the prize; walked around it; smelt at it from a safe distance; walked around it again; grew braver, and took a closer smell; then lifted his lip and tried to seize it carefully, just missing it; made another, and another; began to enjoy the entertainment; lay on its stomach with the beetle between his paws, and continued his experiments; grew tired at last, and then indifferent and absent-minded. His head nodded, and little by little his chin fell and touched the enemy, who seized it. There was a sharp cry, a shaking of the dog's head, and then the beetle fell a couple of yards away, and lay on its back once more. The observers nearby shook with a gentle joy, several faces went behind fans and handkerchiefs, and Tom was entirely happy. The dog looked foolish, and probably felt so; but there was anger hid in heart, too, and a desire for revenge. So he went to the beetle and began a cautious attack on it again; jumping at it from every point of a circle, bringing with his forepaws within an inch of the creature, making even closer snatches at it with his teeth, and shaking both his head and ears. But he grew tired once more, after a while; tried to amuse himself with a fly but found no relief; followed an ant around, with his nose close to the floor,

拘束，叹着气渴望有所改变。它看看甲壳虫，尾巴向上翘着，一晃一晃的。它审视着这份奖赏，绕着它走来走去，站在了一个安全的距离闻了闻；又走开点；胆子大了一些，凑近了些闻，然后张开嘴巴，想要小心翼翼地咬住它，只是没咬上，张开嘴，再咬，再咬；它开始觉得这很有趣；它趴在地上，那只甲壳虫就在他的两个爪子中间，它又试着去咬它，就这样一来一去，小狗变得有些漫不经心，它的头不住地向下点着，下巴一点点地向下，最后碰到了它的敌人，敌人一下夹住了它的下巴。狗尖叫了一声，头狠命摇着，把甲壳虫甩到了几码外的地方，又一次让它仰面朝天。周围观看的人们都被这小小的乐趣逗笑了，身子微微颤着，有几个人用扇子或手帕遮着自己。汤姆非常兴奋。小狗这时看起来傻乎乎的，它自己可能也有这种感觉，可心中还隐藏着愤怒和报仇的欲望，因而又来到甲壳虫旁，准备展开小心翼翼的攻击；它从各个角度扑向它，前爪子落在离虫只有一英寸远的地方；牙齿放得更近去咬它，还一个劲儿地摇着自己的头和耳朵。可过了一会儿，它又累了，试图追逐一只苍蝇为自己解闷；可也没觉得轻松；它又跟着一个蚂蚁转，鼻子紧贴

and quickly tired of that; yawned, sighed, forgot the beetle entirely, and sat down on it. Then there was a wild cry of pain and the poodle dog flew away. At last it moved along the passage in pain and jumped onto his master's lap; the master threw it out of the window and the voice of sadness quickly faded in the distance.

By this time the whole church was red-faced with suppressed laughter. It was a real relief to the whole crowd when the boring sermon was over and the blessing pronounced.

Tom Sawyer went home quite cheerful, thinking to himself that there was some satisfaction about the church service when there was a bit of variety in it. He had but one disturbing thought: he was willing that the dog should play with his pinch bug, but he did not think it was honorable for him to carry it off.

Chapter 6
Tom Meets Becky

Tom Sawyer felt miserable on Monday morning. He always felt so on Monday mornings—because it began another week's slow suffering in school. He always began that day with wishing he had no weekend, since it made the going into suffering and control so much more

着地面，可很快也烦了。小狗打着呵欠，叹着气，把甲壳虫的事忘在了脑后，一屁股坐在了它的上面，紧接着就听到小狗痛苦地嚎叫了一声，猛地一跃逃走了，最后，它难过地沿着过道走到主人身边，跳到了主人的膝上；主人把它扔出了窗外，它那悲伤的呜呜声也很快消失在了远处。

这会儿，整个教堂看了这一幕的人都想笑而不敢笑，憋得满脸通红，当布道结束，宣布了祝福的时候，所有的人才真正地解脱了。

汤姆·索耶高高兴兴地回家，因为有了点儿小作料，他对今天的礼拜活动还有些满意。只是有一件事让他不太畅快：他愿意让小狗和他的夹人虫玩，可又不觉得他的夹人虫获胜了有什么光荣的。

第六章　汤姆与贝琪相识

星期一早晨，汤姆觉得自己挺可怜的，他星期一早晨总有这种感觉——因为这意味着又一周漫长而又折磨人的学校学习开始了。他在这一天总想要是没周末该多好呀，因为愉快的周末会使他更厌烦这种痛苦且又拘束的生活。

boring.

Tom lay thinking. Presently it occurred to him that he wished he was sick; then he could stay home from school. He examined his body. No illness was found, and he examined again. This time he thought he could find some signs showing pain, and he began to encourage them with great hope. But they soon became weak, and presently completely disappeared. He thought further. Suddenly he discovered something. One of his upper front teeth was loose. This was lucky; he was about to begin to groan. But it occurred to him that Aunt could pull it out when she knew it and it would hurt. He put the tooth aside and began to seek other chance. Nothing came to his mind within a short time. Then he remembered hearing the doctor tell about s certain thing that made a patient lay in bed for two or three weeks and threatened to make him lose a finger. So the boy eagerly drew his painful toe from under the sheet and held it up for check. But now he did not know the necessary signs, anyway, he fell to groaning with great spirit.

But Sid slept on unconscious.

Tom groaned louder, and felt that he began to feel pain in the toe.

No result from Sid.

Tom was breathing shortly and quickly with his

汤姆躺在那儿琢磨着，这会儿他真希望要是有病就好了，那他就可以在家里呆着不去学校了，他对自己的全身检查了一番，没发现哪儿有病。他又检查了一遍，这回他想他可以找出几个隐隐作痛的地方，然后又满怀强烈的希望鼓励着这些疼痛能够加剧。可惜很快这几个地儿都不怎么疼了，一会儿甚至完全消失了。他又使劲儿地动着脑筋，突然他发现了什么。他上面的门牙有一颗有点松动，这太好了！他准备开始呻吟，可又一想姨妈若是知道了，一定会给它拔出来，那可就遭罪了。他只好把牙的事放过一边，再去寻找其他的机会，过了一会儿，他还是什么都没发现，这时他记起曾经听医生说过得一种什么病，人可以在床上躺两三周呢，甚至还有可能要割掉一个手指或脚趾，想到这里，汤姆急切地把他那发痛的脚趾取出被子，举起来检查了一番。可他不知道这种病该有什么症状。但不管怎样，他还是可着精神头地躺在床上呻吟起来。

然而赛德还毫无察觉地睡着。

汤姆的呻吟声更大了，而且他感觉到脚趾那儿真疼了。

赛德还是没有反应。

这回汤姆开始短促而急速地呼吸。他休息了

efforts by this time. He took a rest and then continued groaning.

Sid snored on.

Tom was annoyed. He said, "Sid, Sid!" and shook him. This worked well, and Tom began to groan again. Sid yawned, stretched, then brought himself up on his elbow with a snort, and began to stare at Tom. Tom went on groaning. Sid said:

"Tom! Say, Tom!" (No response.) "Here, Tom! Tom! What is the matter, Tom?" And he shook him and looked in his face anxiously.

Tom moaned out:

"Oh, don't, Sid. Don't shake me."

"What's the matter, Tom? I must call auntie."

"No—never mind. It'll be over by and by, maybe. Don't call anybody."

"But I must! Don't groan so, Tom, it's terrible. How long have you been this way?"

"Hours. Ouch! Oh, don't call others, Sid, you'll kill me."

"Tom, why didn't you wake me sooner? Oh, Tom, don't! It makes me feel frightened to hear you. Tom, what is the matter?"

"I forgive you everything, Sid. (Groan) Everything you've ever done to me. When I'm gone—"

一会儿，继续呻吟。

赛德仍旧打着呼噜。

汤姆生气了，他喊"赛德，赛德"！还摇了摇了他，这回奏效了，汤姆继续回去哼哼。赛德打了个呵欠，伸了个懒腰，用胳膊肘把自己撑了起来，还打了个喷嚏。他开始盯着汤姆看，汤姆继续呻吟着。赛德说：

"汤姆！说话，汤姆！"（没有反应）"看这儿，汤姆！汤姆！你怎么啦，汤姆？"他摇着他，焦急地望着他的脸。

汤姆呻吟着说：

"噢，别，赛德，别摇我。"

"你怎么啦，汤姆？我得去叫姨妈。"

"别——不要紧，过一会儿就会好的，或许吧。别叫任何人。"

"可我一定得去！别这么哼哼了，汤姆，太可怕了。你这样多久了？"

"几个小时了，哎哟！噢，别叫别人，赛德，疼死我了。"

"汤姆，为什么你不早点儿把我叫醒呢？噢，汤姆，别这样！我听着害怕，汤姆，怎么啦？"

"我原谅你的一切，赛德，（呻吟着）原谅你对我做过的一切，我走以后——"

"Oh, Tom, you aren't dying, are you? Don't, Tom—oh, don't. Maybe—"

"I forgive everybody, Sid. (Groan) Tell them so, Sid. And, Sid, you give my window sash and my cat with one eye to that new girl that had come to town, and tell her—"

But Sid had seized his clothes and gone. Tom was suffering in reality, now, so well was his imagination working, and so his groans had sounded real.

Sid flew downstairs and said:

"Oh, Aunt Polly, come! Tom's dying!"

"Dying!"

"Yes. Don't wait—come quick!"

"Nonsense! I don't believe it!"

But she fled upstairs, nevertheless, with Sid and Mary following her. And her face grew white, too, and her lip trembled. When she reached the bedside she gasped out:

"You, Tom! Tom, what's the matter with you?"

"Oh, auntie, I'm—"

"What's the matter with you, child?"

"Oh, auntie, my painful toe is swollen!"

The old lady sank down into a chair and laughed a little, then cried a little, then did both together. This helped her recover and she said:

"噢，汤姆，你不会死的，不会吧？不，汤姆——不会死的，或许——"

"我原谅所有的人，赛德，（呻吟着）告诉、他们，赛德，还有，赛德，你把我保存的那只窗框和一只眼的猫给新来咱们镇上的女孩，告诉她——"

可赛德早已抓上衣服跑了，这会儿汤姆真觉得疼了，他的想像力太丰富了，因而他的呻吟也听着是真的了。

赛德飞跑下楼，喊：

"波莉姨妈，快来！汤姆快要死了！"

"快死了？"

"对，别呆在那儿啦——快点儿来！"

"胡说！我不信！"

然而她还是飞奔上楼了，后面跟着赛德和玛丽。她的脸变得惨白，嘴唇也在颤着，跑到汤姆床边，她上气不接下气地问道：

"你，汤姆！汤姆，你怎么啦？"

"噢，姨妈，我——"

"怎么了，孩子？"

"噢，姨妈，我那只发疼的脚趾肿起来了！"

老太太一屁股坐在椅子上，笑了一会儿，又哭了一会儿，然后又哭哭笑笑了一会儿。就这样她回过神来说：

"Tom, what a shock you did give me. Now you shut up that nonsense and climb out of this."

The groans stopped and the pain disappeared from the toe. The boy felt a little foolish, and he said:

"Aunt Polly, it seemed swollen, and it hurt so much that I never minded my tooth at all."

"Your tooth, indeed! What's the matter with your tooth?"

"One of them's loose, and it pains very much."

"There, there, now, don't begin that groaning again. Open your mouth. Well—you tooth is loose, but you're not going to die about that. Mary, get me a silk thread, and some fire out of the kitchen."

Tom said:

"Oh, please, auntie, don't pull it out. It doesn't hurt any more. I wish I may never call anyone if it pains. Please don't, auntie. I don't want to stay home from school."

"Oh, you don't, don't you? So all this trouble you caused was because you thought you'd get to stay home from school and go fishing? Tom, Tom, I love you so, and you seem to try every way you can to break my old heart by doing something unusual." By this time tools for curing teeth pain were ready. The old lady made one end of the silk thread fast to Tom's tooth and tied the other

"汤姆，你可把我吓坏了，现在别胡说八道了，爬起来吧！"

呻吟没有了，脚趾的疼痛也消失了。汤姆觉得自己有点儿傻，他说：

"波莉姨妈，刚才看起来是肿了，而且疼得我都忘了我的牙的事了。"

"你的牙！你牙怎么啦？"

"有一个松动了，特别疼。"

"噢，牙！别哼哼了，张嘴，嗯——你的牙松了，但这也死不了。玛丽，给我取根丝线来，再从厨房弄点儿火。"

汤姆说：

"噢，姨妈，别拔它，现在不疼了，就是真疼的话，我也不叫了。别，姨妈，我可不想在家呆着不上学。"

"噢，你不想，不想吗？你制造的这些麻烦都是因为你想要在家呆着，不上学，好去钓鱼，是吗？汤姆，汤姆，我这样爱着你，可你似乎总要使尽一切招数，闹出点儿没边没沿的事，好让我这老太婆心碎。"说到这儿，治牙疼的工具已经准备好了，老太太把丝线的一头绑在汤姆的牙上，

to the bedpost. Then she seized the fire and suddenly pushed it almost into the boy's face. The tooth hung by the bedpost, now.

But all trials bring their compensations. As Tom went to school after breakfast, he was the envy of every boy he met because the gap in his upper row pf teeth enabled him to spit in a new and admirable way.

Shortly Tom met the young outcast of the village, Huckleberry Finn, son of the town drunkard. Huckleberry was strongly hated and feared by all the mothers of the town, because he was idle and lawless and vulgar and bad—and because all their children admired him so, and delighted in his forbidden society, and wished they dared to be like him. Tom was like the rest of the respectable boys, in that he envied Huckleberry his outcast condition and was under strict orders not to play with him. So he played with him every time he got a chance. Huckleberry Finn was always dressed in the deserted clothes of adults, and his clothes, trousers and hats were always ragged.

Huckleberry might go anywhere as he liked. He slept on door steps in fine weathers and in empty buckets in rainy days; he did not have to go to school or to church, or to call any being master or obey anybody; he could go fishing or swimming when and where he chose,

另一头系在床柱上，然后她抓起火把，突然伸向汤姆，都几乎要撞到他的脸上了，就这样，汤姆的牙掉了，挂在了床柱上。

所有的苦难都会得到补偿。汤姆早饭后去学校的路上，他成了碰到的所有男孩嫉妒的对象，因为他上牙露的这个洞可以使他吐痰的样子新奇别致，令人生羡。

不一会儿，汤姆遇见了村里的小弃儿——哈克贝历·芬恩。他是镇上一个酒鬼的儿子。哈克贝历为镇上所有的母亲所厌恶，因为他又懒又坏，不遵规守法，还粗俗不堪——还因为他们每个人的孩子都为这而羡慕他，都喜欢他的生活圈子，希望自己也敢像他一样，而这是他们的爸妈禁止的。汤姆在这一点上，也像体面的孩子一样，也羡慕哈克贝历是个弃儿，却又奉命不许和他混在一起，因而只要有机会他就会找他玩，哈克贝历·芬恩总穿着大人不要的衣服，而且他的上衣、裤子、帽子总是破破烂烂的。

哈克贝历想去哪儿就可以去哪儿，天气好了，他睡在门口的台阶上；下雨，他就躺在空桶里；他不必去上学，也不必去教堂；他不必称任何人为老师，也不需听谁的话；他可以在他喜欢的任何时间和地点去钓鱼或游泳，想呆多久就多久；

and stay as long as it suited him; nobody forbade him to fight; he could sit up as late as he pleased; he was always the first boy that went barefoot in the spring and the last to wear leather in the fall; he never had to wash, nor put on clean clothes; he could curse wonderfully. In a word, that boy had everything that goes to make life precious. So thought every troubled, respectable boy in St. Petersburg.

Tom called the romantic outcast:

"Hello, Huckleberry!"

After seeing a dead cat Huck brought and knowing that Huck wanted to use the cat to cure the warts on his skin, Tom told Huck the way should be to bring the cat to the graveyard about midnight when somebody that was wicked would be buried; and when it's midnight a devil would come, or maybe two or three, but you could not see them. You Could only hear something like the wind, or maybe hear them talk; and when they're taking that fellow away, you lift your cat after them and say, "Devil follow corpse, cat follow devil, warts follow cat, I'm done with you!" Huck believed and they agreed to try that night.

Then he traded his tooth for a tick with Huckleberry and put it in his box. The boys separated, each feeling wealthier than before.

也没有人阻止他不让他打架；他可以在任何地方想坐多晚就坐多晚；春天里，他总是第一个光脚丫的；秋天里，他总是最后一个穿皮鞋的；他永远不需要洗澡，不需要穿上干净衣裳；他还可以骂人，而且骂得很精彩。总之，这个男孩拥有一切可以使生活更精彩的东西，圣彼兹堡的每一个苦恼的、体面的男孩都这么想。

汤姆喊住了那个富于浪漫色彩的弃儿。

"喂，哈克贝历！"

看到哈克带的一只死猫，得知他要用死猫治他皮肤上的疣子，汤姆就告诉他怎么治："应该是等那个恶人死了，半夜在墓地被埋葬时，你把猫带到那儿去，半夜时有鬼怪会出现，可能还会是两个或三个，可你看不到他们，你只能听到像风一样的声音，或许还会听到他们在说话；等它们把死人抬走的时候，你举着你的猫跟在后面，说：'鬼怪跟着死人走，死猫跟着鬼怪走，疣子跟着死猫走，我浑身什么也没有！'"汤姆相信了，他们说好当天晚上就去试一试。

之后，汤姆用他拔下的那颗牙和哈克交换了一只虱子。他们分手了，各自都觉得比以前更富有了。

When Tom reached the little school-house, he walked in and sat in his seat quickly. The master was sleeping in his armchair caused by the dull hum of study. Tom's coming awakened him.

"Thomas Sawyer!"

Tom knew that when his name was pronounced in full, it meant trouble.

"Sir!"

"Come up here. Now, sir, why are you late again, as usual?"

Tom was about to escape the scolding by telling a lie, when he saw a girl with two long tails of yellow hair that he recognized by the electric sympathy of love; and beside her was the only empty place on the girls' side of the schoolhouse. He instantly said:

"I STOPPED TO TALK WITH HUCKLEBERRY FINN."

The master was dumbfounded, and he stared helplessly. The pupils stopped reading and wondered if this foolishly bold boy had lost his mind. The master said: "You—you did what?"

"Stopped to talk with Huckleberry Finn."

There was no mistaking in the words.

"Thomas Sawyer, this is the most astonishing confession I have ever listened to. Beating is not enough to

汤姆到了学校的小教室，他走了进去。老师正坐在他的扶手椅中，在同学一片乏人的嗡嗡声里睡着了。汤姆本想很快坐下，不想还是吵醒了老师。

　　"托马斯·索耶！"

　　汤姆知道要有人喊他的全名，就意味着麻烦来了。

　　"先生！"

　　"过来，汤姆先生，你为什么像往常一样又迟到了？"

　　汤姆本打算撒个谎，免于被批评，可这时在爱情的火花中他认出了教室里那个黄头发的扎两个长辫的女孩是谁，而且她旁边空着一张座位，这可是全校女生旁边的惟一一个空座位，他马上回答道：

　　"我刚才停下来和哈克贝历·芬恩聊天了。"

　　老师目瞪口呆，他绝望地盯着汤姆，正读书的学生们也都停下来了，都在想这个男孩怎么这么傻大胆。老师又问："你——你干什么了？"

　　"停下来和哈克贝历·芬恩聊天。"

　　话没听错。

　　"托马斯·索耶，你的坦白可太让人吃惊的了。再怎么打你都不足以惩罚你，脱下你的夹克衫。"

punish you. Take off your jacket."

The master's arm moved until it was tired and the stick was broken. Then the order followed: "Now, sir, go and sit with the girls! And let this be a warning to you."

The laughter that spread around the room appeared to make the boy ashamed, but in reality that result was caused rather more by his admiration for his unknown idol and the pleasure. He sat down upon the end of the bench and the girl moved quickly away from him with a shaking of her head. Nudges, and winks and whispers spread the room, but Tom sat still, with his arms upon the long, low desk before him, and seemed to study his book.

By and by the pupils no longer noticed him, and the familiar school murmur rose upon the dull air once more. Presently the boy began to glance at the girl secretly. She observed it, "made a mouth" at him and gave him the back of her head for a minute. When she cautiously faced around again, a peach lay before her. She pushed it away. Tom gently put it back. She pushed it away again, but with less dislike. Tom patiently returned it to its place. Then she let it remain. Tom wrote on his slate, "Please take it—I got more." The girl glanced at the words, but made no sign. Now the boy

老师的手开始挥舞，直打得他觉得累了，棍子也断了，接着他命令汤姆："现在，先生，去和好孩子坐在一起！警告，警告你。"

教室周围发出的笑声似乎使男孩觉得有些羞愧，可事实上，这个结果是他出于爱慕那个不知名的偶像，为了追求快乐而自找的。他在凳子的一头坐下了，女孩摇着头很快朝她那边挪了挪。整个教室的同学们都在相互用肘碰碰，眨眨眼，咬咬耳朵，相互示意瞅瞅汤姆他们俩，可汤姆却一动不动地坐着，胳膊放在面前的课桌上，俨然一副学习的样子。

过了一会儿，同学们不再注意他了，整个教室又沉浸在那熟悉而又乏味的嗡嗡的读书声中。这会儿，男孩偷偷地瞥了一眼女孩，被她注意到了。她向他撇了撇嘴，又给他晾了足有一分钟的后脑勺。当她小心翼翼地转过来时，一个桃子已经摆在她面前了。她推开了桃子，汤姆又轻轻地放了回来。她把它又推走了，但不那么讨厌了。汤姆耐心地又把它放了回来。这回她再没推开。汤姆在石板上写着，"请拿上——我还有很多。"女孩瞥了瞥他写的，没有反应。现在男孩开始在石板

began to draw something on the slate, hiding his work with his left hand. For a time the girl refused to notice, but her human curiosity presently began to show. The boy worked on, apparently unconscious. The girl tried secretly to see it, but the boy did not show that he was aware of it. At last, she gave in and hesitantly whispered:

"Let me see it."

Tom partly uncovered a gloomy picture of a house with smoke rising from the chimney. Then the girl began to be interested in the work and had forgot everything else. When it was finished, she looked at it for a moment, then whispered:

"It's nice—make a man."

The artist drew a man in the front yard; she was satisfied with it, and whispered:

"It's a beautiful man—now make me come along."

Tom drew it. The girl said:

"It's ever so nice—I wish I could draw."

"It's easy," whispered Tom, "I'll teach you."

"Oh, will you? When?"

"At noon. Do you go home to dinner?"

"I'll stay if you'll."

"Good. What's your name?"

"Becky Thatcher. What's yours? Oh, I know. It's

上画起什么，还用左手遮着。好一会儿，女孩都不去看。最终，好奇心开始发挥作用了。男孩继续画着，似乎没觉察到他旁边的变化。女孩试着偷偷地望去，男孩还是没有表现出来他已经觉察到了。最后，女孩屈服了，犹犹豫豫地小声说：

"让我看看。"

汤姆把他那张忧伤的图画露出了一部分。这是一间带着烟囱的房子，炊烟袅袅。女孩对这幅画开始表现出兴趣，其他一切都抛在脑后了。画片画完了，她看了一会儿，低声说：

"真好——画上去个男人。"

艺术家在前院里画个男人；她很满意，又低声说：

"这个男人真帅——现在让我走在他旁边。"

汤姆画上去了，女孩说：

"真好——我希望我也会画。"

"这很容易，"汤姆低声道，"我教你。"

"噢，你教我？什么时候？"

"中午，你中午回家吃饭吗？"

"如果你在这儿呆着，我就不用了。"

"好，你叫什么名字？"

"贝琪·撒切尔，你呢？噢，我知道了，是托

Thomas Sawyer."

"That's the name they call when they scold me or beat me. I'm Tom when I'm good. You call me Tom, will you?

"Yes."

Now Tom began to write something on the slate, hiding the words from the girl. She begged to see. Tom said:

"Oh, it isn't anything."

"Yes, it is."

"No, it isn't. You don't want to see."

"Yes, I do, indeed I do. Please let me see."

"You'll tell."

"No, I won't."

"You won't tell anybody at all? Ever, as long as you live?"

"No, I won't ever tell anybody. Now let me see." And she put her small hand upon his hand and a little struggle followed, Tom pretended to resist but let his hands slip till these words were shown: "I love you."

"Oh, you bad thing!" And she hit his hand a blow, but reddened and looked pleased, nevertheless.

Just at this moment the boy felt a slow, fateful grip closing on his ear, pulling him to stand up. In that grip he was pulled through the house and placed in his own

马斯·索耶。"

"这名字是他们批评我或揍我时才叫的，一般情况下，我叫汤姆，你叫我汤姆吧，好吗？"

"好的。"

现在汤姆开始在石板上写着什么，又把它遮着，不让女孩看到。她求他，让她看看，汤姆说：

"没什么。"

"肯定有什么。"

"没什么，你不想看的。"

"我想，我真想，请让我看看。"

"你会告诉别人的。"

"不，我不会的。"

"你一定谁也不说？永远，永远？"

"是的，我谁也不说，现在让我看看吧。"她把手放在他的手上，俩人争了一会儿，汤姆假装阻拦却又把手滑了下去，露出几个字："我爱你。"

"噢，你这个坏东西！"她打了一下他的手，脸红了，可看着还挺高兴的。

就在这时，男孩感到大事不好，有人在慢慢地拧着他的耳朵，把他拽了起来，在全校同学讨

seat, under an annoying fire of laughter from the whole school. Then the master stood over him during a few terrible moments, and finally moving away to his seat without saying a word. But although Tom's ear was painful, his heart was happy.

As the school quieted Tom made an honest effort to study, but the excitement within him was so great that he could not make a good performance in the following classes.

Chapter 7
Tick – Running and a Heartbreak

The harder Tom tried to concentrate on his book, the more his ideas wandered. So, at last, with a sigh and a yawn, he gave it up. It seemed that the noon would never come. It was the sleepiest of sleepy days. Away off in the sunshine, Cardiff Hill showed its green sides, a few birds flying in the air; no other living thing was visible but some cows, and they were asleep. Tom was eager to be free, or else to have something of interest to do to pass the boring time. His hand entered his pocket and his face lit up. Then secretly the box came out. He released the tick and put him on the long flat desk.

厌的笑声中穿过教室，让他坐在了自己的位置上。之后老师挺吓人地在他旁边站了一会儿，就没说一句话地回到了他的座位上，虽然汤姆觉得耳朵有些疼，但他的心情还是非常愉快的。

学校里安静了下来，汤姆想踏踏实实地学习，可他内心激动得不行，使得他在上课的时候无法循规蹈矩。

第七章　玩虱子与伤心的爱情故事

汤姆越使劲儿地集中精力看书，他就越容易走神。最后，他吸了几口气，打了个呵欠，干脆放弃努力了，觉得中午似乎总也不到。这些日子人总爱犯困，而这会儿则是最让人瞌睡的时间。远处，阳光下的卡迪夫山显得树木茂密。几只鸟在天空中飞翔；除了几只还在睡觉的奶牛外，再也没有什么活物了。汤姆渴望自由，或者有其他什么有趣的事可做，以消磨这无聊的时光。他的手塞进了兜里，脸上顿时有了光彩。他偷偷地把盒子取了出来，把里面的虱子——放在了又长又平的课桌上。

Tom's bosom friend sat next him, suffering just as Tom had been, and now he was deeply and gratefully interested in this entertainment in an instant. This bosom friend was Joe Harper. In order to have the full joy of the tick, Tom put Joe's slate on the desk and drew a line down the middle of it from the top to bottom.

"Now," said he, "as long as he is on your side you can stir him up and I'll let him alone; but if you let him get away and get on my side, you're to leave him alone as long as I can keep him from crossing over."

"All right, go ahead; start him up."

However, not long after the tick went to Joe's side, Tom could not resist the temptation and used his pin to stir the tick. Joe was angry in a moment. Said he:

"Tom, you let him alone."

"I only just want to stir him up a little, Joe."

"No, sir, it isn't fair; you just let him alone."

"Look here, Joe Harper, whose is that tick?"

"I don't care whose tick he is—he's on my side of the line and you shan't touch him."

"Well, I'll just bet I will, though. He's my tick and I'll do what I like with him, or die!"

A heavy blow came down on Tom's shoulders and then on Joe's. The boys had been too absorbed to notice

汤姆的知心朋友坐在他旁边，正和刚才的汤姆一样闷闷不乐。看到这好玩的东西也立刻产生了浓厚的兴趣，对汤姆充满了感激。他的知心朋友名叫乔·哈普。为了能够玩得尽兴，汤姆把乔的石板放在课桌上，在中间从上到下划了一条线。

"现在，"他说，"只要它爬到你那边，我就不动它；但如果你让它爬到我这边，只要我能让它不过去，你就别碰它。"

"好的，开始吧；动它。"

然而，玩了一会儿，虫爬到乔那边没多大一会儿，汤姆就忍不住了，用他的别针去捅了虫一下，乔很生气，他说：

"汤姆，你别动它。"

"我只是想逗它一会儿，乔。"

"不行，先生，这不公平；你别动它。"

"看看，乔·哈普，这是谁的虫？"

"我不管这是谁的——它在我这边，你就不该动它。"

"哼，可我就是动定了，这是我的虫，我爱怎么着它，我就怎么着！"

这时，汤姆的肩膀被重重地打了一下，紧接着乔也挨了一下子，两个孩子太专心致志地玩虫，

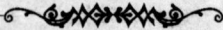

the silence when the master came tiptoeing down the room and stood over them. He had watched them for a long time.

When school broke up at noon, Tom flew to Becky Thatcher and whispered in her ear:

"You pretend you're going home, when you get to the corner let them go and you turn down through the lane and come back. I'll go the other way and come back."

So the one went off with one group of students, and the other with another. In a little while the two met and reached the school where there were no others. Then they sat together, with a slate before them, and Tom gave Becky the pencil and held her hand in his, guiding it, and so created another surprising house. When the interest in art began to fade, the two began talking. Tom was swimming in happiness. He said:

"Do you love rats?"

"No! I hate them!"

"Well, I do, too—live one. But I mean dead ones."

"No, I don't care for rats much, anyway. What I like is chewing gum."

"Oh, I should say so. I wish I had some now."

"Do you? I've got some. I'll let you chew it for a

他们根本没注意教室已变得寂静无声，老师已经踮着脚走下来，站到他们跟前，看他们已经很久了。

学校中午一放学，汤姆就飞奔到贝琪那儿，在她耳边悄悄说：

"你假装回家，走到拐角那儿，让他们先走，你沿着小巷子拐回来，我从另一条路走回来。"

俩人各跟了一帮同学离开了，不一会儿，就相继回到了空无一人的学校，他们坐在一起，把石板摆在面前。汤姆给贝琪了一支笔，手把手地教他，就这样盖起了一幢令人吃惊的房子。慢慢地，俩人对艺术的兴趣消退了，开始聊天。汤姆在欢乐的海洋中畅游，他说：

"你喜欢老鼠吗？"

"不，我讨厌老鼠。"

"嗯，我也是——活的。但我问你的是死老鼠。"

"不，不管什么样的，我都不喜欢；我喜欢嚼口香糖。"

"噢，我应该说也是这样，我真希望我现在有一些。"

"你喜欢？我有一些，我让你嚼一会儿，可你

while, but you must give it back to me."

That was pleasant.

"Becky, were you ever engaged?"

"What's that?"

"Why, engaged to be married."

"No."

"Would you like to?"

"I think so. I don't know. What is it like?"

"Like? Why, it isn't like anything. You only just tell a boy you won't ever have anybody but him, ever and ever, and then you kiss and that's all. Anybody can do it."

"Kiss? What do you kiss for?"

"Why, that, you know, is to—well, they always do that."

"Everybody?"

"Why, yes, everybody that's in love with each other. Do you remember what I wrote on the slate?"

"Ye – es."

"What is it?"

"I shan't tell you."

"Shall I tell you?"

"Ye – yes – but some other time."

"No, now."

"No, not now—tomorrow."

必须得还给我。"

这很好。

"贝琪，你订婚了吗？"

"什么叫订婚？"

"嗯，就是约订好要结婚。"

"没。"

"你想订婚吗？"

"我想我愿意吧，我不知道，这像什么呢？"

"像什么？不像什么，你只是告诉一个男孩你除了他永远不会再有其他人了，永远，永远，永远，然后你们互相吻一下，就好了，谁都可以这么做。"

"吻？吻什么呀？"

"嗯，你知道，就是——嗯，他们都这样。"

"每个人？"

"嗯，是，每一个与别人恋爱的人，你还记得我在石板上给你写的什么吗？"

"记——得。"

"什么？"

"我不告诉你。"

"那要我告诉你吗？"

"好——吧——等以后吧。"

"不，现在。"

"不，别现在——明天。"

"Oh, now, now. Please, Becky—I'll whisper it, I'll whisper it ever so easy."

Becky hesitating, Tom took silence for satisfaction and passed his arm about her waist and whispered the words ever so softly, with his mouth close to her ear. And then he added:

"Now, you whisper it to me—just the same."

She resisted for a while, and then said:

"You turn your face away so you can't see, and then I will. But you mustn't ever tell anybody—will you, Tom? Now you won't, will you?"

"No, indeed, indeed I won't. Now, Becky."

He turned his face away. She whispered, "I – love – you!"

Then she sprang away and ran around and around the desks and benches, with Tom after her. She escaped to a corner at last with her little white apron on her face. Tom clasped her about her neck ad pleaded:

"Now, Becky, it's all done—all over but the kiss. Don't you be afraid of that—it isn't anything at all. Please, Becky." And he pulled her apron and her hands.

By and by she gave up, and let her hands drop; her face came up. Tom kissed the red lips and said:

"Now, it's all done, Becky. And always after

"噢，现在，现在，让我告诉你吧，贝琪——我小声说，我会说得很自然的。"

贝琪犹豫着，汤姆把她的沉默当成了赞许，就搂起她的腰，嘴巴贴近她的耳朵，温柔地低声向她说了那句话。他又接着说：

"现在，你把这句话悄悄告诉我——和我一样。"

她反抗了一会儿，说：

"你把脸转过去，别看着我，我就说，但你一定不许告诉任何人——好吗，汤姆？你不会告诉别人吧？"

"好，没问题。我真的不会告诉别人的，开始吧，贝琪。"

他转过了脸，她低声说："我——爱——你！"

说完她就跳走了，围着桌子跑着，后面汤姆追着。她最后逃到了一个角落里，用她的小白围裙遮着脸，汤姆搂着她的脖子，求她说：

"现在，贝琪，一切都做完了——除了吻。你不害怕吧——根本就没什么，请吧，贝琪，"说着他拽着贝琪的小围裙和手。

逐渐地贝琪投降了，手放了下来，露出了脸，汤姆吻了她的红嘴唇，说：

"现在好啦，贝琪，你一定不要忘了我们举行

this, you know, you aren't ever to love anybody but me, and you aren't ever to marry anybody but me, never, never and forever. Will you?"

"No, I'll never love anybody but you, Tom, and I'll never marry anybody but you—and you aren't to ever marry anybody but me, either."

"Certainly. Of course. And always coming to school or when we're going home, you're to walk with me, when there isn't anybody looking—and you choose me and I choose you at parties, because that's the way you do when you're engaged."

"It's so nice. I never heard of it before."

"Oh, it's so joyful! Why, me and Amy Lawrence—"

The big eyes told Tom his mistake and he stopped, confused.

"Oh, Tom! Then I'm not the first you've ever been engaged to!"

The child began to cry. Tom said:

"Oh, don't cry, Becky, I don't care for her any more."

"Yes, you do, Tom—you know you do."

Tom tried to put his arm about her neck, but she pushed him away and turned her face to the wall, and went on crying. Tom tried again, with gentle words in

过这样的仪式。你知道，你再也不能爱别人，只能爱我啦。你也不能嫁别人，只能嫁我啦，永远，永远不能，好吗？

"好的，我永远不爱别人，只爱你一个，汤姆，我永远不嫁别人，只嫁你——你也不能再娶别人，只有我。"

"一定，当然。上学或回家的时候，如果没别人看的话，你要一直和我走——在舞会上，你挑我，我挑你，因为订过婚的人都这样做。"

"太好了，我以前从没听说过。"

"噢，这可有意思了。我的艾米·劳伦斯——"

贝琪瞪大的眼睛告诉了汤姆他说错话了，他忙打住，不知所措。

"噢，汤姆！那么我不是你第一个订婚的人！"

女孩子开始哭，汤姆说：

"噢，别哭，贝琪，我现在再也不喜欢她了。"

"不，你喜欢，汤姆——你知道你喜欢她。"

汤姆试图搂着她的脖子，却被推开了。她将脸转向墙，继续哭着，汤姆又试着去搂贝琪，嘴

his mouth, and was rejected again. Then his pride was up, and he went outside. He stood about, restless and uneasy, for a while, glancing at the door every now and then, hoping she would regret and come to find him. But she did not. Then he began to feel badly and fear that he was in the wrong. It was a hard struggle with him to make new advances, now, but he encouraged himself and entered. She was still standing back there in the corner, sobbing, with her face to the wall. He went to her and stood a moment, not knowing exactly how to go on. Then he said hesitatingly:

"Becky, I – I don't care for anybody but you."

No reply—but sobs.

"Becky"—pleadingly. "Becky, won't you say something?"

More sobs.

Tom got out his best jewel—a brass knob, and passed it around her so that she could see it, and said:

"Please, Becky, won't you take it?"

She struck it to the floor. Then Tom marched out of the house and over the hills and far away, to return to school no more that day. Pesently Becky began to doubt. She ran to the door; he was not in sight; she flew around to the playyard; he was not there. Then she called:

"Tom! Come back, Tom!"

里还说着温柔的话，可再次被拒绝。这使得他觉得自尊心受到了伤害，他走了出去，在外面站着。有一段时间觉得烦乱不安。他不时地向门瞥去，希望她会后悔、出来找他，可她没。他心情很糟，担心自己是不是错了。到底还进不进去劝贝琪，他很矛盾，最后还是鼓起勇气，走了进去。她仍然在角落里站着，面朝墙抽泣着。他走向她，站了一会儿，不知到底该怎么办，他不安地说：

"贝琪，我——我除了你谁也不喜欢。"

没有回答——只有抽泣。

"贝琪，"他恳求说，"贝琪，你不说点儿什么吗？"

更猛烈地抽泣。

汤姆取出了他最珍贵的宝物，一个青铜圆柄，绕到她的面前：

"贝琪，你不想要它吗？"

她把它打到地上，见此汤姆大步走出教室，翻过小山，远远地走了，那天再也没回学校。这会儿贝琪开始琢磨汤姆哪儿去了。她跑到门口，没看见他；她跑到操场上，他也没有在那儿。她叫着汤姆的名字：

"汤姆！回来，汤姆！"

She listened eagerly, but there was no answer. She had nothing but silence and loneliness. So she sat down to cry again and scold herself; and by this time the pupils went to school again, and she had to hide her sadness and still her broken heart and spent the long, boring, painful afternoon, with no one to exchange sorrows with.

Chapter 8
A Pirate Bold to Be

Tom went from one lane to another to avoid meeting the returning pupils. Half an hour later he was disappearing behind the Douglas building on the top of Cardiff Hill and the schoolhouse was hardly seen away off in the valley behind him. He entered a dense wood, picked his pathless way to the center of it, and sat down. There was not even a gentle wind; the dead noonday heat had even stilled the songs of the birds. The boy's soul was in depression. He sat long with his elbows on his knees and his chin in his hands, thinking. It seemed to him that life was but a trouble at best, and he more than half envied Jommy Hodges, who so lately died; it must be very peaceful, he thought, to lie and sleep and dream forever and ever, with the wind whispering through the trees and

她急切地听着，可却没有回答，陪伴她的只是沉寂与孤独。她坐在那儿又哭了，开始责备自己；这会儿同学们纷纷回来上学了，她不得不掩饰住她的悲伤和破碎的心，消磨那漫长、无聊而又痛苦的下午时光，无处倾诉她的痛苦。

第八章　勇敢的大盗

汤姆穿过一个又一个巷子，避开那些来上学的同学们，半小时后就消失在位于卡迪夫山顶上道格拉斯家那幢房子后面。身后那位于山谷中的学校几乎已经看不见了。他走进草木繁盛的小林子，穿过草丛走到林子中间坐下了，空气中甚至连一丝微风都没有；在这死气沉沉而且酷热的夏日中午，鸟儿也不唱歌了，男孩的情绪很沮丧。他双肘竖在膝上，手托着下巴，思索着。生活对于他意味着更多的麻烦，他几乎嫉妒起最近才死的乔米·赫奇斯了，他想他可以永远平静地躺在那里。沉睡在梦中，风掠过他墓上的花草，与树儿

touching the grass and flowers over the grave, and nothing to bother and feel sad about, ever any more. Now as to this girl, what had he done? Nothing. He had meant the best in the world, and been treated like a dog—like a very dog. She would be sorry someday—maybe when it was too late. Ah, if he could only die for some time!

But mind of youth can never be attached to one thing. Tom presently began to think about this life. What if he turned his back, now, and disappeared mysteriously? What if he went away—ever so far away, into unknown countries beyond the seas—and never came back any more! How would she feel then! He would be a soldier, and return after long years, quite experienced in wars and famous. No—better still, he would join the Indians, and hunt buffaloes and go on the warpath on the mountains and great plains of the Far West, and in the future come back a great chief, wearing feathers, frightfully painted, and walk into Sunday school, causing uncontrollable envy among the pupils. But no, there was something more marvelous even than this. He would be a pirate! That was it! Now his future lay clear before him, shining with unimaginable splendor. How his name would fill the world, and make people tremble! How proud he would go through plowing the dancing seas, in

低语。再也没有什么可以心烦、难过的了。至于那个姑娘，他做什么了？没什么，他本是出于好意。这种好意简直是无与伦比，然而却被像狗一样对待——就像一条狗。终有一天她会后悔的——或许那已经太晚了。啊，如果他能暂时的死去该多好！

　　然而不管怎样，年轻人的思想是不会永远停留在一件事上的。这会儿，汤姆开始思考他的一生。如果现在他扭过头，神秘地消失了，那会怎样呢？如果他走了会怎样——走得远远的，去了海那边不为人知的国度——永远都不回来！那时，她会有什么感觉！他会当一名战士，磨砺沙场多年后，声名显赫地回来，不——还有更好的，他要加入到印第安人中去，和他们一起猎杀野牛，叱咤在大山里的战场中，驰骋在西部辽阔的草原上。等到将来成为大酋长的时候，他再回到家乡，他身上穿着羽毛衣服，涂着可怕的油彩，走进主日学校里，定会引起学生们的羡慕。不，还有更好的，他要当一个海盗！对！当个海盗！现在他的未来清晰地展现在了他的面前，闪着不可想象的光芒。他的名字会家喻户晓，让人家听到就心惊胆战！他乘着长长的、低矮的"风暴精神号"

his long, low, black ship, the *Spirit of the Storm*, with his horrible flag flying at the head of the ship! And when he was most famous, how he would suddenly appear at the old village and walk into church, brown and weather – beaten, in his black clothes and pants, in his great boots, with his red belt and pistols, his sword at his side, his hat with waving plumes, his black flag with the skull and crossbones on it, and hear with great excitement the whispers, "It's Tom Sawyer the Pirate!"

Yes, it was settled; his career was determined. He would run away from home and enter upon it. He would start the very next morning. Therefore, he must now begin to get ready. He would collect his resources together. He went to a rotten log near at hand and began to dig under one end of it with his knife. When he was making all these preparations, Joe Harper appeared. Tom called:

"Stop! Who comes here into Sherwood Forest without my pass?"

"Guy of Guisborne wants no man's pass. Who are you that—that—"

"Dares to say such words," said Tom, —for they talked "by the book," from memory.

"Who are you that dares to say such words?"

黑色轮船，船头上还有飘扬着恐怖的旗子，在颠簸的大海中穿行，劫取财宝，那是何等的荣耀！等他闻名遐迩之日，他会突然出现在这古老的村子里，久经风雨的他拥有一身棕褐色的皮肤，穿着一身黑衣，脚蹬一双大靴子，系着红腰带，插着手枪，旁边还别了一把剑，帽子上挥舞着羽毛，还有一面骷髅旗。他走进教堂，人们激动不已，他们在小声嘀咕："这就是海盗汤姆·索耶！"

是啊，这就妥了！他的事业定了，他将从家里逃出来，开始这项事业，他明天一早就出发，所以他现在必须开始准备了，他要开始收集那些有用的东西。他走到旁边的一块烂木头旁，开始用他的小刀在木头一头的地上挖着。就在他做这些准备工作时，乔·哈普出现了，汤姆叫道：

"别动！谁未经我的许可闯到舍伍德森林了？①"

"吉斯堡的人② 是不要谁的许可的，你——你是谁？"

"居然敢这么说，"汤姆说道。他们是在背书中的"台词"。

"你居然敢这么说，你是谁？"

---

① 舍伍德森林：英国传说中绿林好汉罗宾汉的驻地。
② 吉斯堡的人：罗宾汉的自称。

"I, indeed! I am Robin Hood."[①]

Then they talked and fought as Robin Hood stories had told.

When they went off they felt sad that there were no outlaws like Robin Hood any more, and wondered what modern civilization could claim to have done to compensate for their loss. They said they would rather be outlaws a year in Sherwood Forest than President of the United States forever.

Chapter 9
Tragedy in the Graveyard

At half past nine, that night, Tom and Sid were sent to bed, as usual. They said their prayers, and Sid was soon asleep. Tom lay awake and waited, in restless impatience. When it seemed to him that it must be nearly daylight, he heard the clock strike ten! This was despair. He would have turned from side to side, as his nerves demanded, but he was afraid he might wake Sid. So he lay still, and stared up into the dark. Everything was still. At last he fell asleep, in spite of himself; the clock knocked eleven, but he did not hear it. The rais-

---

① Robin Hood:罗宾汉(英国民间传说中劫富济贫的绿林好汉)。

"我，我是真正的罗宾汉。"

接着，他们又像罗宾汉故事中讲的那样说着，打着。

离开小树林的时候，他们都觉得挺难过的，因为现在再也没有罗宾汉那样的绿林好汉了。俩人还琢磨着现代文明怎能补偿他们的损失，他们说自己宁愿在舍伍德森林里做一年的绿林好汉，也不当一世的美国总统。

第九章　墓地悲剧

那晚九点半的时候，汤姆和赛德像往常一样被打发上了床。祷告之后，赛德很快入睡了。汤姆躺在那儿，毫无睡意，烦躁不安地等着，当他觉得一定都该天亮时，钟才敲响十点钟！他有些绝望了。不安的他总想翻来覆去，可又怕吵醒赛德，因而只好一动不动，在黑暗与寂静中两眼向上瞪着，最后他还是睡着了;钟敲响了十一点，他

ing of a neighboring window disturbed him. A cry of "Go away! You devil!" and the crash of an empty bottle against the back of his aunt's room brought him wide awake, and a single minute later he was dressed and out of the window and creeping along the roof on all fours. He "meow'd" with caution once or twice, as he went; then jumped to the ground. Huckleberry Finn was there, with his dead cat. The boys moved off and disappeared in the dark. At the end of half an hour they were walking through the tall grass of the graveyard.

It was a graveyard of the old-fashioned western kind. It was on a hill, about a mile and a half from the village. A faint wind moaned through the trees, and Tom feared it might be the spirits of the dead, complaining of being disturbed. The boys talked little, and only under their breath, for the time and the place and the seriousness and silence oppressed their spirits. They found the sharp new heap they were seeking, and stayed under the protection of three great elms within a few feet of the grave.

Then they waited in silence for what seemed a long time. Tom felt more oppressive. He must force some talk. So he said in a whisper:

"Huck, do you believe the dead people like us to be here?"

没听着。隔壁窗户拉起的声音吵醒了他。紧接着一声大喊:"快滚!你这个混蛋!"一声空瓶子砸到他姨妈房子后面打碎的声音让他彻底清醒了。只一分钟之后他就穿好了衣服,爬出了窗户,上了屋顶。他边爬边小心翼翼地喵了一两声,接着跳到了地面上。哈克就在那儿,还有他的死猫。孩子们走远了,消失在黑暗当中,半小时后他们已在墓地高高的草丛中穿行了。

这是西方老式的墓地,坐落在离村一英里半的小山上。微风在树林中呻吟,汤姆忧心忡忡,觉得这可能是死人的鬼魂在抱怨被吵着了,孩子们很少说话,就是说,声音也压得很低。因为这时间、这地点、这事情的严重性,以及周围的寂静都太压抑了。他们找到了他们正在寻找的那堆土,很明显是新的。为了安全起见,他们在离墓地几英尺外的三棵大橡树下呆了一会儿。

他们静静等了似乎很长时间,汤姆的心情越来越沉重,他必须强迫自己说点儿什么。所以他低声说:

"哈克,你觉得死人喜欢我们在这儿吗?"

"I wish I know. It's very solemn here, isn't it?"

"I bet it is."

There was a long pause, while the boys thought about this matter in their heart. Then Tom whispered:

"Say, Huck—do you think Hoss Williams hears us talking?"

"Of course he does. At least his spirit does."

Tom, after a pause:

"I wish I'd said Mister Williams. But I never meant any harm. Everybody calls him Hoss."

"A body can't be too particular about how they talk about these dead people, Tom."

Then the conversation died again.

Presently Tom seized his comrade's arm and said: "Sh!"

"What is it, Tom?" And the two clung together with beating hearts.

"Sh! There it is again! Didn't you hear it?"

"I—"

"There! Now you hear it."

"Lord, Tom, they're coming! They're coming sure. What'll we do?"

"Oh, Tom, they can see in the dark, same as cats. I wish I hadn't come."

"Oh, don't be afraid. I don't believe they'll

"我要是知道就好了。这儿静得可怕，不是吗？"

"的确是这样。"

又是一段长时间的沉寂，孩子们各自在心中想着这回事，汤姆低声说：

"你说，哈克——你觉得豪斯·威廉姆斯能听到我们说话吗？"

"当然能，至少他的魂能。"

稍停片刻，汤姆说：

"我希望我刚说的是威廉姆斯先生。可不论怎样我没什么恶意。每个人都叫他豪斯。"

"死人最在意别人怎么称呼他们了，汤姆。"之后谈话中断了。

这时汤姆抓住同伴的胳膊，说：

"嘘！"

"怎么啦，汤姆？"两个人紧紧抱着，心怦怦乱跳。

"嘘！又有声音了！你听到没有。"

"我——"

"在那儿！你听到了吧。"

"上帝，汤姆，他们来了！一定是他们来了，我们该怎么办？"

"噢，汤姆，他们即使晚上也什么都能看见，就像猫似的。我真希望我没来这儿。"

"别害怕，我相信他们不会惹咱们的，我们又

bother us. We aren't doing any harm. If we keep perfectly still, maybe they won't notice us at all."

"I'll try to, Tom, but, Lord, I'm all of a shiver."

"Listen!"

The boys bent their heads together and hardly breathed. A low sound of voices rose up from the far end of the graveyard.

"Look! See there!" whispered Tom. "What is it?"

"It's devil-fire. Oh, Tom, this is terrible."

Some vague figures came here from the dark, lifting an old-fashioned lantern. Presently Huckleberry whispered with a shiver:

"They're the devils, sure enough. Three of them! Lord, Tom, we're going to die! Can you pray?"

"I'll try, but don't you be afraid. They aren't going to hurt us. Now I lay me down to sleep, I—"

"Sh!"

"What is it, Huck?"

"They're humans! One of them is, anyway. One of them is Old Muff Potter's voice."

"No—it isn't so, is it?"

"I bet I know it. Don't you stir nor move. He isn't sharp enough to notice us. Maybe he is drunk as usual."

没伤害他们。如果我们一动不动地在这儿呆着，或许他们压根儿注意不到咱们。"

"我尽量不动吧，汤姆。可是，上帝呀，我浑身抖得慌。"

"听！"

孩子们一起把头低下，几乎屏住了呼吸，墓地那边远远地传来了低低的声音。

"看！看那儿！"汤姆悄声说，"那是什么？"

"是鬼火，噢，汤姆，太可怕了。"

几个模模糊糊的身影在黑暗中走来，手里还拎着一个老式灯笼，这时哈克贝历颤抖着说：

"他们一定是鬼，一共三个！上帝，汤姆，我们要死了！你能祈祷吗？"

"我可以试试，但你别怕，他们不会伤害我们的。现在我躺倒睡觉，我——"

"嘘！"

"什么，哈克？"

"他们是人！至少有一个是，有一个人的声音是老穆夫·波特的。"

"不像啊，不是吗？"

"肯定是的。你不要再动了。他没有注意到我们，也许他像平常一样喝多了。"

"All right, I'll keep quiet. Say, Huck, I know another's voice; it's Injun Joe."

"That's so. What can they be up to?"

The whisper died wholly out, now, for the three men had reached the grave and stood within a few feet of the boys' hiding place.

"Here it is," said the third voice; and the speaker held the lantern up and showed the face to young Dr. Robinson.

Potter and Injun Joe were carrying a handbarrow with a rope and several shovels on it. They began to open the grave.

"Hurry, men!" he said in a low voice; "the moon might come out at any moment."

They answered and went on digging. Finally a spade struck upon the coffin and within another minute or two the men had raised it out on the ground. They opened the lid with their shovels, got out the body and threw it rudely on the ground. The moon drifted from behind the clouds and exposed the pale face. The barrow was ready and the corpse was placed on it, covered with a blanket, and bound to its place with the rope.

"Now the cursed thing is ready, and you'll give me another five, or here she stays."said Potter.

"That's the subject!" said Injun Joe.

"好吧，我不动了。嗨，哈克，我听出另一个人的声音，是印第安人乔。"

"是，他们到这儿干吗？"

现在他们连小声嘀咕也不多了，因为三个男人已经来到墓旁，距离孩子们的藏身之地只有几英尺远。

"就是这儿。"第三个人的声音说道，说话人举起了灯笼，照亮了他的脸庞，那是年轻的罗宾森医生。

波特和印第安人乔正推着一个小车，上面放了一根绳子和几把铁锹。他们开始挖墓了。

"快点儿，伙计们！"他低声说，"月亮随时都可能出来。"

他们应了一声，继续挖着。最后铁锹终于碰到了棺材，一两分钟之后，棺材已经被抬到了地面上。他们用铁锹打开了棺材盖，取出尸体，粗鲁地扔到了地上。月亮从云中探了出来，照在死人苍白的脸上。手推车已经准备好了，尸体放在了上面，用一条毛毯盖着，用绳子捆上，固定住。

"现在这该死的东西准备好了，你得再给我五个金币，否则就得让她在这儿躺着了，"波特说。

"说得对！"印第安人乔附和道。

"What does it mean?" said the doctor. "You required your pay in advance, and I've paid you."

"Yes, and you have done more than that," said Injun Joe, coming to the doctor. "Five years ago you drove me away from your father's kitchen one night, when I came to ask for something to eat, and you said I wasn't there for any good; and when I swore I'd take revenge if it took a hundred years, your father put me to prison. Did you think I'd forget? The Injun blood isn't in me for nothing. And now I've got you and you got to settle it, you know!"

He was threatening the doctor, with his fist in his face, by this time. The doctor struck out suddenly and knocked the man on the ground. Potter dropped his knife, and shouted:

"Here, now, don't you hit my friend!" and the next moment he had fought with the doctor and the two were struggling. Injun Joe sprang to his feet, his eyes burning with passion, seized Potter's knife, and went creeping, catlike and bending, round and round about the two, looking for a chance. All at once the doctor flung himself free, seized the heavy headboard of Williams's grave, and knocked Potter to the earth with it— and in the same instant Joe saw his chance and drove the knife in the young man's breast. He swayed and fell

"什么意思?"医生问,"你们要求提前把钱付清,我已经给你们了。"

"是啊。你做的还不止这些呢!"印第安人乔说着,走向医生,"五年前的一天晚上,我求你给我点儿吃的时候,你把我从厨房赶了出来,还说我在你那儿真一无是处;正当我发誓我要报仇,哪怕需要一百年的时候,你爸爸把我送进了监狱。你认为我会忘了这一切吗?印第安人的血在我身上不是白流的,要知道现在你栽到我手上了,这事你得摆平了。"

他威胁着医生,在他面前挥着拳头。医生突然出手,将他打倒在地。波特扔掉他的刀子,喊道:

"好哇,你打我的朋友!"接着他就去搂医生,俩人扭打在了一起,印第安人乔跳了起来,眼里冒着火,抓起波特的刀,像猫一样弓着身,慢慢地,悄悄地,围着那两个人转呀,转呀,寻找着机会,突然医生猛地脱了身,抓起威廉姆斯坟上的一块重木牌,把波特砸倒在地——就在同时,乔看到了自己的机会,把刀戳向那位年轻人的胸部。医生晃了晃,身子倒了下去,压在了波特身

partly upon Potter, and his blood flew over him. The two frightened boys went fast away in the dark.

Presently, when the moon appeared again, Injun Joe was standing over the two bodies, thinking. The doctor murmured and gave a long gasp or two and was still. Joe said:

"I've settled it—damn you."

Then he robbed the body, after which he put the fatal knife in Potter's open right hand, and sat down. Three – four – five minutes passed, and then Potter began to stir and moan. His hand closed upon the knife; he raised it, glanced at it, and let it fall, with a shudder. Then he sat up, pushing the body from him, and gazed at it, and then looked around him, confusedly. His eyes met Joe's.

"Lord, how is this, Joe?" he said.

"It's a dirty business," said Joe, without moving. "What did you do it for?"

"I! I never did it!"

"Look here! That can't be removed."

Potter trembled and grew white.

"I thought I'd got clear-minded. Joe, tell me how it was, Joe. Oh, it's terrible."

"Why, you two were fighting, and he beat you with the stone and you fell down; and then up you came, all

上，血也流在了他的身上。两个受惊的男孩在黑暗中飞速离开了。

不一会儿，月亮又出来了，印第安人乔站在两个人的身旁，沉思着，医生哼哼了几声，长长地吐了一两口气，就一动不动了。乔说：

"我已经摆平了——他妈的。"

他在医生身上搜了搜，又把那致命的小刀放在波特打开的右手里，坐下了。三分钟、四分钟、五分钟过去了，波特动了动，呻吟着。他用手握紧了刀；起身瞥了一眼，吓得浑身发抖，松手把刀扔掉了。他坐了起来，把死人推开，瞪着眼看了看，又迷惑地环视了四周，他的目光对上了乔的。

"上帝呀，这是怎么回事，乔？"他说。

"这事干得可够拙劣的，"乔不动声色地说，"你这是干吗呀？"

"我！我没干过这档子事！"

"看看这儿！铁证如山！"

波特全身战栗着，脸都白了。

"我想我得头脑清醒一点儿，乔，告诉我这是怎么回事。噢，太可怕了。"

"嗯，你们俩人在打架，他用木牌把你砸倒了，之后你又摇摇晃晃地起来。就在他又要砸你

swaying, and seized the knife and jammed it into him, just as he knocked on you—and you've laid there."

"Oh, I didn't know what I was doing. I wish I may die this minute if I did. It was all because of whisky and the excitement, I think. I never used a weapon in my life before, Joe. Don't tell! Say you won't tell, Joe. I always liked you, Joe, and stood up for you, too. Don't you remember? You won't tell, will you, Joe?" And the poor creature dropped on his knees before the cold murderer.

"I won't reject you. That's as fair as a man can say."

"Oh, Joe, you're an angel. I'll bless you for this the longest day I live." And Potter began to cry.

"Come now, that's enough of that. This isn't the time for crying. You leave here that way and I'll clear this. Move, now, don't leave any tracks behind you."

Potter started to run. Joe stood looking after him.

Two or three minutes later the murdered man, the blanketed corpse, the lidless coffin, and the open grave were under no inspection but the moon's. The stillness was complete again, too.

的时候，你抓了刀子，捅向他——之后你们就都躺在这儿了。"

"噢，我真不知道我都干了些什么。如果是我干的，我恨不能立刻死掉，都怨这威士忌，害得我酒后发疯，我这辈子还从未使过任何凶器呢。乔，别告诉别人，说你不告诉别人，乔。我一向很喜欢你，乔，我一直站在你一边，你不记得吗？你不告诉别人，好吗，乔？"可怜的家伙扑通跪在了冷酷的杀手面前。

"我不会抛弃你的，这不公平。"

"噢，你真是一个天使，我一辈子都会为你祝福，"波特开始哭了。

"好了，够了，这不是哭的时候，你走那条路离开这儿。我来清理现场，快走，现在，别留下任何痕迹。"

波特跑了，乔站在后面看着他。

两三分钟后，被杀的人，毛毯裹着的尸体，没盖的棺材，打开的墓都留在了月亮的审视之下。这儿又恢复了宁静。

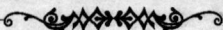

Chapter 10
Terrible Prediction of the Howling Dog

The two boys flew on and on, toward the village, speechless with horror. They glanced backward over their shoulders from time to time, frightened, as if they feared they might be followed. Every stump in their path seemed a man and an enemy, and made them catch their breath; and as they ran by some remote cottages that lay near the village, the barking of the aroused watchdogs seemed to give wings to their feet.

"If we can only get to the old tannery before we break down!" whispered Tom, in short catches between breaths. "I can't stand it much longer."

Huckleberry's hard breaths were his only reply. At last, breast to breast, they burst through the open door and fell thankful and rather tired. By and by their pulses slowed down, and Tom whispered:

"Huckleberry, what do you think will come of this?"

"If Dr. Robinson dies, I think hanging'll come of it."[1]

---

[1] hanging'll come of it: 凶手最终会被绞死。

第十章 野狗嚎叫，恐怖预兆

两个男孩飞快地朝村子跑呀，跑呀，吓得一句话都不说。他们不时惊恐地扭过头向后瞥去，惟恐有什么会追着他们。面前出现的每个树桩都像个人，像个敌人，吓得他们透不上气。他们跑过村子附近偏僻的农舍时，听到看门狗被吵醒后汪汪的叫声。这下更像插上了翅膀一样。

"但愿咱们累趴下之前，能到那个老制菜坊！"汤姆趁喘气的当中气喘吁吁地说："我实在受不了了。"

哈克贝历的惟一回答就是呼呼的喘气声了。最后，他们肩并肩一同冲入了老制菜坊那扇打开的门，躺倒在地，疲惫不堪，为能活着到这儿感到欣慰极了。渐渐地，脉搏缓和了下来，汤姆低声说：

"哈克贝历，你觉得那事儿会怎样？"

"我想如果罗宾森医生死了的话，凶手最终会被绞死的。"

Tom thought awhile, then he said:

"Who'll tell? We?"

"What are you talking about? Suppose something happened and Injun Joe didn't hang? Why, he'd kill us some time or other."

"That's just what I was thinking to myself, Huck."

"If anybody tells, let Muff Potter do it, if he's foolish enough. He's generally drunk enough."

Tom said nothing—went on thinking. Presently he whispered:

"Huck, Muff Potter didn't know it. How can he tell?"

"What's the reason he didn't know it?"

"Because he'd just got that blow when Injun Joe did it. Do you think he could see anything? Do you think he knew anything?"

Then they pricked their thumbs and used their blood to sign their initials to swear they could keep silent about the matter.

A figure crept secretly through break in the other end of the ruined building, now, but they did not notice it.

They continued to whisper for some little time. Presently a dog sent up a long, sad howl just outside—

汤姆想了一会儿，说：

"谁会说出来呢，我们吗？"

"你说什么呢？想想万一发生点儿什么事，印第安人乔没被绞死呢？他非得在哪一天把我们杀了不可。"

"这也正是我想的，哈克。"

"如果有人说，就让穆夫·波特说吧，如果他真那么愚蠢的话。他总是醉醺醺的。"

汤姆没吭声——继续思考着，之后他小声说：

"哈克，穆夫·波特不知道发生的一切，他怎么说？"

"他为什么不知道？"

"因为印第安人乔杀人时，他已经被砸昏了，你觉得他能看到什么吗？你觉得他能知道什么吗？"

随后他们把各自的大拇指扎破，用血写下各自名字的第一个字母，以此发誓他们对此事保持沉默。

这时，有个身影从破房子另一头的豁口悄悄地爬了进来，他们没注意到。

他们继续小声嘀咕了一会儿，突然距离他们

within ten feet of them. The boys held each other suddenly, in a pain of fright.

"Which of us does he mean?" gasped Huckleberry.

"I don't know—look through the hole. Quick!"

"No, you, Tom!"

"I can't—I can't do it, Huck!"

"Please, Tom. There it is again!"

Tom, trembling with fear, gave in, and put his eyes to the hole. His whisper was hardly heard when he said:

"Oh, Huck, IT'S A STRAY DOG!"

"Quick, Tom, quick! Who does he mean?"

"Huck, he must mean us both—we're right together."

"Oh, Tom, I think we're going to die. I think I have been so wicked."

And Tom began to sob a little.

And Huckleberry began to sob too.

Tom choked off and whispered:

"Look, Huck, look! He's got his back to us!"

Huck looked, with joy in his heart.

The howling stopped. Tom pricked up his ears.

"Sh! What's that?" he whispered.

"Sounds like—like pigs grunting. No—it's somebody snoring, Tom."

十英尺之外的一条狗在外面发出一声长长的悲伤的嚎叫，俩人吓得急忙搂住了对方。

"它冲的是咱们俩谁？"哈克喘着气。

"我不知道——从这个小洞向那边看，快！"

"不，你看，汤姆！"

"我不行——我不行，哈克！"

"求你了，汤姆，又叫了！"

汤姆吓得浑身发抖，可他还是屈服了，眼睛放在了洞上，他说话的声音小得几乎都听不见：

"噢，哈克，是条野狗！"

"快点，汤姆，快看看冲谁叫呢？"

"哈克，它肯定冲的咱们俩——咱们在一起呢。"

"噢，汤姆，我觉得咱们难逃一死了，可能是我过去坏事干太多了。"

汤姆开始抽泣。

哈克贝历也开始哭了。

一会儿，汤姆停下了抽泣，低声说：

"看，哈克，看，它现在背对我们啦！"

哈克一看，心中一阵喜悦。

嚎叫停下来了，汤姆竖起了耳朵。

"嘘！什么声？"他悄声问。

"听起来像——像猪打哼哼，不——是有人在打呼噜，汤姆。"

"That is it! Where is it, Huck?"

"I believe it's down at the other end."

The spirit of adventure rose in the boy's souls once more.

"Huck, do you dare to go if I lead?"

"I don't like to, much. Tom, suppose it's Injun Joe!"

Tom trembled. But presently the temptation rose up strong again and the boys agreed to try, with the understanding that they would take to their heels if the snoring stopped. So they went tiptoeing secretly down, the one behind the other. When they had got to within five steps of the snorer, Tom stepped on a stick, and it broke with a sharp noise. The man moaned and his face came into the moonlight. It was Mutter Potter. The boys' hearts had stood still, and their hopes too, when the man moved, but their fears passed away now. They tiptoed out, and stood at a little distance to exchange a parting word.

"Oh! It's him!" said both boys, in a breath.

Tom said: "They say when a stray dog howls, someone is going to die. I'm sure Muff Potter is going to die, Huck."

Then they separated, thinking. When Tom crept in at his bedroom window the night was almost spent. He

"没错！在哪儿呢，哈克？"

"肯定在房子的那一头。"

那股冒险劲儿又在孩子们身上滋生起来。

"哈克，如果我打头，你敢去吗？"

"我不太想去，汤姆，想想如果那是印第安人乔呢！"

汤姆战栗了一下，然而过了一会儿，俩人却抵挡不住诱惑，都同意去看一看，都明白如果呼噜声停下来，他们会拔脚就跑，俩人偷偷地踮着脚向前走，一个跟一个。就在他们走到离打呼噜的人还有五英尺的时候，汤姆踩到了一根棍上，"啪"的一声，棍子折断了，声音很清脆，那个人哼了一下转了过来，暴露在月光下，是穆夫·波特。就在他转身时，孩子们的心都揪住了，以为自己这下完了，可一看是波特，他们的恐惧消失了。俩人又踮着脚出来了，站在稍远的地方作临别前的交谈。

"是他！"俩孩子异口同声地说道。

汤姆说："人们常说如果一条野狗嚎叫的话，就意味着有人要死了，我担保穆夫·波特要送命了。"

说完俩人就分手了，各自心事重重。当汤姆悄悄地从窗口爬进卧室时，天快要亮了。他小心

undressed very cautiously, and fell asleep congratulating himself that nobody knew of his escaping. He was not aware that the gently snoring Sid was awake, and had been so for an hour.

When Tom awoke, Sid was dressed and gone. He was amazed. Why had he not been called, as usual? Within five minutes he was dressed and downstairs, feeling painful and sleepy. The family were still at table, but they had finished breakfast. There was no voice of scolding, but they avoided looking at him and there was a silence and an air of seriousness that frightened Tom. He sat down and tried to seem happy, but it was uphill work; it roused no smile, no response, and he became silent and let his heart sink down to the depths.

After breakfast his aunt took him aside. His aunt wept over him and asked him how he could go and break her old heart so; and finally told him to go on, and ruin himself and bring her gray hairs with sorrow to the grave, for it was no use for her to try any more. This was worse than a thousand whippings, and Tom's heart was more painful now than his body. He cried, he pleaded for forgiveness, promised to improve over and over again, and then received his dismissal.

He left the presence too miserable to even feel revengeful toward Sid; and so the latter's quick escape

翼翼地脱下衣服睡觉，庆幸没人知道他曾逃走了。他不知轻轻打呼噜的赛德实际醒着呢，而且醒了一个小时了。

第二天，汤姆醒来时，赛德已经穿好衣服，走了。他有点吃惊，怎么没人叫他。五分钟后穿好了衣服，下了楼，感到浑身发疼，还很困。一家人已经吃过饭了，正坐在桌前，没人责备他，可谁也不看他。那种沉寂和严肃的气氛让汤姆很害怕。他坐下来，试图表现得很高兴，这如上山一样困难；没人因此向他微笑，或者作出任何反应。他也开始一声不吭，任由自己的心情变糟。

早饭后，姨妈把他拉到了一边，哭着问他怎么可以这样伤她一位老人的心；最后告诉他，既然她无论怎么努力帮他都无济于事，就让他这样下去吧，毁了自己，让姨妈也愁白了头，带着悲伤走进坟墓。这话可比用鞭子抽他一千下都疼。他哭了，恳求姨妈的原谅，一再许诺要改好。就这样，姨妈让他走了。

他离开了家，心情非常难过，根本没想着要报复赛德。可赛德一见到他，立刻从后门溜了，

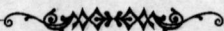

through the back gate was unnecessary. He went to school sadly, and took his beating, together with Joe Harper, for playing truant the day before. Then he took his seat and his heart broke when he saw the knob he had given to Becky.

Chapter 11
Conscience Tortures Tom

Close upon the hour of noon the whole village was suddenly electrified with the terrible news. The tale flew from man to man, from group to group, from house to house, with little less than telegraphic speed. Of course the school-master gave holiday for that afternoon; the town would have thought strangely of him if he had not.

A knife had been found close the murdered man, and it had been recognized by somebody as belonging to Muff Potter. And it was said that a man had seen Potter washing himself in the "stream" about one or two o' clock in the morning, and that Potter had at once escaped—the washing was not a habit with Potter. It was also said that the town had been searched for this "murderer" (the public was not slow in the matter of finding evidence and arriving at a verdict), but that he could not be found.

这真是大可不必。他悲伤地来到学校，因为昨天逃学一事和乔·哈普一起挨打了。回到座位上，看到了他送贝琪的圆柄，心都碎了。

第十一章　良心不安的汤姆

接近中午的时候，一个消息传遍了整个村子，人们都震惊了。消息一传十，十传百，速度一点都不亚于电报。当然，学校老师也给学生们放了一下午假，否则，镇上的人会认为他好奇怪。

人们在被害人身边发现了一把刀，有人认出那是穆夫·波特的。据说有人半夜一两点时看到波特在小溪洗澡，而波特一看到有人就跑了——洗澡可不是他的习惯。还有人说整个镇子都找遍了，都没找着波特。①

---

① 老百姓寻找证据、作出判断一点也不慢。

All the town was drifting toward the graveyard. Tom's heartbreak disappeared and he joined the procession, not because he would not a thousand times rather go anywhere else, but because an awful, unaccountable fascination drew him on. Arriving at the dreadful place, he wormed his small body through the crowd and saw the sad scene. It seemed to him an age since he was there before. Somebody pinched his arm. He turned, and his eyes met Huckleberry's. Then both looked elsewhere at once, and wondered if anybody had noticed anything in their mutual glance. But everybody was talking, and intent upon the horrible scene before them.

"Poor fellow!" "Poor young fellow!" "Muff Potter'll hang for this if they catch him!" This was the chief subject of remark; and the clergyman said, "It was a judgment; his hand is here."

Now Tom shivered from head to heel; for his eye fell upon the cold face of Injun Joe. At this moment the crowd began to sway and struggle, and voices shouted, "It's him! It's him! He was coming himself!"

"Who? Who?" from twenty voices.

"Muff Potter!"

"He's stopped!—Look out, he's turning! Don't let him get away!"

People in the branches of the trees over Tom's head

全镇的人都来到墓地，汤姆这会儿也不再难过了，他加入了去墓地的队伍，并不是因为他不愿去其他地方，而是有一种难以形容的诱惑强烈地吸引着他。来到这个可怕的地方后，他小小的身子在人群中穿来穿去。来到了前面，汤姆看到了那悲伤的一幕。他觉得自己离开这块地方似乎很长时间了。这时有人拧了他一下。他转过身，目光与哈克贝历相遇。俩人立刻又朝别处望去，看看是否有人注意到了他们相互对视，好在每个人都正关注着眼前可怕的景象，互相讨论着，没人注意到他们。

"可怜的家伙！""可怜的年轻小伙子！""穆夫·波特如果被抓住的话，他肯定会被绞死的！"这是谈话的主题。牧师说："这是报应呀！他的手纹在这儿呢。"

这时汤姆从头到脚都开始哆嗦；因为他看到了印第安人乔那冷酷的脸。一会儿，人群开始涌动，拥挤。有人喊："是他！是他！他自己来了！"

"谁？谁？"很多人问。

"穆夫·波特！"

"他停住了！——小心，他转身了！别让他跑了！"

站在汤姆头顶上方树杈上的人说，他没有企

said he wasn't trying to get away——he only looked doubt-ful and puzzled.

The crowd fell apart, now, and the sheriff came through, leading Potter by the arm. The poor fellow's face looked tired, and his eyes showed the fear. When he stood before the murdered man, he began to tremble and he put his face in his hands and burst into tears.

"I didn't do it, friends," he sobbed.

Potter lifted his face and looked around him with a miserable hopelessness in his eyes. He saw Injun Joe, and shouted:

"Oh, Injun Joe, you promised me you'd never——"

"Is that your knife?"

Potter would have fallen if they had not caught him and eased him to the ground.

Huckleberry and Tom stood dumb and staring, and heard the stonyhearted liar make his calm statement, they expecting every moment that the clear sky would de-liver God's lightening upon his head and wondering to see how long the stroke was delayed. And when he had finished and still stood alive and whole, their impulse to break their oath and save the poor betrayed prisoner's life faded and disappeared, for obviously it would be fa-tal to be against that villain.

Tom's fearful secret and distressing conscience dis

图逃跑——他只是看着，不知所措，挺怀疑发生在这的一切。

人群让出了一条道，治安官拽着波特走了过来，这个可怜的家伙看起来很疲惫，眼神中显露出恐惧。当站在被害人面前时，他开始颤抖，双手捧住了脸，又哭起来。

"这事不是我干的，朋友们。"他抽泣着。

波特抬起脸，向四周环视，一副可怜无助的样子。他看到了印第安人乔，喊道：

"噢，印第安人乔。你向我许诺过的，你永远不会——"

"那可是你的刀？"

如果不是旁边有人扶住他，把他放在地上，他早已瘫那儿了。

哈克贝历和汤姆目瞪口呆地望着这一切，听着那个铁石心肠的骗子冷静地讲所发生的一切。他们无时不希望上帝能够在晴天来一声霹雳，击死这个骗子；可又纳闷这一切为什么迟迟不来。他们原本冲动着不再信守誓言，挽救那可怜的波特。他已遭朋友抛弃，马上就要锒铛入狱。可当乔说完话，仍毛发未损活生生地站那儿时，他们那冲动也慢慢地淡了，消失了，因为很明显，与这个恶棍作对——会让他们丢命的。

汤姆保守的秘密令他惊恐，良知令他痛苦，在

turbed his sleep for as much as a week after this; and at breakfast one morning Sid said:

"Tom, you turn around and around and talk in your sleep so much that you keep me awake half the time."

Tom turned pale and dropped his eyes.

"It's a bad sign," said Aunt Polly seriously. "What did you get on your mind, Tom?"

"Nothing." But the boy's hand shook so that he spilled his coffee.

"And you do talk such things," Sid said. "Last night you said, 'It's blood, it's blood, that's what it is!' You said that over and over. And you said, 'Don't torment me so—I'll tell!' Tell what? What is it you'll tell?"

Everything was swimming before Tom. There is no telling what might have happened now, but luckily the concern passed out of Aunt Polly's face and she came to Tom's relief without knowing it. She said:

"It's that dreadful murder. I dreamed about it almost every night myself. Sometimes I dreamed it's me that did it."

Mary said she had been affected much the same way. Sid seemed satisfied. Tom got out of the presence as quickly as he could, and after that he complained of toothache for a week, and tied up his jaws every night.

这之后整整一周的睡梦中都折磨着他；一天早饭时，赛德说：

"汤姆，你睡觉的时候翻过来覆过去的，还不停地说话，搅得我半宿都睡不着。"

汤姆的脸变得灰白，低下了眼睛。

"这可是不好的迹象，"波莉姨妈严肃地说，"你脑子都在想什么呢，汤姆？"

"没什么，"可这男孩的手却不停地抖着，把咖啡都洒了。

"你还说这些话了，"赛德说，"昨晚你说'是血，是血，就是血！'你不停地说呀说。你还说，'别这样折磨我了——我说！'说什么？你要说什么么？"

所有的一切都在汤姆眼前闪现。他不知道将会发生什么。可幸运的是，听到这些话，波莉姨妈脸上的焦虑消失了。她替汤姆解了围，自己却没意识到。她说：

"都是那场可怕的谋杀。我自己每天晚上梦的最多的都是这个。有时我还梦到自己就是杀人犯呢。"

玛丽说她自己也一样受到影响。赛德似乎满意了，汤姆尽快地离开了饭桌。这之后的一个星期他不停地诉苦说牙疼，因而每晚睡觉的时候都

He never knew that Sid lay nightly watching, and frequently slipped the bandage free and then leaned on his elbow listening a long time, and afterward slipped the bandage back to its place again. Tom's distress of mind wore off gradually and the toothache grew annoying and was discarded. If Sid really managed to make everything out of Tom's broken words, he kept it to himself.

It seemed to Tom that his schoolmates never would stop playing with ingves ts or the dead cats, and thus keeping his trouble present to his mind. Sid noticed that Tom never showed himself off at these questions and always avoided them though it had been his habit to take the lead in all new things. Sid was surprised, but said nothing.

Every day or two, during this time of sorrow, Tom watched his chance and went to the little jail window and offered small comforts through to the "murderer". These offerings greatly helped to ease Tom's conscience.

The villagers had a strong desire to wrap Injun Joe with tar and feather and make him walk on the street, for stealing corpse, but so frightening was his character that nobody could be found who was willing to take the lead in the matter, so it was given up. He had been careful to begin both of his inquest statements with the fight, without confessing the grave robbery that went before it;

把下巴绑了起来。他根本不知道赛德每晚都躺在那儿看他呢，还时不时地把他的绷带放开，胳膊枕着脑袋听汤姆说梦话，听很长时间之后把绷带再绑回去。逐渐地汤姆精神上的痛苦消失了，他也觉得牙疼怪麻烦的，就把牙疼这事还有绷带什么的扔一边了。如果赛德真要从汤姆断断续续的梦话了解到一切，他是不会告诉别人的。

汤姆觉得他的同学似乎不停地玩活死猫验尸的把戏，搞得他脑子里总摆脱不掉那件烦心事。赛德注意到对那些问题，汤姆再也不显能了，总在试图回避，可以往汤姆最爱在新鲜事儿面前领个头，赛德觉得很奇怪，却没说什么。

在那段磨人的日子里，每过一两天，汤姆都会寻找机会到那个小监狱，从窗口将他带来的小小慰问品递给"凶手"。因为只有这样，汤姆才觉得不安的良心能得到很多安慰。

村里的人都特别希望能给印第安人乔这个盗尸贼浑身浇上沥青，插上羽毛，让他当街示众。可他的性格太可怕了，没人愿意带头干这件事，因而只好放弃了。乔每次回答有关那场争斗的询问时都非常谨慎，不坦白发生在那之前的盗尸事

therefore it was thought wisest not to try the case in the court at present.

Chapter 12
The Cat and the Painkiller

One of the reasons why Tom's mind had drifted away from its secret troubles was that it had found a new and important matter to interest itself about. Becky Thatcher had stopped coming to school. Tom had struggled with his pride a few days, and tried to "whistle her down the wind," but failed. He began to find himself hanging around her father's house at nights, and feeling very miserable. She was ill. What if she should die! He no longer took an interest in war, nor even in piracy. The charm of life was gone; there was nothing but sadness left. He put his toys away; there was no joy in them any more. His aunt was concerned. She began to try all ways to cure him. She was one of those people who love to try all new ways of producing health or mending it she learned. But she never doubted she was not an angel of curing to the suffering people.

After being treated in various ways, Tom grew more and more unhappy and pale. The boy had become indifferent to cruel treatment by this time. This filled the old

件；因而目前让谋杀案上庭还不是明智之举。

第十二章　猫咪与止痛药

汤姆之所以不再为他要保守的秘密而烦乱不安是因为他有新的、更重要的事情要关注。贝琪最近一直没来学校，头几天他为顾全自尊心而矛盾着，试图让自己满不在乎，可却不行。后来他开始发现自己晚上的时候总可怜巴巴地在她爸爸屋子周围晃悠。他得知她病了，担心如果她死了怎么办？这会儿，他对什么战争啦，甚至是当海盗啦都不感兴趣了。生活的魅力没有了；剩下的只是忧伤。他把他的小玩意儿也扔到了一边，因为他觉得这些东西也没意思了。他的姨妈对此忧心忡忡。她开始试着用各种方法为他治病，她这种女人喜欢尝试所有新学来的各种治病健身方法，却从不怀疑对于那些遭受病痛之苦的人，自己是不是治愈的天使。

在接受了各种各样的治疗方法之后，汤姆变得更加郁闷苍白了。现在他对于各种针对他的治疗方法都已经无动于衷了，这使得老太太焦虑不

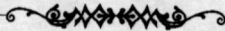

lady's heart with anxiety. This indifference must be broken up at any cost. Now she heard of painkiller for the first time. She bought a lot at once. She tasted it and was filled with thankfulness. It was simply fire in a liquid form. She gave Tom a teaspoonful and watched with the deepest anxiety for the result. Her troubles were instantly at rest, her soul at peace again, for the "indifference" was broken up. The boy could not have shown a wilder, heartier interest if she had built a fire under him.

Tom felt that it was time to wake up. So he thought over various plans for relief, and finally hit upon that of claiming to be fond of painkiller. He asked for it so often that he became troublesome, and his aunt ended by telling him to help himself and stop bothering her. She found that the medicine did really reduce, but it did not occur to her that the boy was mending a crack in the floor with it.

One day Tom was filling the crack with painkiller when his aunt's yellow cat came along, purring, eying the teaspoon, and begging for a taste. Tom said:

"Don't ask for it unless you want it, Peter."

But Peter showed that he did want it.

"You'd better make sure."

Peter was sure.

安，她要不惜代价地打破这种无动于衷。这时，她平生第一次听说了止痛药，立刻买了许多。她尝了尝，心中无限感激，那药尝起来就像火一样，只不过是液体的，她给汤姆喝了满满一勺，异常焦虑地观望着会发生的结果。然后她的不安立刻消失了，她的灵魂又恢复了平静。因为她看到汤姆不再无动于衷了，他又变得生气勃勃了，就是给他屁股底下点团火，他也不会比现在更疯狂了。

汤姆觉得他该清醒了，随即想到了几种为自己解围的方案。最后决定他要宣称自己喜欢止痛药，要不停地要这种药吃。对此姨妈都觉得烦了，最后告诉他自己去拿，别烦她了。她发现药确实少了，但没有想到这孩子在用药补地板上的裂缝。

一天，正当汤姆用药补地板缝时，姨妈的黄猫喵喵地走来了，盯着那药勺，企求尝尝。汤姆说：

"如果你不想吃就不要尝了，彼得。"

可彼得表示它的确需要。

"你最好确信一下。"

彼得确信自己需要。

"Now you've asked for it, and I'll give it to you, because there isn't anything mean about me; but if you find you don't like it, you mustn't scold anybody but your own self."

Peter was agreeable. So Tom opened his mouth and poured down the painkiller. Peter sprang a couple of yards in the air, and then delivered a war-cry and set off round and round the room, banging against furniture, upsetting flowerpots, and making general damage. Next he rose on his hind feet and jumped around, in wild enjoyment, with his head over his shoulder and his voice showing his unappeasable happiness. Then he went tearing around the house again spreading chaos and destruction in his path. Aunt Polly entered and stood dumbfounded, peering over her glasses; Tom lay on the floor dying with laughter.

"Tom, what on earth troubles that cat?"

"I don't know, aunt." gasped the boy.

"Why, I never see anything like it. What did make him act so?"

"Indeed I don't know, Aunt Polly; cats always act so when they're having a good time."

"They do, do they?"

The old lady was bending down. Too late he discovered her direction of attention. The handle of the tea-

"既然你要，我就给你。我可没什么卑鄙的；可如果你发现自己不喜欢，你可不能怪任何人，只能赖你自己。"

彼得欣然同意了，汤姆打开了它的嘴，把止痛药灌了下去。就看见彼得在空中跳得有几码高，发出了如参战时的那种吼叫，在屋子里转呀转，撞得家具砰砰响，还掀翻了花盆，把屋里搞得一塌糊涂。紧接着它后脚撑地站了起来，头倚着肩膀跳来跳去，声音中显露出难以平静的狂喜。他在房子里奔来跳去，所到之处，大搞破坏，一片狼藉。波莉姨妈走了进来，目瞪口呆地站在那儿，从眼镜上方望着这一切。汤姆躺在地板上都要笑死了。

"汤姆，到底什么把这只猫惹着了?"
"我不知道，姨妈。"孩子喘着气回答着。
"我可从来没见过它这样。到底什么惹得它这样?"

"我真不知道，姨妈，猫高兴的时候都这样。"

"真的吗?"
老太太垂下了腰，等到他发现她已经注意到那儿时已太晚了，床底下的茶匙柄就露在外面。

spoon was visible under the bed. Aunt Polly took it, and he dropped his eyes. Aunt Polly raised him by the usual handle—his ear—and cracked his head soundly with her thimble.

"Now, sir, what did you want to treat that poor dumb beast so for?"

"I did it out of pity—because he hadn't any aunt,"

"Hadn't any aunt! —you numskull. What has that got to do with it?"

"A lot. Because if he had had one she would have burnt him herself! She would have roasted his bones out of him without any more feeling than if he was a human!"

Aunt Polly felt a sudden pain of regret. What was cruelty to a cat might be cruelty to a boy too. She began to soften; she felt sorry. Her eyes watered a little, and she put her hand on Tom's head and said gently:

"I was meaning for the best, Tom. And, Tom, it did do you good."

"I know you were meaning for the best, auntie, and so was I with Peter. It did him good, too. I never saw him get around so since—"

"Oh, go along with you, Tom, before you annoy me again. And you try and see if you can't be a good

波莉姨妈拿起了它，汤姆低下了眼睛。波莉姨妈抓起她常使的汤姆的那个耳朵，把汤姆拎了起来。用顶针把汤姆的头敲得啪啪直响。

"先生，你这样对待那只不会说话的可怜小动物是为了什么？"

"我是可怜它——因为它没有姨妈。"

"没有姨妈——你这傻瓜蛋，这跟没有姨妈有什么关系？"

"关系大了。因为如果它有姨妈，它姨妈就会给它喂那像火一样的药，烧它的五脏六腑，就像它是个人一样，丝毫不可怜它。"

波莉姨妈突然感到悔恨，心中一阵痛楚。对一只猫是残忍的做法，对一个男孩也一样。她开始变得温和起来。心中一阵难过，眼睛也有些湿润，她将手放在汤姆头上，温柔地说：

"我真是出于好意，汤姆。而且，汤姆，这种方法确实起作用了。"

"我知道你是为我好，姨妈，我也是为彼得好，而且也对它起作用了。我从未见过它这样兴高采烈的。"

"噢，快走吧，汤姆，趁你这会儿还没有惹恼我。你试着看看自己能不能成为一个好男孩，哪

boy, for once, and you needn't take any more medicine."

Tom reached school ahead of time. It was noticed that this strange thing had been occurring every day lately. And now, he hung about the gate of the schoolyard instead of playing with his comrades. He was sick, he said, and he was like it. He tried to seem to be looking everywhere but he really was looking—down the road. Presently Jeff Thatcher appeared in sight, and Tom's face lighted; he gazed a moment, and then turned sorrowfully away. When Jeff arrived, Tom spoke to him, and "led up" cautiously to opportunities for words about Becky, but the man never could see the bait. Tom watched and watched, hoping whenever a living dress came in sight, and hating the owner of it as soon as he saw she was not the right one. At last dresses stopped to appear, and he entered the empty schoolhouse hopelessly and sat down to suffer. Then one more dress passed in at the gate, and Tom's heart gave a great bound. The next instant he was out, and "going on" like an Indian; yelling, laughing, chasing boys, jumping over the fence at risk of life, throwing handsprings, standing on his head—doing all the heroic things he could imagine, and keeping a secretive eye out, all the while, to see if Becky Thatcher was noticing. But she seemed to be un-

怕只一次。你现在不必吃药了。"

　　汤姆早早地来到了学校。大家注意到，最近汤姆每天都来得很早，真奇怪，这会儿，他没有和伙伴们玩，却在校门口转来转去，他对大家说，他病了。他尽量表现出他在四处张望，但事实上他只是沿着校门口的路望去。这会儿，杰夫·撒切尔出现在他的视野中，汤姆的脸上焕发出一阵光彩；他盯了一会儿，然后就失望地转身走了。杰夫到门口时，汤姆走去跟他搭讪，小心翼翼地想引他说说贝琪，可那个人却不上套。汤姆又望啊望，希望随时都会有一个穿裙子的活生生的人出现，可只要一看到裙子的主人不是他盼的那一个，心中就生起了厌恶。最后再没有裙子出现了，他心灰意冷地走进教室，坐下来，等待受苦受难的上课时间的到来。这时又有一条裙子穿过校门，汤姆的心猛的跳了一下，紧接着他已经出去了，像印第安人一样表演着；大喊大笑，追逐男孩，冒着生命危险在篱笆墙上蹦来跳去，翻筋斗，拿大顶——卖弄各种动作，以显示他的英勇，就在同时他还一直乜斜着一只眼，看贝琪·撒切尔是否

conscious of it all; she never looked. Could it be possible that she was not aware that he was there? He showed himself immediately before her, came war-crying around, seized a boy's cap, threw it to the roof of the school-house, broke through a group of boys, pushing them in every direction, and fell lying himself, under Becky's nose, almost upsetting her—and she turned, with her nose in the air, and he heard her say: "Mf! Some people think they're smart always showing off!"

Tom's cheeks burned. He gathered himself and sneaked off, crushed and discouraged.

Chapter 13
The Pirate Crew Set Sail

Tom's mind was made up now. He was sad and very disappointed. He was a deserted, friendless boy, he said; nobody loved him; when they found out what they had driven him to, perhaps they would be sorry; he had tried to do right and get along, but they would not let him; since nothing would please them but to get rid of him, let it be so; and let them blame him for the consequences—why shouldn't they? What right had the friendless boys to complain? Yes, they had forced him to it at last: he would lead a life of crime. There was no

在注意他。可她似乎没意识到这一切，根本不朝
这边看。难道她还没注意到他在那儿？汤姆想着，
马上走到她跟前展示自己，转来转去，如打仗般
地吼叫，抓起一个男孩的帽子扔到教室屋顶上，
又冲进一堆男孩，把他们赶得哪都是，还躺倒在
贝琪的鼻子尖下，搞得她都快烦了——贝琪转过
身，鼻子翘得高高的。他听到她说："哼！有人自
以为自己挺聪明的——总在显能!"

汤姆的脸烧了起来。他强打起精神，偷偷溜
走了，一副遭受打击后垂头丧气的样子。

第十三章　海盗结帮扬帆远航

悲伤失望的汤姆认定自己成了一个没有朋友，
被人抛弃的男孩，没人爱他。汤姆想等有一天他
们发现自己把这个男孩逼到什么地步，可能他们
会难过。他尽量不让自己做错事，可就连这机会
他们都不给他，既然他们只想赶他走，就由着他
们来吧；随他们批评他做错这做错那，凭什么阻
止人家呢？没有朋友的男孩有什么权利抱怨呢？
是啊，是他们把他最终逼成这样的，他的一生将
罪行累累，因为他别无选择。

choice.

By this time he was far down Meadow Lane, and the bell for school tinkled faintly upon his ear. He sobbed, now, to think he should never, never hear that old familiar sound any more—it was very hard, but it was forced on him; since he was driven out into the cold world, he must accept—but he forgave them. Then the sobs came thick and fast.

Just at this point he met his soul's sworn comrade, Joe Harper—hard-eyed, and with evidently a great and sad purpose in his heart. Plainly here were "two souls with but a single thought." Tom, wiping his eyes with his sleeve, began to say something about a decision to escape from strict rules and lack of sympathy at home by wandering abroad into the great world never to return; and ended by hoping that Joe would not forget him.

But it occurred that this was a request which Joe had just been going to make to Tom, and had come to look for him for that purpose. His mother had beaten him for drinking some cream which he had never tasted and knew nothing about; it was clear that she was tired of him and wished him to go; if she felt that way, there was nothing for him to do but obey; he hoped she would be happy, and never regret having driven her poor boy out into the cold world to suffer and die.

这会儿，他沿着麦道巷走得很远了，学校的铃声在他耳边模模糊糊地响起。他哭了，想自己永远永远都听不到这陈旧却又熟悉的声音了——他很痛苦，却又无奈；既然他被驱逐到这冰冷的世界，就必须接受这一切——可他会原谅他们的。想到这儿，他哭得更凶了。

就在这时，他遇到了自己的知心朋友——乔·哈普——他看上去也满腹悲伤，显然心中也计划着什么悲壮之举，很明显。这俩难兄难弟走到一起来了。汤姆用袖子擦了擦眼睛，说出了他的决定。他要逃离这充满清规戒律的生活，逃离那没有同情的家庭，流落异乡，去那伟大的国度，永不回来；最后还说希望乔不要忘了他。

可没想到，这正是乔要问汤姆的，也正是他来找汤姆的目的。他妈妈因为怀疑他偷吃奶油而打了他，而他压根儿没有尝过，甚至就不知道这回事。显而易见，她腻味他了，希望他走得远远的；如果她那么觉着，那他别无选择，只有服从了。他希望她过得快乐，永远不会后悔把她可怜的孩子赶到这冷漠的世界，让他受罪，然后死。

As the two boys walked sorrowing along, they made a new compact to stay by each other and be brothers and never separate till death relieved them of their troubles. Then they began to make their plans. Joe was for being a hermit, and living on stones in a remote cave, and dying, sometime, of cold and want and sadness; but after listening to Tom, he agreed that there were some obvious advantages about a life of crime, and so he agreed to be a pirate.

Three miles below St. Petersburg, at a point where the Mississippi River was a little over a mile wide, there was a long, narrow, wooded island, with a shallow bar at the head of it. No people lived here and far away there was a dense and almost wholly unpeopled forest. So Jackson's Island was chosen. Who were to be the subjects of their piracies was a matter that did not occur to them. Then they hunted up Huckleberry Finn, and he joined them quickly. They presently separated to meet at a lonely spot on the river—bank two miles above the village at the favorite hour—which was midnight. There was a small log raft there which they meant to seize. Each would bring hooks and lines, and such necessary things as he could steal in the most dark and mysterious

两个男孩一边难过地走着，一边达成协定：他们要相互支持，互为兄弟，永不分离，直到死去摆脱这尘世的烦恼。接着俩人就开始制订计划。乔赞成去做一个隐士，住在遥远的山洞里，在寒冷、饥饿、悲伤中死去。然而听了汤姆的计划后，他同意犯罪的生活更要有许多明显的好处，所以他同意当一个海盗。

向下三英里处的密西西比河不过一英里多宽。那儿有一座又长又宽的岛屿，上面郁郁葱葱，岛端还有一个浅浅的海湾，那儿没人居住，更远处是一座茂密的森林，更是人迹罕见。这样，他们就选好了他们的杰克森岛。谁将会成为他们偷盗的对象呢！这个问题他们还没考虑过。之后他们找到哈克贝历·芬恩。他很快加入了进来。一会儿仁人分手了，相约在他们最喜欢的时间——半夜再见。地点就是村子向上两英里处河岸上的一处偏僻地方。那儿有一个小独木筏子，他们准备弄到手。每个人都要带来鱼钩、鱼线，以及其他可以最隐秘、最神秘的方式偷到的有用的东西——

way—as became[①] outlaws. And before the afternoon was done they had all managed to enjoy the sweet glory of spreading the fact that pretty soon the town would "hear something." All who got this vague hint were cautioned to "be silent and wait."

About midnight Tom arrived with a boiled ham and a few other small things, and stopped in dense bushes on a small cliff overlooking the meeting place. It was starlight, and very still. The powerful river lay like an ocean at rest. Tom listened a moment, but no sound disturbed the quiet. Then he gave a low, clear whistle. It was answered from under the cliff. Tom whistled twice more; these signals were answered in the same way. Then a cautious voice said:

"Who goes there?"

"Tom Sawyer, the Black Avenger of the Spanish Main. Name your names."

"Huck Finn the Red-Handed, and Joe Harper the Terror of the Seas." Tom had offered these titles, from his favorite literature.

"Well. Give the countersign."

Two hoarse whispers delivered the same awful word at the same time:

---

① become: 与……相称。

这样做才配一个海盗之名。下午快过完的时候，他们四处散布，说镇上的人很快会听到点什么。所有得到这模模糊糊暗示的人都被警告说要不吭一声地等待事情的发生。而他们仨则沉浸在散布此事带来的甜蜜与得意之中。

大约半夜时分，汤姆带着一个煮火腿和其他几样小东西到了，在会面地点上面的小山崖那稠密的树丛中等待着。河流水势凶猛，就好像平静的大海。汤姆听了一会儿，却没有什么声音扰乱这寂静，接着他又低低地吹出清晰的口哨声。山崖下有了回声，汤姆又吹了两遍，他发出的信号得到了同样的回应。这时一个声音小心翼翼地问道：

"谁在上面？"

"汤姆·索耶，西班牙海上黑衣侠盗，报上你的姓名。"

"赤手大盗哈克贝历·芬恩；海上恐怖大盗乔·哈普。"汤姆从他最喜欢的文学故事中给他们各自选了一个称号。

"好。请给口令。"

俩人嘶哑着嗓子低声发出同样一个可怕的词：

"BLOOD!"

Then Tom threw his ham over the cliff and let himself down after it, tearing both skin and clothes to some extent in the effort. There was an easy, comfortable path along the shore under the cliff, but lacked the advantages of difficulty and danger so valued by a pirate.

The Terror of the Seas had brought a side of bacon, and had about worn himself out with getting it there. Finn the Red-Handed had stolen a frying-pan and leaf tobacco, and also brought a few corncobs to make pipes with. But none of the pirates smoked or "chewed" but himself.

They pushed their raft off the shore presently, Tom in command, Huck at the after oar and Joe at the forward. Tom stood in the middle with a sad face and folded arms, and gave his orders in a low, serious whisper:

"Luff, and bring her to the wind!"

"Aye – aye, sir!"

"Steady, steady – y – y – y!"

"Let her go off a point!"

"Point it is, sir!"

Now the raft was passing before the distant town. Two or three glimmering lights showed where it lay, peacefully sleeping, unconscious of the great event that was happening. The Black Avenger stood still with fold-

"血！"

接着汤姆从山崖上扔下他的火腿，自己也顺着滚了下来，划破了皮肤，撕破了衣裳。其实崖下沿着海岸有一条挺好走的捷径，然而走那条路却有一样不好，缺乏海盗重视的艰难险阻。

海上恐怖大盗带来了一扇烤肉，可把他累坏了。赤手大盗偷来了一个煎锅，一些烟叶，还有几个玉米秆做的烟斗。那俩海盗可是既不抽烟，也不嚼烟的。

他们把筏子推下河岸。汤姆负责发布命令，哈克划后桨，乔划前桨。汤姆双臂叠起站在船中央，脸色忧郁，低声严肃地命令：

"掉转船头，顺风行驶。"

"是——是，船长！"

"保持航向，保持——"

"转向！"

"转向了，船长！"

此时，筏子正漂过远处的村镇，镇上闪烁的两三盏灯显示了其方位。小镇此时已安详地睡着了，不知正在发生的这件大事。黑衣侠盗双臂交

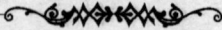

ed arms, "looking his last" upon the scene of his former joys and his later sufferings, and wishing "she" could see him now, abroad on the wild sea, facing danger and death with brave heart, going to his doom with a courageous smile on his lips. He "looked his last" with a broken and satisfied heart. The other pirates were looking their last, too; and they all looked so long that they came near letting the current drift them out of the range of the island. But they discovered the danger in time, and made shift to avoid it. About two o'clock in the morning the raft grounded on the bar two hundred yards above the head of the island, and they waded back and forth until they had landed their things. Part of the little raft's belongings consisted of an old sail, and this they spread in the bushes for a tent to protect their things; but they themselves would sleep in the open air in good weather, as became outlaws.

They built a fire against the side of a great log twenty or thirty feet long in the depths of the forest, and then cooked some bacon in the frying pan for supper, and used up half of the corn bread they had brought. It seemed glorious sport to be holding a grand meal in the virgin forest where no men came, and they said they never would return to civilization.

When the last crisp slice of bacon was gone and the

叉，一动不动地站着，向曾经给他带来快乐，后又带来痛苦的地方望去最后一眼。他真希望"她"现在能看到他已漂泊在凶猛的大海上，正以一颗勇敢的心面对困难与危险，嘴边带着勇敢的微笑面对死亡。他向那个地方望去最后一眼，心中既充满了悲伤，又洋溢着满足。其他两位海盗也在望去最后一眼。他们看的时间太长了，水流都快要把他们的筏子冲出小岛的水域了。幸亏仁人及时地发现了危险，调转了方向。大约凌晨两点钟的时候，他们的筏子停泊在了两百码外的一个沙洲上。仁人涉水跑了几趟，卸下了他们的财产，其中包括一个旧帆，用来铺在树丛上做帐篷，遮盖他们的东西。而他们自己呢，为了与海盗这个头衔相称，天好的时候就在露天宿营。

他们在林子二三十英尺深处的一个大圆木边点起了一堆火。准备晚餐。三人用煎锅做了一些烤肉，还把他们带来的玉米面包吃掉了大半。在这个没有人烟的森林里举行如此盛大的晚宴，真是了不起极了。他们说他们再也不会回归文明世界了。

最后一片烤肉享受了，最后一份玉米面包也

last allowance of corn bread eaten, the boys stretched themselves out on the grass, filled with satisfaction.

"Isn't it happy?" said Joe.

"Terrific!" said Tom. "What would the boys say if they could see us?"

"Say? Well, they'd just die to be here—hey, Hucky!"

"I think so," said Huckleberry; "anyway, I'm suited. I don't want anything better than this. I didn't ever get enough to eat, generally—and here they can't come and bully me."

"It's just the life for me," said Tom. "You don't have to get up in mornings and you don't have to go to school, and wash, and do all those follish things. You see a pirate doesn't have to do anything, Joe, when he's ashore, but a hermit has to be praying a lot, and then he docsn't have any fun, anyway, all by himself that way."

"Oh, yes, that's so," said Joe, "but I hadn't thought much about it, you know. I'd a good deal rather be a pirate, now that I've tried it."

Now the Red – Handed was blowing a cloud of fragrant smoke—he was in the full bloom of luxurious satisfaction. The other pirates envied him this majestic vice, and secretly determined to learn it shortly. Presently

吃了之后，他们躺在草丛中，伸展着身子，满足极了。

"高兴吧?"乔说。

"好极了!"汤姆说，"如果那帮男孩看到咱们这样，会说什么?"

"说什么? 哼，他们巴不得也在这儿呢——嘿，哈克!"

"我想也是，反正这儿挺适合我。这可是我求之不得的。平时，我食不裹腹，吃不饱肚子。在这儿，他们就无法来欺负我了。

"这也正是我要过的生活，"汤姆说，"你不必大早起床，不必上学，不必洗脸，不必干所有那些愚蠢的事儿。乔，你看，海盗上岸以后什么都不需要干，不像隐士，他还得不停地祷告，而且没什么有意思的; 不论怎样，他总是一个人孤独地生活。"

"噢，对，没错，"乔说，"可是我以前没想那么多，你知道的，现在我已经感觉到了我更愿意做一个海盗。"

这会儿，哈克正在吞云吐雾，烟味还挺香的——他心满意足得要命，他感觉这太舒服了。另两个海盗羡慕他这种辉煌的恶行，暗自下定决心要很快学会。这时，哈克说:

Huck said:

"What do pirates have to do?"

Tom said:

"Oh, they have just a good time—take ships and burn them, and get the money and bury it in horrible places in their island where there're ghosts and things to watch it, and kill everybody in the ships—make them drown."

"And they carry the women to the island," said Joe; "they don't kill the women."

"No," agreed Tom, "they don't kill the women—they're too noble. And the women're always beautiful, too."

"And don't they wear the most magnificent clothes! Oh, no! All gold and silver and diamonds," said Joe, with enthusiasm.

"Who?" said Huck.

"Why, the pirates."

Huck glanced at his own clothing sadly.

"I think I'm not dressed fit for a pirate," said he, with a regretful pity in his voice; "but I have got none but these."

But the other boys told him the fine clothes would come fast enough, after they should have begun their adventures. They made him understand that his poor rags

"海盗都要干什么呢?"

汤姆说:

"噢,他们总是很快乐——劫船,烧船,拿上钱,藏到他们岛上有鬼和其他什么可以看住钱的可怕地方。然后杀掉船上所有人——让他们淹死。"

"他们还把女人带到岸上!"乔说,"他们不杀女人。"

"对,"汤姆也同意,"他们不杀女人——他们非常高尚,况且女人也总是很美丽的。"

"他们还穿着最华丽的衣裳!噢,全身都贴满了金子、银子,挂满了钻石。"乔激动地说:

"谁?"哈克问。

"海盗。"

哈克哀伤地看了看自己的衣服。

"我想我穿的这身不配海盗的身份,"他说着,流露出一种遗憾的语气,"可我再没别的穿了。"

另两个孩子告诉他,只要他们一开始自己的冒险事业,好衣服很快就会来的。他们使他明白

would do to begin with, though wealthy pirates usually started with a proper wardrobe.

Gradually their talk died out and sleepiness began to steal upon the eyelids of the little boys. The pipe dropped from the fingers of the Red-Handed, and he fell asleep. The Terror of the Seas and the Black Avenger of the Spanish Main had more difficulty in getting to sleep. They said their prayers inwardly, lying down, since there was nobody there ordering to make them kneel and recite aloud. Then at once they reached and hovered upon the verge of sleep—but an intruder came. It was conscience. They began to feel a vague fear that they had been doing wrong to run away; and next they thought of the stolen meat, and then the real torture came. They tried to argue it away that they had stolen sweetmeats and apples many times; but conscience was not to be calmed down by such thin excuse; it seemed to them that taking sweetmeats was only "hooking," while taking bacon and hams and such valuables was plain simple stealing—and there was a command against that in the Bible. So they inwardly decided that so long as they remained in the business, their piracies should not again be ruined with the crime of stealing. Then conscience stopped struggling, and these curiously changeable pirates fell peacefully to sleep.

尽管有钱的海盗通常一开始就穿着体面的衣裳，他那一身破烂刚开始也行。

慢慢地，聊天停下了，困意袭来，这些男孩眼睛都快睁不开了。哈克手中的烟管掉了，他睡着了，海上恐怖大盗和西班牙海上黑衣侠盗入睡则有些困难。这儿再也没人命令他们跪下来大声祷告了，可他们自觉地在内心做着祷告，然后躺下，很快就游到了梦乡之岸——这时，有东西来侵扰他们了，那就是良知。他们隐隐约约有些害怕，觉得逃跑是件错事，然后他们又想到自己偷的肉，他们的良心真的开始受到折磨。他们试图为自己辩白，告诉自己曾经多次偷过甜肉和苹果，然而这一点儿说服力都没有，他们的良心无法得到平衡，他们觉得拿甜肉似乎只能称为"钓"，而拿熏肉、火腿等值钱的东西显然就是偷——况且《圣经》中有一条戒律是禁止这样的。所以他们暗下决心，只要干上海盗这一行，他们就决不让偷盗这一罪行毁了自己。良知远离他们而去了，这些情绪多变让人摸不透的海盗平静地睡着了。

Chapter 14
Happy Camp of the Freebooters

When Tom awoke in the morning, he wondered where he was. He sat up and rubbed his eyes and looked around. Then he understood. It was the cool gray dawn, and there was a delicious sense of peace in the deep silence of the woods. Joe and Huck still slept.

Gradually the cool dim gray of the morning whitened, and as gradually sounds increased and life showed itself. Tom stirred up the other pirates and they all ran away with a shout, and in a minute or two were naked and chasing after and rolling over each other in the shallow water of the white sand bar. They felt no longing for the little village sleeping in the distance beyond water. A slight rise in the water had carried off their raft, but this only satisfied them, since its going was something like burning the bridge between them and civilization.

They came back to camp wonderfully refreshed, glad-hearted, and hungry; and they soon had the campfire burning again. Huck found a spring of clear cold water close by, and the boys made cups of broad oak leaves and felt that water, sweetened with such a wildwood charm as that, would be a good enough substitute for

第十四章 海盗们快乐的营地

汤姆早晨醒来时，琢磨着自己在哪儿呢，他坐了起来，揉了揉眼睛，向四周望望。随后就明白了。这会儿还是凉爽的黎明时分，天空一片灰白，树林深深的沉寂中有一种怡人的祥和之感。乔和哈克还在睡觉。

慢慢地，随着凉爽清晨的到来，灰暗的天空泛出了鱼肚白。各种声音也响了起来，生命开始复苏。汤姆叫醒其他两位海盗。他们大喊了一声，跑了出去。一两分钟就脱光了衣服在白色沙洲的浅水域翻滚着，互相追逐着。他们不再向往远处水那边还在沉睡的小村子了。稍稍上涨的水已经漂走了他们的筏子，这更使他们高兴了，因为这意味着联系他们与文明世界的桥被烧断了。

他们回到营地，精神抖擞，心神愉快，却已经饿了。很快他们就点着了营火。哈克在附近找到了一眼清澈凉爽的泉水。孩子们用宽橡树叶卷成杯子品尝泉水，他们发现泉水具有森林魅力的

coffee. While Joe was cutting bacon for breakfast, Tom and Huck asked him to hold on a minute; they went to the riverbank and threw in their lines; almost immediately they had reward. Very quickly they got enough fish for even a family. They fried the fish with the bacon, and were astonished, for no fish had ever seemed so delicious before. They did not know that the quicker a fresh-water fish is on the fire after he is caught the better he is; and they rarely realized what a sauce open-air sleep, open-air exercises, bathing, and a large ingredient of hunger makes, too.

They lay around in the shade, after breakfast, and then went off through the woods on an adventure. Now and then they came upon comfortable places carpeted with grass and jeweled with flowers.

They took a swim about every hour, so it was close upon the middle of the afternoon when they got back to camp. They were too hungry to stop to fish, but they had a splendid meal upon cold ham and then threw themselves down in the shade to talk. But the talk soon began to drag, and then died. The stillness, the solemnity in the woods, and the sense of loneliness began to fall upon the spirits of the boys. They fell to thinking. A sort of vague longing crept upon them. It was increasing homesickness. But they were all ashamed of their weakness,

甘甜足以取代咖啡了。乔为早餐切熏肉时，汤姆和哈克让他稍等片刻。他们来到河岸边扔下鱼线，立刻就得到了回报。不一会儿，他们钓上了足够一家子吃的鱼。他们把鱼和肉放在一起煎，惊奇地发现以前吃的鱼怎么没这么鲜。他们不知道淡水鱼钓上来后烹得越早，味道就越好；他们也难能意识到露天睡觉、露天嬉戏、游泳，尤其是他们此刻的饥饿是多么好的作料啊。

早饭后，三人在树阴下聊了一会儿，然后就穿过森林冒险去了，不时地他们会看到许多怡人的地方，草丛有如地毯，而各种鲜花则像镶嵌上去的珠宝。

他们几乎每个小时都会游一次泳，所以回到营地时都快下午三四点了。他们太饿了，根本等不及去钓鱼，就拿冷火腿做了一顿丰盛的晚餐。然后，躺倒在树阴中聊天。不久，聊天变得平淡无奇，最后没有了。村子的宁静肃穆还有那种孤寂感开始袭上孩子们的心头。他们躺在那儿，各自想着心事，一种模糊的渴望悄然而升。那是一种越来越强烈的想家的念头。然而他们都为自己

and none was brave enough to speak his thought.

Presently one mysterious sound became more and more noticeable and drew the boys' attention. The boys started, glanced at each other, and then each assumed a listening attitude. There was a long silence, deep and unbroken; then a deep, gloomy sound came floating down out of the distance.

"Let's go and see."

They sprang to their feet and hurried to the shore toward the town. They parted the bushes on the bank and peered out over the water. The little steam ferry-boat was about a mile below the village, drifting with the current. Her broad deck seemed crowded with people. There were a great many boats rowing about or floating with the stream near the ferryboat, but the boys could not determine what the men in them were doing. Presently a great jet of white smoke burst from the ferryboat's side.

"I know now!" shouted Tom; "somebody's drowned!"

The boys listened and watched. Presently a thought flashed through Tom's mind, and he shouted:

"Boys, I know who's drowned—it's us!"

They felt like heroes in an instant. Here was a magnificent victory; they were missed; they were

的这种脆弱感到羞耻，谁也不敢说出心里的想法。

这时一种奇怪的声音变得越来越明显了，吸引了孩子们的注意力。他们很吃惊，互相瞥了一眼，都决定再听一听。随之而来的是长时间的寂静；紧接着一种深深的悲伤的声音从远处传来。

"咱们去看看。"

他们跳起来，急忙跑到朝村镇的那边河岸，拨开河岸上的树丛，朝水那边窥视。他们看到离村子约一英里的水上有一艘小蒸汽渡船，随着水流漂浮着，宽宽的甲板似乎挤满了人。渡船周围还有许多只小船在划行或是随水漂流，然而男孩们无法确定船上的人在干什么。这时，一股白烟从渡船的一边喷射出来。

"我现在知道了！"汤姆喊道，"有人溺水了！"

孩子们听着，看着。这时，汤姆恍然大悟，他大喊：

"伙伴们，我知道谁溺水了——是我们！"

立时，他们感觉自己就要像英雄一样。他们的名声大了，这对他们而言，简直是辉煌的胜利；

mourned; hearts were breaking for them; tears were being shed; accusing memories of unkindness to these poor lost boys were rising up, and useless regrets were being allowed; and best of all, the lost boys were the talk of the whole town, and the envy of all the boys, as far as this shining fame was concerned. This was fine. It was worthwhile to be a pirate, after all.

As twilight drew on, the ferryboat went back to her familiar business and the boats disappeared. The pirates returned to camp. They were happy with vanity over their new pride and the famous trouble they were making. They caught fish, cooked supper and ate it, and then fell to guessing at what the village was thinking and saying about them; and the pictures they drew of the public sadness for them were satisfying to look upon—from their point of view. But when the shadows of night closed them in, they gradually stopped talking, and sat gazing into the fire, with their minds wandering elsewhere. The excitement was gone now, and Tom and Joe could not keep back thoughts of certain persons at home who were not enjoying this joy as much as they were. Worries came; they grew troubled and unhappy; a sigh or two escaped, unawared. By and by Joe timidly ventured upon a roundabout "feeler" as to how the others might look upon a return to civilization—not right now, but—

他们不见了，人们在为他们悲伤；多少颗心在为他们破碎；眼泪为他们而流；人们为没有善待这些可怜的失踪的孩子而开始自责，尽由自己无用地悔恨；最棒的是，这些失踪的男孩成了整个镇子议论的中心，成了所有男孩羡慕的对象。这太好了，不管怎样，当一个海盗还是值得的。

随着暮色的降临，渡船又开始回到它往日的工作中，那些小船也不见了。海盗们回到了营地，制造了为那么多人瞩目的麻烦，又带来了新的自豪。他们的虚荣心得到了满足。快乐极了。他们去钓鱼，做晚餐，吃完后就躺在那儿猜测着村子里的人们会怎么想，怎么说他们；他们想象着大家会如何为他们痛苦，他们感到很满意——至少在他们看来。但是当夜幕将裹住他们时，三人渐渐地不再说话了，坐在那儿，凝视着篝火，脑子已经云游他处了。那种激动已经过去了。汤姆和乔禁不住地想到家里的某些人。他们是不会和他们一样享受这快乐的，俩孩子开始担忧，变得不安，不快；不经意间发出一两声叹息。后来，乔拐弯抹角怯生生地冒险问大家对回归文明世界怎么看——当然不是立刻；却是——

Tom defeated him with despise! Huck joined with Tom, and the waverer quickly "explained," and was glad to get out of the awkward situation with as little chickenhearted homesickness as he could.

As the night deepened, Huck began to nod, and presently to snore. Joe followed next. Tom lay upon his elbow motionless, for some time, watching the two intently. At last he got up cautiously, on his knees, and went writing something on two pieces of wood. One he rolled up and put in his jacket pocket, and the other he put in Joe's hat and removed it to a little distance from the owner. And he also put into the hat certain schoolboy treasures of almost inestimable value—among them a lump of chalk, an India-rubber ball, three fishhooks, and one of that kind of marbles quite like crystal. Then he tiptoed his way cautiously among the trees till he felt that he was out of hearing, and ran quickly in the direction of the sand bar.

Chapter 15
Tom's Secret Visit Home

A few minutes later Tom was wading toward the Illinois shore. Shortly before ten o'clock he came out into an open place opposite the village. Everything was quiet

汤姆用鄙视的目光击败了他！哈克也站在汤姆一边，动摇者很快作以解释，庆幸自己摆脱了这种尴尬的局面，胆怯、想家的感觉也几乎没有了。

夜渐渐深了，哈克开始不住地点头，后来就打起呼噜了。乔也紧跟着。汤姆躺在自己的肘上，好一会儿一动不动，密切关注着那两位。最后他小心翼翼地站了起来，在两片木头上写了点什么。一片他卷了起来，放在他的夹克衫里，另一片他放在乔的帽子里，把他拿到离主人稍远的地方。他还在帽子里放入了一些对上学的孩子来说不可估价的宝物——有一堆粉笔、一个印第安橡胶球、三个鱼钩，还有一种像水晶一样的大理石。随后他蹑手蹑脚、小心翼翼地走在树丛中，走到他觉得他们听不见他了，才开始向沙洲方向飞快地跑去。

第十五章　汤姆秘密探家

几分钟之后汤姆就涉水朝伊利诺斯河岸走去。快到十点钟时，他上岸来到村子对面的一块空旷地带，星光闪烁下的小镇一切都很宁静。

under the blinking stars.

He flew along empty alleys, and shortly found himself at his aunt's back fence. He climbed over, and looked in at the sitting-room window, for a light was burning there. There sat Aunt Polly, Sid, Mary, and Joe Harper's mother, grouped together, talking. They were by the bed, and the bed was between them and the door. Tom went to the door and began to softly lift the latch; then he pressed gently, and the door yielded a crack; he continued pushing cautiously, till he judged he might squeeze through on his knees; so he put his head through and began, cautiously.

Tom disappeared under the bed. He lay and "breathed" himself for a time, and then crept to where he could almost touch his aunt's foot.

"But as I was saying," said Aunt Polly, "he wasn't bad, so to say—only naughty. Only just fond of excitement, and reckless, you know. He was always responsible. He never meant any harm, and he was the best-hearted boy that ever was"—and she began to cry.

"It was just so with my Joe—always full of deviltment and up to every kind of mischief, but he was just as unselfish and kind as he could be—and laws bless me, to think I went and whipped him for taking that cream, never once remembering that I threw it out myself

他沿着空无一人的巷子跑着，很快就到了他姨妈家后院的篱笆墙下。汤姆爬过去，看到起居室里灯亮着，他就透过窗户向里望去，看到波莉姨妈、赛德、玛丽，还有乔·哈普的妈妈围坐在一起说话呢。他们坐在床边，床的另一边则正对着门。汤姆走到门口，轻轻地抬起门闩，又轻轻地压下来，门被推开了一条缝；他又继续小心推着，直到他觉得自己能爬着挤过去，汤姆先把头探了过去，随后身子，小心翼翼地。

他爬到了床底下，在那儿躺了一会儿，让自己的呼吸平静下来。随后又悄悄地爬到了几乎能触到他姨妈脚的地方。

"可是就像我刚提的，"波莉姨妈说，"可以说，他不坏——只是淘气。喜欢搞点刺激的事儿，有些冒冒失失。可他责任感很强，对人从没有坏心眼，他心地最善良了——"说着说着，她就哭起来。

"我家乔也是这样——总是很淘气。换着花样搞恶作剧。可他一点也不自私，非常善良——想想，我以为他偷了奶油打了他，却一点儿也没记起是我因它酸了，自己把它扔了，从此我再也见

because it was sour, and I never saw him again in this world, never, never, never, poor boy!" And Mrs. Harper sobbed as if her heart would break.

"I hope Tom's better off where he is," said Sid, "but if he'd been better in some ways—"

"Sid!" Tom felt the glare of the old lady's eye, though he could not see it. "Not a word against my Tom, now that he's gone! God'll take care of him— never you trouble yourself, sir! Oh, Mrs. Harper, I don't know how to give him up! I don't know how to give him up! He was such a comfort to me, although he tormented my old heart most."

"Only last Saturday my Joe busted a firecracker right under my nose and I knocked him. Little did I know then how soon—oh, if it was to do over again I'd hug him and bless him for it."

"Yes, yes, yes, I know just how you feel, Mrs. Harper, I know just exactly how you feel. No longer ago than yesterday noon my Tom took and filled the cat full of painkiller, and I did think the creature would tear the house down. And God forgive me, I cracked Tom's head with my thimble, poor boy, poor dead boy. But he's out of all his troubles now. And the last words I ever heard him say were scold—"

But this memory was too much for the old lady, and

不到他了，再也见不到了，再也见不到，再也见不到了。可怜的孩子!"哈普太太哭得仿佛心都碎了。

"我希望汤姆在他那边过得更幸福。"赛德说，"可如果他过去能在某些方面好些——"

"赛德!"汤姆尽管看不到，但能感到老太太正怒视着赛德，"既然他现在已经走了，你不许说一句他的坏话!上帝会照顾他的——你不必自找麻烦，先生!噢，哈普太太，我真不知如何才能忘记他!我不知道如何才能忘记他!尽管他总是让我难过，可却是我莫大的安慰。"

"就在上个星期，因为我的乔在我鼻子底下放了一个炮，我打了他。我那会儿哪能知道这么快——如果他还这么干的话，我非得搂着他，夸他放得好。"

"对，对，对，我很理解你的心情，哈普太太，我完全理解你的感受。就在昨天中午我的汤姆给猫灌了一肚子止痛药，我那会儿的确觉得那小家伙会把房子都踢踏碎。上帝宽恕我，我拿我的顶针敲了他的头。可怜的孩子，可怜的死去的孩子，他现在完全摆脱了这所有的烦恼，我听到他说的最后一句话就是：批评——"

这段回忆对老太太来说太痛苦了。她情绪完

she broke entirely down. Tom was sobbing now, himself—and more in pity of himself than anybody else. He could hear Mary crying, and putting in a kind word for him from time to time. He began to have a nobler opinion of himself than ever before. Still, he was sufficiently touched by his aunt's sadness to long to rush out from under the bed and give her joy—and the theatrical magnificence of the thing appealed strongly to his nature, too, but he resisted and lay still.

He went on listening, and gathered by odds and ends that it was guessed at first that the boys had got drowned while taking a swim; the small raft had been missed; next, certain boys said the missing boys had promised that the village should "hear something" soon; the wiseheads had "put this and that together" and decided that the boys had gone off on that raft and would turn up at the next town below, presently; but toward noon the raft had been found, lodged against the Missouri shore some five or six miles below the village—and then hope died; they must be drowned, else hunger would have driven them home by nightfall if not sooner. It was believed that the search for the bodies had been a fruitless effort merely because the drowning must have occurred in mid-channel, since the boys, being good swimmers, would otherwise have escaped to shore. This

全失去了控制，大哭起来，此时的汤姆哽咽着
——更怜惜的不是别人，而是他自己，他能听到
玛丽也在哭，还时不时说一两句汤姆的好话。他
现在比以往更认为自己高尚了。他仍然为他姨妈
的悲痛而特别感动，渴望自己能从床下冲出去让
她高兴——况且这种富于戏剧性的不凡之举正符
合他的个性，强烈地吸引着他。可他还是控制住
了自己，一动不动地躺在那儿。

　　汤姆继续听着，零零碎碎地了解到了他走后
发生的事情——村里的人们刚开始猜测孩子们肯
定是游泳时溺水了，然后发现小筏子丢了；后来，
一些男孩们说丢失的小孩们曾经向他们许诺说村
子里的人很快会"听到什么事"！那些聪明的人就
"把这、那联系起来"，认为孩子们是乘筏子走的，
那会儿应该到了下游的镇子；可到中午时筏子找
到了，停靠在村子下游五六英里处的密索里河岸
——这样一看觉得没希望了，孩子们一定是淹死
了。否则至多到傍晚之后，饿极了的孩子们也会
回家填肚子的。人们觉得再费劲儿打捞孩子们的
尸体也是徒劳的，因为他们一定是在水流中间淹
死的，早被冲走了，要不这些谙习水性的孩子们，
一定会逃到岸边的。这会儿是星期三晚上，

was Wednesday night. If the bodies continued missing until Sunday, all hope would be given over and the funerals would be preached on that morning. Tom shuddered.

Mrs. Harper gave a sobbing good night and turned to go. Then with a mutual impulse the two sad women flung themselves into each other's arms and had a good, consoling cry, and then parted. Aunt Polly was tender far beyond her usual way, in her good night to Sid and Mary. Sid sobbed a bit and Mary went off crying with all her heart.

Aunt Polly knelt down and prayed for Tom so touchingly, so appealing, and with such measureless love in her words and her old trembling voice, that he was in tears long before she was through.

He had to keep still long after she went to bed, for she kept making brokenhearted cries from time to time, turning over and over unrestfully. But at last she was still, only moaning a little in her sleep. Now the boy stole out, rose gradually by the bedside, shaded the candlelight with his hand, and stood looking at her. His heart was full of pity for her. He took out that piece of wood and placed it by the candle. But something occurred to him, and he hesitated. His face lighted with a happy solution of his thought; he put it rapidly in his

如果尸体到星期日还找不着的话，那是真的没希望了。葬礼将在那天早晨举行，汤姆听了全身战栗了一下。

哈普太太哭着与大家道晚安，转身要走。就在这时，两位伤心的老人都情不自禁地投向对方怀抱，大哭了一场，相互表示安慰，随后就分手了，波莉姨妈向赛德和玛丽说晚安时，也比平时温柔多了。赛德也抽搭了一会儿，而玛丽在回屋时又痛哭了一场。

波莉姨妈跪了下来为汤姆祈祷，她的祈祷那么感人，那么动听，话中充满了无尽之爱。加之她那苍老而又颤抖的声音，使得汤姆在她没说完时就已泪水涟涟了。

姨妈上床已经很长时间了，汤姆还一动不动地躺在那儿，因为她不时地发出心碎的哭声，不停地辗转反侧，最后她终于平静下来了，偶尔在睡梦中发出一两声呻吟。这时汤姆偷偷爬出来，在她的床边慢慢站起来，一边用手挡着烛火，一边凝视着姨妈。他取出了那片木头，放在了蜡烛旁边，又想起了什么，犹豫了一会儿，想出了一个有趣的解决办法后，汤姆的脸又焕发出了光彩。

pocket. Then he bent over and kissed the faded lips, and left secretly.

He went back to the riverbank. Finding nobody there, he untied the boat and rowed to the island.

The night was far spent. He rested again until the sun was well up and gliding the great river with its splendor, and then he swam in the stream. A little later he heard Joe say:

"No, Tom's true, Huck, and he'll come back. He won't desert us. He knows that would be a disgrace to a pirate, and Tom's too proud for that sort of thing. He's up to something or other."

"Here I am!" shouted Tom, with fine dramatic effect, stepping grandly into camp.

A splendid breakfast of bacon and fish was shortly provided. Tom told his adventures. Then Tom hid himself away in a shady place to sleep till noon, and the other pirates got ready to fish and travel.

Chapter 16
First Pipes—"I've Lost My Knife"

After dinner all the boys turned out to hunt for turtle eggs on the bar. They went about pushing sticks into the sand, and when they found a soft place they went

他很快把木片塞进了兜里，随后弯下腰，吻了吻姨妈那惨白的嘴唇，悄悄地走了。

他回到岸边，看见没人，就解开了一艘小船，向小岛划去。

夜晚很快过去了，他一直睡到太阳爬得老高，大河已是金波粼粼了，他起来到河里去游泳，不一会儿就听到乔说：

"不，汤姆是真正的，哈克，他会回来的，他不会抛弃我们。他知道那样做有辱一个海盗的名声。汤姆对这名声可自豪了，他一定是有别的什么事。"

"我在这儿呢！"汤姆喊道，自豪地走进了营地，一切颇富戏剧性的效果。

很快，一顿用烤肉和鱼做的盛大早餐准备好了。汤姆向他们讲述了他的冒险经历，然后，就躲在一个阴凉地儿躺下，一直睡到中午。另两个海盗则准备去钓鱼，旅行。

第十六章　初尝烟斗——"我把我的刀丢了"

午饭后孩子们都去沙洲上找乌龟蛋了。他们用棍子在沙洲上到处捅，只要碰到软软的地方，

down on their knees and dug with their hands. They had a famous fried-egg dinner that night, and another on Friday morning.

After breakfast they went shouting and jumping out on the bar, and chased each other round and round. Now and then they splashed water in each other's faces with their palms.

When they were well tired, they would lie on the dry, hot sand, and cover themselves up with it, and by and by break for the water.

They gradually wandered apart, and fell to gazing longingly across the wide river to where the village lay in the sun. Tom found himself writing "Becky" in the sand with his big toe; he wrote it out, and was angry with himself for his weakness. But he wrote it again, nevertheless; he could not help it. He erased it once more and then took himself out of temptation by driving the other boys together and joining them.

But Joe's spirits had gone down almost beyond hope. He was so homesick that he could hardly bear the misery of it. The tears lay very near the surface. Huck was sad, too. Tom was in low spirits, but tried hard not to show it. He had a secret which he was not ready to tell, yet, but if this rebellious depression was not broken up soon, he would have to bring it out. He said, with a

就跪下来用手挖。那天晚上他们吃了一顿美味的煎乌龟蛋，星期五早晨又继续吃了一顿。

早饭后孩子们在沙洲上又蹦又喊，绕着圈子互相追逐，不时地用棕榈叶互相往脸上泼水。

一会儿玩累了，三个人就躺在了干热的沙子上，用沙子把全身埋起来，然后再又爬起来跳到水里。

慢慢地三人走散了，各自躺在地上凝望着大河对面阳光下的村子，满心渴望。汤姆发现他自己在沙子上用大脚指头写"贝琪"，写完后又生气自己的脆弱。可他还是无法控制，又写了一遍，之后又擦掉。为了让自己摆脱这种诱惑，汤姆跑去追逐另两个男孩，加入了他们的行列。

可乔的情绪低落到了极点，他特别想家，简直痛苦得受不了了。泪水在他眼眶里打转。哈克也很难过。汤姆心情虽也不好，可他尽力不表现出来。他有个秘密，却不打算现在说出来，可如果这样危险的消沉局面不能很快打破，他就得说出来。他尽量表现得很高兴。

show of cheerfulness:

"I bet there'd been pirates on this island before, boys. We'll find it again. They'd hid treasures here somewhere. How'd you feel to find a rotten box full of gold and silver—hey?"

But it roused only a little interest, which faded out with no reply. Tom tried one or two other seductions; but they failed, too. It was discouraging work. Joe looked very gloomy. Finally he said:

"Oh, boys, let's give it up. I want to go home. It's so lonesome."

"Oh, no, Joe, you'll feel better by and by." said Tom. "Just think of the fishing that's here."

"I don't care for fishing. I want to go home."

"But, Joe, there isn't such another swimming place anywhere."

"Swimming's no good. I don't seem to care for it, somehow, when there isn't anybody to say I shouldn't go. I mean to go home."

"Oh! Baby! You want to see your mother, I think."

"Yes, I do want to see my mother—and you would, too, if you had one. I'm not any more baby than you are." And Joe sobbed a little.

"Well, we'll let the crybaby go home to his moth-

"我打赌这个岛上以前肯定有海盗，伙计们，咱们很快会发现的。他们肯定在这个岛上的哪儿藏着宝呢。想一想，如果你找到一个烂盒子，里面装的都是金子、银子，会有什么感觉，嗯？"

可这也只勾起了他们的一点点兴趣，还没等吱声呢，那点儿兴趣就已经消失了。汤姆又试着说了一两样其他的事情，想吸引他们的注意力，可都没用。这太令人泄气了，乔看着很难过，最后他说：

"噢，伙计们，咱们别当海盗了，我想回家，呆这儿太寂寞了。"

"噢，不，乔，你慢慢就会适应的，"汤姆说，"想想咱们在这儿可以钓鱼。"

"我不喜欢钓鱼，我想回家。"

"可是，乔，哪儿也没有这儿这么好的地方让咱们游泳啊！"

"游泳没什么好，如果没人说不让我游的时候。我发现我好像也不怎么喜欢游泳了。我打算回家。"

"噢！你可真是妈妈的宝宝！你想回去看妈妈，是吧。"

"嗯，我就是想回家看我妈——如果你有妈的话，你也会这样的。我是宝宝，你也不比我强，"乔开始有些抽搭。

"哼，我们让这个爱哭的宝宝回家找他妈吧，

er, won't we, Huck? Poor thing—does it want to see its mother? And so it shall. You like it here, don't you, Huck? We'll stay, won't we?"

Huck said "Y – e – s"—without any heart in it.

"I'll never speak to you again as long as I live," said Joe, rising. "There now!" And he moved sadly away and began to dress himself.

"Who cares!" said Tom. "Nobody wants you to. Go along home and get laughed at. Oh, you're a nice pirate. Huck and me aren't crybabies. We'll stay, won't we, Huck? Let him go if he wants to. I think we can get along without him, perhaps."

Presently, without a parting word, Joe began to wade off toward the Illinois shore. Tom's heart began to sink. He glanced at Huck. Huck could not bear the look, and dropped his eyes. Then he said:

"I want to go too, Tom. It was getting so lonesome anyway, and now it'll be worse. Let us go, too, Tom."

"I won't! You can all go, if you want to. I mean to stay."

"Tom, I'd better go."

"Well, go along—who's preventing you?"

Huck began to pick up his clothes. He said:

"Tom, I wish you'd come too. Now you think it over. We'll wait for you when we get to shore."

好吗，哈克？可怜的家伙——他想着他的妈妈，那他去吧，你喜欢呆这儿，是吗，哈克？我们在这儿呆着，不好吗？"

哈克拖拖拉拉地说了"是"，却没有什么诚意。

"我这辈子再也不跟你说话了，"乔说着，站了起来，"就从现在开始!"他难过地走开了，开始穿衣服。

"谁在乎呀!"汤姆说，"没人要你跟我说话。回家吧，让人笑掉大牙吧。噢，你还是个海盗呢。哈克和我可不是爱哭的小宝宝，我们在这儿呆着，好吗，哈克？如果他要走，让他走，我想或许我们没他一样能行。"

这会儿，乔没说一句告别的话，就开始趟水向伊利诺斯河岸走去。汤姆的心开始下沉。他瞥了一眼哈克，哈克受不了这一瞥，他低下了眼睛，说：

"我也想走，汤姆。不管怎样，太寂寞了，现在乔一走，更没意思了。咱们一起走吧，汤姆。"

"我不走! 如果你们要走，你们可以都走哇! 我打算在这儿呆着。"

"汤姆，那我最好还是走了。"

"嗯，走吧——谁挡你了？"

哈克开始拾起他的衣服，他说：

"汤姆，我希望你也能来。你现在想一想，我们到岸边会等你的。"

Tom hoped the boys would stop, but they still waded slowly on. He suddenly felt that it became very lonely and still. He made one final struggle with his pride, and then rushed after his comrades, shouting:

"Wait! Wait! I want to tell you something!"

They presently stopped and turned around. When he got to where they were, he began telling his secret, and they listened till at last they saw the interest, and then they applauded and said it was "splendid!" and said if he had told them at first they wouldn't have started away. He made a reasonable excuse; but his real reason had been the fear that not even the secret would keep them with him for a long time, and so he had planed to hold it as a last seduction.

The boys came happily back. After a delicious egg and fish dinner, Tom said he wanted to learn to smoke, now. Joe said he would like to try too. So Huck made pipes and filled them. Now they stretched themselves out on their elbow and began to puff, carefully, and with slight confidence. The smoke had an unpleasant taste, and they gagged a little, but Tom said:

"Why, it's just so easy! If I'd have known this was all, I'd have learned long ago."

"So would I," said Joe. "It's just nothing."

"Why, many a time I've looked at people smok-

汤姆希望他们会停下来，可他们还在慢慢地涉水向前走着。他突然觉得这儿变得那么寂寞，安静。他最后一次和自己的自尊心作了斗争，然后，就奔向他的伙伴们，喊道：

"等等！等等！我有话告诉你们！"

他们停下来，转过身。汤姆跑到他们跟前，开始讲他的秘密。他们听着，听着，就听出了乐趣。接着两人就鼓起掌来，喊着"太棒了！"说如果他早告诉他们，他们就不会走了。汤姆找了一个合适的借口，可没说真实的原因却是害怕即便这个秘密也不能让他们多呆些时候，因而，他计划把这作为最后一招来使。

孩子们高高兴兴地回来了，吃了一顿可口的蛋和鱼后，汤姆说他现在想学着抽烟，乔说他也想试试。哈克就给他们准备了烟斗，装满了烟叶，他们伸展了身子，倚在自己的肘上，开始认真地吸烟，心里却一点底儿都没有。烟的味道很不好，令他们觉得恶心，可汤姆却说：

"啊，这太简单了！如果我早知道就这样的话，我早就学了。"

"我也一样，"乔说，"这没什么。"

"好多次我看别人抽烟时，都在想我要是能抽

ing, and thought well I wish I could do that; but I never thought I could," said Tom.

"I believe I could smoke this pipe all day," said Joe. "I don't feel sick."

"Neither do I," said Tom. "I could smoke it all day. But I bet you Jeff Thatcher couldn't."

"Jeff Thatcher! Why, he'd fall down just with two draws. Just let him try it once. He'd see!"

"I bet he would. And Jonny Miller—I wish I could see Jonny Miller deal with it once."

"Oh, I bet just one little breath would blow him."

"Joe, say—I wish the boys could see us now."

"So do I."

"Say—boys, don't say anything about it, and sometime when they're around, I'll come up to you and say, 'Joe, got a pipe? I want a smoke.' And you'll say, kind of careless like, as if it wasn't anything, you'll say, 'Yes, I got my old pipe, and another one, but my tobacco isn't very good.' And I'll say, 'Oh, that's all right, if it's strong enough.' And then you'll bring out the pipes, and we'll light up just calmly, and then just see their look!"

"Oh, that'll be happy, Tom! I wish it were now!"

"So do I! And when we tell them we learned it when we were of pirating, won't they wish they'd been

就好了。可从来没想过我真能抽。"汤姆说。

"我想我能抽上一整天,"乔说,"我一点也不觉得难受。"

"我也不觉得,"汤姆说,"我也能抽一整天,可我跟你打赌杰夫·撒切尔不行。"

"杰夫·撒切尔!噢!他抽两口就躺倒了,让他试一次,就知道了!"

"我打赌他肯定得趴倒,还有乔尼·米勒——我真想看看乔尼·米勒也抽上一次。"

"噢,我担保一小口就得要他的命。"

"乔,我说——我特希望那些男孩能看到咱们现在抽烟的样子。"

"我也是。"

"我说——假设那些男孩都在这儿。咱俩不说什么,等他们聚到咱周围时,我就到你跟前,说,'乔,有烟斗吗?我想抽烟。'你呢,带着那种不经意的样子,好像这不是什么事,说,'有,有个旧的,另外还有一个。可我的烟草不怎么好。'然后我就说,'没事,只有劲儿够。'然后你就把烟斗取出来,咱们若无其事地点上,然后你就看他们的表情吧!"

"噢,太有意思了,汤姆,我希望现在就行!"

"我也是!如果咱们告诉他们抽烟是在当海盗时学的,他们难道不希望他们当初也能跟咱们来

along?"

"Oh, I'll just bet they will!"

So the talk ran on. But presently the silences widened. They felt very sick and wanted to vomit all the time. Both boys looked very pale and miserable, now. Joe's pipe dropped from his nerveless fingers. Tom's followed. Joe said weakly: "I've lost my knife. I think I'd better go and find it."

Tom said, with trembling lips:

"I'll help you. You go over that way and I'll hunt around by the spring. No, you needn't come, Huck— we can find it."

So Huck sat down again, and waited an hour. Then he found it lonesome, and went to find his comrades. They were far from each other in the woods, both very pale, both fast asleep.

They were not talkative at supper that night. They had a poor look, and when Huck prepared his pipe after the meal and was going to prepare theirs, they said no, they were not feeling very well—something they ate at dinner had disagreed with them.

About midnight Joe awoke, and called the boys. There was an oppressiveness in the air that seemed to show something. The boys huddled themselves together and sat still, intent and waiting. Now a flash turned

吗?"

"我打赌他们肯定这么想!"

他们说啊说,可一会儿,沉默的时间就越来越长了。俩人都觉得特别恶心,直想吐,脸上一点血色都没有,一副可怜兮兮的样子。乔的烟从他那双无力的手指中掉了下去,汤姆的也掉了。乔无力地说:"我把小刀丢了,我想我最好去找找。"

汤姆嘴唇颤抖着说:

"我帮你,你走那边,我到山泉周围找找。不,你不必来,哈克——我们能找到的。"

因此,哈克又坐下来了。等了一个小时,他觉得寂寞,就去找他的同志了。那两个人在林子里相互离得很远,脸色都很苍白,正昏昏沉沉地睡着呢。

那天晚上吃饭时他们话不多,俩人看着仍是可怜巴巴的。饭后哈克给自己装烟管,也打算给他们俩装时,他们说不了,因为感觉不太舒服——可能吃饭时吃的什么东西不对劲儿。

大约半夜乔醒了,把两个孩子也叫了起来。空气很闷,仿佛有什么要发作。孩子们挤在一起坐着,一动不动,神情专注,像在等待着什么。

night into day. And it showed three white, surprised faces, too. A deep thunder went rolling and tumbling down the heavens in the distance. They clung together in terror. A few big raindrops fell upon the leaves.

"Quick, boys! Go for the tent!" shouted Tom.

They sprang away. One blinding flash after another came, and one deafening thunder after another. And now a drenching rain poured down and the rising hurricane drove along the ground. One by one the boys took shelter under the tent, cold, frightened, and streaming with water; but to have friends in misery seemed something to be thankful for. They could not talk, the old sail flapped so violently. The tempest rose higher and higher, and presently the sail tore loose from its fastenings and went away. The boys seized each other's hand and fled to the shelter of a great oak that stood upon the riverbank. The storm was at its highest that seemed likely to tear the island to pieces, burn it up, drown it to the treetops, blow it away, deafen every creature in it, all at one and the same moment. It was a wild night for homeless young heads to be out in.

But at last the battle was done. The boys went back to camp, but they found there was still something to be thankful for, because the big tree—the shelter of their beds was a ruin now, blasted by the lightening, and they

这时，一道闪电将黑夜变成了白天，也照亮了三张苍白、惊愕的面孔。远处天际边深沉的雷声轰隆隆地响起。他们非常怕，相互紧紧抱着，几颗大雨点落在了树叶上。

"快跑，伙计们！快到帐篷里躺着！"汤姆喊道。

他们跳起来跑走了。一道道令人目眩的闪电劈下来，一声声震耳欲聋的雷声响起来，天上下起了倾盆大雨，愈演愈烈的飓风沿着地面吹起。孩子们一个接一个地进了帐篷躲雨，浑身发冷，满心恐惧，头上身上还不停地往下滴着雨水，可他们觉得特别欣慰，因为还有朋友患难与共。他们不能说话，因为那个旧帐篷被风吹得猛烈地摆动着。暴风雨越来越猛烈了，帐篷的绑角处被风刮松了，紧接着，帐篷就给刮跑了，孩子们互相拉着手，飞奔到河岸的大橡树下避雨。此时的暴风雨到了极致，小岛似乎被撕成碎片，要被燃烧起来，要被淹得只剩树尖，岛上的每一样活物都要被刮走，震聋。对于这些未归家的孩子们来说，这真是一个可怕的夜晚。

最终，与暴风雨的斗争结束了，孩子们回到了营地，发现他们真的该感谢上帝。因为替他们遮雨挡风的大树已经被雷劈了，而这天灾发生时，

were not under it when the disaster happened.

Everything in camp was wet. They made the fire burn again. They dried their boiled ham and had a dinner, and after that they sat by the fire and glorified their midnight adventure until morning, for there was not a dry place to sleep on, anywhere around.

As the sun began to steal in upon the boys, sleepiness came over them and they went out on the sand bar and lay down to sleep. After breakfast, they were attracted by the idea of being Indians for a change instead of being pirates; so it was not long before they were naked, and fought against each other. They gathered in camp toward suppertime, hungry and happy; but now a difficulty arose—Indians could not start dinner together without smoking a pipe of peace. Two of the boys almost wished they remained pirates. However, there was no other way; so with such show of cheerfulness as they could they called for the pipe and took their pipe. They were glad when they found that they could now smoke a little without having to go and hunt for a lost knife; they did not get sick enough to be seriously uncomfortable. They practiced cautiously, after supper, with right fair success, and so they spent a happy evening. They were in their wild pride and happiness in their new acquirement. We will leave them to smoke and chatter and

他们没躺在下面。

营地里到处都是湿的。他们又点起了火，烘干了火腿，吃了一顿饭，之后就坐在火旁，吹嘘着半夜的冒险经历，直到清晨。因为周围没有一块干地可让他们睡觉。

太阳悄悄地爬了上来，困意向他们袭来，三人走到沙洲上，躺下睡觉，早饭后，他们想换换口味，不当海盗了，扮印第安人。这个想法强烈地吸引着他们；很快三人就脱光了身子，互相打斗了起来，直到晚饭他们才一起回到营地。肚子虽然饿了，心情却很愉快，可这会儿他们又碰到了一个难题——印第安人吃饭前必须抽一管象征和平的烟。那两个男孩真希望自己一直是海盗就好了。可却没有办法，只好尽量表现得很高兴的样子，要来了一管烟拿上了。当他们发现自己可以抽一点儿而不需再找丢失的小刀时，他们很兴奋，俩人也不觉得恶心了，也不觉得特别难受。晚饭后他们又接着练习抽烟。取得了伟大的胜利，因而晚上过得挺快乐，为自己掌握了这个新本事而特别自豪、欣喜。我们先留他们在这儿抽烟，聊天，吹牛吧，因为我们接下来的事暂时不需要他们了。

brag, since we have no further use for them at present.

Chapter 17
Pirates at Their Own Funeral

But there was no joy in the little town that same peaceful Saturday afternoon. The Harpers and Aunt Polly's family were being put into mourning, with great grief and many tears. The village was unusually quiet, although it was ordinarily quiet enough, in all conscience. The Saturday holiday seemed a burden to the children. They had no heart in their sports, and gradually gave them up.

In the afternoon Becky Thatcher was crying in the empty schoolhouse yard, and feeling very sad. But she found nothing there to comfort her. She said to herself: "Oh, if I only had a knob again! But I haven't got anything now to remember him by." And she choked back a little sob.

Presently she stopped, and said:

"It was right here. Oh, if it was to do over again, I wouldn't say that—I wouldn't say it for the whole world. But he's gone now; I'll never never never see him any more."

This thought broke her down and she wandered

第十七章　海盗们出席自己的葬礼

可在同样宁静的那个星期六下午,小镇找不到一丝快乐的气息。哈普和波莉姨妈两家人已穿上丧服,大家沉浸在一片悲痛和泪水中。村子尽管平时也是宁静的,可今天的宁静却异乎寻常。星期六的假日对孩子们来说似乎成了负担。他们没心思玩什么游戏,慢慢地都不玩了。

下午,贝琪在空荡荡的校园里哭着,特别难过。可她却无以慰藉。她对自己说:"噢,哪怕我还能有一个圆柄就好了! 可现在我什么纪念他的都没有,"她哽咽着。

一会儿她不哭了,自言自语道:
"就是在这儿,如果一切可以重来,我就不会那么说了——就是把整个世界给我,我也不会说那种话了。可他现在走了,我永远永远永远都再也看不到他了。"
想到这儿,她不禁大哭起来,慢慢地走远了。

away, with the tears rolling down her cheeks. Then quite a group of boys and girls—playmates of Tom's and Joe's—came by, and stood looking over the paling fence and talking in respectful tones of how Tom did so—and—so, the last time they saw him, and how Joe said this and that small things—and each speaker pointed out the exact place where the lost boys stood at the time, and then added something like "and I was standing just so—just as I am now, and as if you were him—I was as close as that—and he smiled, just that way—and then something seemed to go all over me, like—terrible, you know—and I never thought what it meant, of course, but I can see now!"

When the Sunday-school hour was finished, the next morning, the bell began to toll, instead of ringing in the usual way. The villagers began to gather and whisper about the sad event. But there was no whispering in the house. None could remember when the little church had been so full before. There was finally a waiting pause, and then Aunt Polly entered, followed by Sid and Mary, and they by the Harper family, all in deep black, and all the people, the old clergyman as well, rose respectfully and stood until the mourners were seated in the front seats. There was another silence, broken at intervals by sobs, and then the clergyman spread his hands

眼泪还不停地顺着脸颊流下来，一群男孩、女孩们——汤姆和乔的玩伴走过来，站在曾经粉刷过的篱笆旁看着。用尊重的语气谈论汤姆曾经怎么怎么了，他们最后一次见他怎么了。对于这样那样的小事，乔说过什么——每一个说话的人都确切地指出失踪的孩子当时在哪儿，然后加了些证明如下的话。"我就那样站着——就像我现在；你呢，就是他——我和他就这么近——他笑着，就像那样——然后我浑身有一种，似乎有一种感觉。就像——太可怕了，你知道——我那会儿从未想过，这意味着什么，但我现在明白了。"

第二天早晨，主日学校结束，钟声就缓慢而有节奏地响起来，绝不是平时的那种清脆的玲玲声。村里人开始聚在一起，低声谈论着这件悲痛的事，一走进教堂，大家就都不说话了，谁也记不起小教堂什么时候像今天这样有这么多人。最后在大家的等待中，波莉姨妈走进来了，后面跟着赛德和玛丽，后面是哈普一家，都穿着深黑色的丧服。所有的人，包括老牧师，尊敬地站了起来，这些哀悼亲人的人们在前排就座。又是一阵沉默，偶尔传出几声啜泣。牧师伸出他的手，开

and prayed. A moving hymn was sung, and the text followed: "I am the Resurrection and the life."

As the service went on, the clergyman showed his regret for only having seen the faults and flaws in the poor boys. He related many touching incidents in the lives of the lost boys, too, which showed their sweet, generous characters. The people became more and more moved, as the sad tale went on, till at last all broke down and joined the weeping mourners, the clergyman himself giving way to his feelings and crying.

There was a rustle in the passage, which nobody noticed; a moment later the church door creaked; the clergyman raised his streaming eyes above his handkerchief, and stood dumbfounded! First one and then another pair of eyes followed the clergyman's, and then almost within one second, all the people rose and stared while the three dead boys came marching up the passage, Tom in the lead, Joe next, and Huck, in rags, walking shyly in the back! They had hid in the passage listening to their own funeral speech!

Aunt Polly, Mary, and the Harpers threw themselves upon their boys, almost killed them with kisses and poured out thanksgivings, while poor Huck stood shyly and uncomfortable, not knowing exactly what to do or where to hide from so many unwelcoming eyes. He

始祈祷，然后唱了赞美诗，又朗读了名为"我的复活与生命"的经文。

仪式继续进行着，牧师表达了自己的忏悔，他说自己过去光看到可怜的孩子身上的缺点而实际上那些孩子们温和可爱，慷慨大方。借此，他讲了他们的许多感人的事情。听着这些故事，人们越来越感动了，最后所有的人都和死者家属一起大哭，牧师自己也抑制不住自己的情感，哭了。

走道发出一阵窸窸窣窣的声音，可没人注意到；一会儿教堂的门就开了；牧师从手帕中抬起他的泪眼，顿时目瞪口呆！接着一双，又一双眼睛跟着牧师望去，几乎不到一秒钟，所有的人都站了起来，瞪着眼睛。三个死去的男孩沿着走道大踏步走来，汤姆在先，乔跟着，一身破烂的哈克害羞地走在后面！他们一直躲在走道后面听着自己的葬礼致词。

波莉姨妈、玛丽、哈普一家扑向他们的孩子，亲来亲去，嘴里不停地说着"感谢上帝"的话，几乎都快让孩子们窒息了。可怜的哈克不好意思地站在一旁，很别扭，不知道面对这么多双不欢迎的眼睛，自己该干什么，该躲到哪儿去。他犹

hesitated, and started to go away, but Tom seized him and said:

"Aunt Polly, it isn't fair. Somebody's got to be glad to see Huck."

"And so they shall. I'm glad to see him, poor motherless thing!" And the loving attentions of Aunt Polly made him more uncomfortable than he was before.

Suddenly the clergyman shouted at the top of his voice: "Praise God from whom all blessings flow—sing and put your hearts in it!"

And they did. Tom Sawyer the Pirate looked around upon the envying boys about him and admitted in his heart that this was the proudest moment of his life.

Chapter 18
Tom Tells His Dream Secret

That was Tom's great secret—the plan to return home with his brother pirates and attend their own funerals.

At breakfast, Monday morning, Aunt Polly and Mary were very loving to Tom, and very attentive to his wants. There was an unusual amount of talk. In the course of it Aunt Polly said:

"Well, I don't say it wasn't a fine joke, Tom, to keep everybody suffering almost a week while you boys

豫着，准备离去，可汤姆抓住他，说：

"波莉姨妈，这不公平，有人应该高兴又见到哈克。"

"是这样，我很高兴见到他，可怜的没妈的东西！"波莉姨妈向他投来的爱意与注意力让他比以前更不自在了。

突然，牧师高声喊道，声音压过了所有的人："赞美上帝，是他给予我们所有的幸福——让我们全心全意地为他歌唱吧！"

众人跟着唱了起来，海盗汤姆·索耶环顾四周，望了望那些羡慕他的男孩们，由衷地认为这是他一生中最自豪的时刻了。

第十八章　汤姆借梦吐露秘密

这就是汤姆那了不起的秘密——与他的海盗兄弟一起回家，参加他们自己的葬礼。

星期一早饭的时候，波莉姨妈和玛丽仍然对汤姆爱个不够，特别留心他想要什么。大家聊了很多。波莉姨妈说：

"我可不能说你这个玩笑开得很好，汤姆，让所有的人为你难过了快一个星期而你们却玩得高

had a good time, but it is a pity you could be so hard-hearted as to let me suffer so. If you could have come over and given me a hint someway that you wasn't dead, and then run off. Say, now, would you, if you'd thought of it?"

"I—well, I don't know."

"Tom, you'll look back, someday, when it's too late, and wish you'd cared a little more for me when it would have cost you so little."

"Now, auntie, you know I do care for you," said Tom.

"I'd know it better if you acted more like it."

"I wish now I'd thought of it," said Tom, with a respectful tone; "but I dreamed about you, anyway. That's something, isn't it?"

"It isn't much—a cat does that much—but it's better than nothing. What did you dream?"

"Why, Wednesday night I dreamt that you were sitting over there by the bed, and Sid was sitting by the woodbox, and Mary next to him."

"Well, so we did. So we always do. I'm glad your dreams could take even that much trouble over us."

"And I dreamt that Joe Harper's mother was here."

"Why, she was here! Did you dream any more?"

高兴兴。我很伤心，你心肠怎么这么硬，舍得让我这样为你悲痛。如果你当时能回来一下，用什么方法暗示暗示我，说明你没死，只是跑走了那就好了。说，现在，如果你当时想到了，你会不会那么做呢？"

"我——嗯，我不知道。"

"汤姆，终有一天等你回忆过去时，你会想当时能多关心姨妈一点儿就好了，这样做费不了什么事，可那会儿想起就太晚了。"

"姨妈，你知道我的确关心你。"

"如果你能在行动上表现出来，我就更明白了。"

"我现在希望我当时能想到那么做了。"汤姆带着一种尊敬的语气说，"可不管怎样，我梦到你了，这也行，不是吗？"

"这并不够——猫也能做到这点——可这总比什么都没做强。你梦到什么啦？"

"嗯，星期三晚上我梦到你在床那儿坐着，赛德坐在木箱旁，玛丽在他旁边。"

"没错，我们总这样坐，我很高兴，你做梦还能不嫌麻烦地想到我们。"

"我梦到乔·哈普的妈妈也在这儿。"

"她是在这儿！你还梦到什么啦？"

"Oh, lots. But it's so dim, now."

"Well, try to remember it—can't you?"

Tom pressed his fingers on his forehead an anxious minute, and then said:

"I've got it now! I've got it now! It blew the candle!"

"Mercy on us! Go on, Tom—go on!"

"You made Sid shut the door."

"Well, for the land's sake! I never heard anything as surprising as that in all my days! I shall tell Sereny Harper immediately. I'd like to see her get around this about superstition. Go on, Tom!"

"Oh, it's all getting as bright as day, now. Next you said I wasn't bad, only naughty and reckless."

"And so it was! Well, goodness gracious! Go on, Tom!"

"And then you began to cry."

"So I did. So I did. Not the first time, neither. And then—"

"Then Mrs Harper began to cry, and said Joe was just the same, and she wished she hadn't beaten him for taking cream when she threw it out her own self—"

"Tom! The spirit was upon you! You were prophesying—that's what you were doing! Land alive, go on,

"可多了。但现在都记不清楚了。"

"试试看能不能想起来——行吗？"

汤姆焦急地用手指在额头上压了一会儿，说：

"我现在想起来了！我现在想起来了！风吹着烛了！"

"天哪！继续说，汤姆——继续！"

"你让赛德去关门。"

"哎呀！我这辈子还没听过这么新奇的事！我要马上告诉瑟瑞妮·哈普，看看她用迷信怎么解释这事。继续，汤姆！"

"噢，现在一切都跟白天一样清楚了。然后你说我不坏，只是淘气、冒失。"

"对。啧啧！继续，汤姆！"

"然后你就开始哭了。"

"我是哭了，我是哭了。不是第一次哭，那后来——"

"后来，哈普太太也开始哭了，说乔也一样。她真希望自己没有错以为乔偷吃奶油而打他，因为奶油是她自己扔掉的——"

"汤姆！你一定是神灵附身了！神灵一直在启示你呀！上帝！继续，汤姆！"

Tom!"

"Then Sid he said—he said—"

"I don't think I said anything," said Sid.

"Shut your mouth and let Tom go on! What did he say, Tom?"

"He said—I think he said he hoped I was better off where I was gone to, but if I'd been better sometimes— And you shut him up sharp."

"I did! There must have been an angel there."

"And Mrs Harper told about Joe frightening her with a firecracker, and you told about Peter and the painkiller—"

"Just as true as I live!"

"And then there was a lot of talk about us, and about having the funeral on Sunday, and then you and old Miss Harper hugged and cried, and she went."

"It happened just so! Tom, you couldn't tell it more like, if you'd seen it! And then what? Go on, Tom!"

"Then I thought you prayed for me—and I could see you and hear every word you said. And you went to bed, and I was so sorry, that I took and wrote on a piece of wood, 'we aren't dead—we are only off being pirates.' and put it on the table by the candle, and then you looked so good, laying there asleep, that I thought I

"然后赛德说——说——"

"我记得我没说什么。"赛德说。

"闭上你的嘴，让汤姆继续说，他说什么，汤姆？"

"他说——我记得他说他希望我在另一个世界过得更好，可如果我过去能好一点儿的话——这时你就突然让他闭上嘴了！"

"没错！你那会儿身边一定有个天使！"

"然后哈普太太讲到乔用鞭炮吓她，你说到了彼得和止痛药——"

"分毫不差。"

"你们说了很多关于我的事情。还有星期天举行葬礼的事。之后，你和哈普太太互相拥抱，又哭了一场，然后她走了。"

"当时就是这样的！汤姆，就是你亲眼看到，也不可能比这讲得更像了！然后怎么样？继续，汤姆！"

"然后我记得你为我祈祷——我在梦里可以看到你，听到你说的每一句话！后来你就上床了，我特别难过，就拿出一片木头，在上面写了'我们没死——只是去当海盗了。'把它放在桌上蜡烛旁。你躺在那儿睡着了，看着很安详。我还走到

227

went and leaned over and kissed you on the lips."

"Did you, Tom, did you! I just forgive you everything for that!" And she hugged the boy so tightly that made him feel like the guiltiest of villains.

"It was very kind, even though it was only a dream," Sid said.

"Shut up, Sid! A body does just the same in a dream as he'd do if he was awake. Here's a big apple I've been saving for you, Tom. I'm thankful to the good God and Father of us all I've got you back."

What a hero Tom became, now! He did not go jumping, but moved as dignified as a pirate who felt that the public eye was on him. And indeed it was: he tried not to seem to see the looks or hear the words as he passed along, but they were food and drink to him. Smaller boys than himself followed his heels, as proud to be seen with him. Boys of his own size pretended not to know he had been away at all; but they were envious, nevertheless.

At school the two heroes began to tell their adventures to hungry listeners. And finally, when they got out their pipes and went calmly puffing around, the very peak of glory was reached.

Tom decided that he could be independent of Becky Thatcher now. Glory was enough. He would live for glo-

你面前，弯下身，亲了亲你的嘴唇。"

"是吗？汤姆，是吗？就冲这，我原谅你的一切！"她紧紧地搂着男孩，让他感觉无地自容，简直是个恶棍了。

"你真好，可惜这只是个梦。"赛德说。

"闭嘴，赛德！一个人清醒时怎么做的，他在梦里就会是什么样。拿上这个我一直给你留的大苹果，汤姆，感谢上帝你回来了。"

汤姆现在真是变成了个英雄！他不再去蹦蹦跳跳，他感觉到大家都在注视着他，所以走起路来，就像一个高贵的强盗。事实也是这样，他走路时，总是试图表现得根本就没看见别人的表情或听见别人说什么话，然而这些对于他来说有如食粮。年龄小一些的孩子们跟在他脚后跟，因为让别人看到他和汤姆在一起是很自豪的。和汤姆差不多大的男孩则装着根本就不知道他曾经离开过这里，可心里对汤姆则羡慕不已。

在学校里两位英雄开始向那些如饥似渴的听众们讲述他的冒险经历。最后，当他们取出烟斗平静地吞云吐雾时，那种荣耀感真是到了极致。

汤姆觉得他现在可以没有贝琪·撒切尔而生活了。围绕在他身边的光环就足够了。他将为这种

ry. Now that he was famous, maybe she would be wanting to win his favor. Presently she arrived. Tom pretended not to see her. He moved away and joined a group of boys and girls and began to talk. Soon he observed that she was running back and forth with red face and dancing eyes, pretending to be busy running after schoolmates, and screaming with laughter when she seized someone; but he noticed that she always seized someone near him. This made him more proud. In her secret and longing glance, Becky observed that now Tom was talking more particularly to Amy Lawrence than to any else. She felt a sharp pang and grew upset and uneasy at once. She tried to go away, but her feet were against her, and carried her to the group instead. She said to a girl almost at Tom's elbow:

"Mary Austin! My ma's going to let me have one picnic."

"Oh, won't it be fun! You are going to have all the girls and boys?"

"Yes, everyone that's friend to me—or wants to be"; and she glanced ever so secretly at Tom, but he talked right along to Amy Lawrence about the terrible storm on the island, and how the lightening tore the great tree all to pieces while he was "standing within three feet of it."

荣耀而活。既然他已经出名了，或许她需要赢得他的青睐。这会儿贝琪来了，汤姆假装没看到她。他走开了，来到一群男孩女孩中间，与他们聊天。很快他观察到她正跑前跑后，假装忙于追逐同学。她满脸通红、顾盼流离，一旦抓到谁，又笑又叫的。可他注意到她抓到的人总在他周围。这更使他得意了。她带着渴盼的心情偷偷地瞥了瞥汤姆，发现他正跟艾米·劳伦斯说话；说得比跟谁的时间都长。她强烈地感到一阵痛苦，马上变得难过、不安了。她想走开，脚却不听话，硬是把她带到了那堆孩子中。她站在跟汤姆几乎只有一寸之隔的地方，对一个女孩说：

"玛丽·奥斯汀！我妈妈准备让我举办一次野餐会。"

"噢，太好了！你打算把所有的男孩、女孩都请去吗？"

"是，所有和我是朋友——或要跟我做朋友的人。"她又非常隐秘地瞥了一眼汤姆，可他却一直在给艾米·劳伦斯讲他在岛上遭遇的暴风雨，讲闪电是如何把大树劈成碎片的，而他当时就站在三英尺外的地方。

"Oh, may I come?" Said Gracie Miller.

"Yes."

"And me?" said Sally Rogers.

"Yes."

"And me too?" said Susy Harper. "And Joe?"

"Yes."

And so on, with clapping of joyful hands, till all the group had begged for invitations but Tom and Amy. Then Tom turned coolly away, still talking, and took Amy with him. Becky's lips trembled and the tears came to her eyes; she hid these signs with a forced happiness and went on chattering; she got away as soon as she could and hid herself and had what her sex call "a good cry." Then she sat sadly, with wounded pride, till the bell rang. She rose up now and said she knew what she'd do.

Tom continued his talk with Amy with self satisfaction. And he kept drifting about to find Becky. At last he found her which gave him great disappointment. She was sitting cozily on a little bench behind the schoolhouse looking at a picture book with Alfred Temple—and so absorbed were they, and their heads so close together over the book, that they did not seem to be conscious of anything in the world besides. Jealousy ran red-hot through Tom's veins. He began to hate himself for

"噢，我也可以去吗?"格瑞瑟·米勒问。

"可以。"

"我呢?"沙莉·罗切斯问。

"行。"

"我也行吗?"苏珊·哈普问,"还有乔?"

"行。"

一个接一个,大家高兴地拍着手,直到最后,这堆孩子都请求了贝琪,得到了邀请,除了汤姆和艾米。汤姆满不在乎地走了,还带着艾米边走边跟她说着话。贝琪的嘴唇颤抖着,眼泪已经到了眼眶,她遮掩住这些,强作欢颜,继续聊着天;可一有机会她就很快地走掉了,躲在一个地方,就像女孩子们常说的那样"大哭了一场"。她难过地坐在那儿,感到自尊心受到了伤害。直到上课铃响了,她才站了起来,告诉自己知道该怎么做了。

汤姆带着一种自我满足感,继续和艾米聊着天。他从这儿挪到那儿,从那儿挪到这儿,想要找到贝琪。最后他终于看到她了,却非常失望。她正暖洋洋地坐在教室后面的一个小凳上,和艾弗瑞德·泰普一起看画册呢——他们是那么地投入,头挨得那么近,似乎根本意识不到周围的一切。强烈的嫉妒心使汤姆的血在血管里奔腾。他

throwing away the chance Becky had offered for a reconciliation. He called himself a fool, and all the hard names he could think of. He wanted to cry. Amy chatted happily along, as they walked, for her heart was singing, but Tom's tongue had lost its function. He did not hear what Amy was saying. He kept drifting to the back of the schoolhouse, again and again, to burn his eyeballs with the hateful scene there. He could not help it. Becky knew she was winning her fight and was glad to see him suffer as she had suffered.

Amy's happy talk became intolerable. Tom hinted he had to do something now. But in vain—the girl still talked. Tom thought, "Oh, hang her, am I ever going to get rid of her?" At last he must be doing something— and she said artlessly that she would be waiting for him. And he hurried away, hating her for it.

Grinding his teeth, Tom thought, "Any boy in the whole town but that Alfred Temple thinks that he dresses so fine and noble! Oh, all right, I beat you the first day you ever saw this town, mister, and I'll beat you again! You just wait till I catch you out!"

And he went through the actions of beating an imaginary boy—kicking and hitting.

Tom fled home at noon. His conscience could not bear any more of Amy's thankful happiness, and his

开始恨自己丢掉了贝琪刚才给他的一个和解机会。他骂自己是个傻瓜，以及所有他能想到的讨厌的称呼。他想哭，可艾米却边走边叽叽喳喳兴奋地说个不停，因为她的心在歌唱，而汤姆的舌头却转不动了。他没有听艾米说了些什么。他不断地走到教室后面。看着那可憎的一幕，他的眼睛都要喷火了，可还是禁不住想去看看。贝琪知道在这场斗争中她赢了，得意地看着他正像刚才的她一样痛苦。

艾米那快乐的言语现在变得简直难以忍受了。汤姆暗示说他现在得干点儿什么事了。可没用——那个女孩继续唠叨着。汤姆想："噢，让她上吊吧，我怎么都摆脱不了她了？"最后他说他必须要去干点什么事了。可她的心眼儿却那么实在，说她等他。他急忙跑掉了，对她说这样的话感到腻味透了。

汤姆恨恨地咬着牙，想，"这镇上所有的男孩里就艾弗瑞德·泰普觉得自己穿得体面，高贵！哼，好哇，你看到这个镇子的第一天我就收拾过你，先生，我还会揍你的！你就等着什么时候栽到我手里吧！"

他在自己面前虚构了一个男孩，接着完成了一套动作——拳打脚踢。

中午时分汤姆飞快地回家了。他的良心让他无法面对艾米那充满感激、兴奋无比的神情。他

jealousy could bear no more of the other sadness. Becky went on reading her picture book with Alfred, but as the time went on and no Tom came to suffer, her victory began to lose and she lost interest; two or three minutes she pricked up her ear at a footstep, but it was a false hope; no Tom came. At last she grew entirely miserable and wished she hadn't done it so far. When poor Alfred, seeing that he was losing her, he did not know how, kept shouting: "Oh, here's a funny one! Look at this!" she lost patience at last, and said, "Oh, don't bother me! I don't care for them!" and burst into tears, and got up and walked away.

Alfred was going to try to comfort her, but she said:

"Go away and leave me alone, can't you! I hate you!"

So the boy stopped, wondering what he could have done—for she had said she would look at pictures all through the noon—and she walked on, crying. Then Alfred went thoughtfully into the empty schoolhouse. He was ashamed and angry. He easily guessed his way to the truth—the girl had simply made use of him to show her anger upon Tom Sawyer. He hated Tom when this thought occurred to him. He wished there was some way to get that boy into trouble without much risk to himself.

的嫉妒心使他再也无法忍受其他的悲伤事了。贝琪继续和艾弗瑞德看着画册，可时间一点一点过去，再也看不到汤姆那份难过样子，她的胜利感开始消退，对这种把戏也没兴趣了，隔两三分钟她只要听到脚步声就竖起耳朵，可希望却不停地破灭，来人总不是汤姆。最后，她觉得特别难过，觉得自己不该这么过分。可怜的艾弗瑞德看出自己在失去她，却不知所措，只有不住地喊叫："噢，这张有趣！快看！"贝琪最后实在不耐烦了，说："别烦我！我不喜欢这些东西！"说着泪水就涌了出来，她站起身，走开了。

艾弗瑞德想试着安慰她，可她却说：

"滚开！让我一个人呆会儿不行吗？我讨厌你！"

男孩只好停下了，琢磨自己究竟做错了什么——因为是她说的她要一中午都看画片的——贝琪继续走着、哭着。艾弗瑞德若有所思地走进空荡荡的教室。他感到耻辱、生气。不费什么劲儿他就猜到了到底是怎么回事——女孩子只是利用他来表达对汤姆·索耶的不满。想到这儿，他对汤姆的憎恨油然而生。他希望有什么办法可以让那个男孩惹上一身麻烦，而自己不用冒什么险。汤

Tom's spelling book fell under his eye. Here was his chance. He opened to the lesson for the afternoon and poured ink upon the page.

Becky, glancing in at a window behind him at the moment, saw the act, and moved on pretending not to see. She started homeward, now, intending to find Tom and tell him; Tom would be thankful and their troubles would be healed. Before she was halfway home, however, she had changed her mind. The thought of Tom's treatment of her when she was talking about her picnic came painfully back and filled her with shame. She decided to let him get beaten for ruined spelling book, and to hate him forever.

Chapter 19
The Cruelty of "I Didn't Think"

Tom arrived at home in a low mood, and heard his aunt say to him:

"Tom, I've an idea to skin you alive!"

"Auntie, what have I done?"

"Well, you've done enough. Here I went over to Sereny Harper, expecting I'm going to make her believe all that about that dream, when she found out from Joe that you were over here and heard all the talk we had

姆的拼写书映入他的眼帘。他的机会来了，他翻到下午要学的那一课，把墨水泼了上去。

贝琪此时正站在他身后的窗外向里瞥，看见了这一幕。她继续向前走，假装没看到，然后就朝回家的方向走去，想要找到汤姆，告诉他这件事；汤姆一定会很感激的，他们之间的矛盾就会消除的。然而她还没走到一半时，就改变主意了。贝琪又想到了当她谈论她的野餐会时汤姆是如何对待她的，悲伤与羞耻又袭上心头。她决定就让他为那本弄脏了的拼写书挨鞭子吧，而且她要永远恨他。

第十九章　无情的"我没想到"

汤姆情绪低落地回到了家，听到他姨妈冲他嚷道：

"汤姆，我真想活剥了你的皮！"

"姨妈，我做什么啦？"

"哼，够了。我去瑟瑞妮·哈普那儿了，想着要让她相信你梦到的一切，她却从乔那儿得知你那天晚上回来了，听到我们谈话了。汤姆，做出

that night. Tom, I don't know what is to become of a boy that will act like that. It makes me feel so bad to think you could let me go to Serenry Harper and make such a fool of myself and never say a word."

His smartness of the morning had seemed to Tom a good joke before. It only looked mean now. He hung his head and could not think of anything to say for a moment. Then he said:

"Auntie, I wish I hadn't done it."

"Oh, child, you could think to come all the way over here from Jackson's Island in the night to laugh at our troubles, and you could think to fool me with a lie about a dream; but you couldn't ever think to pity us and save us from sorrow."

"Auntie, I didn't come over here to laugh at you that night."

"What did you come for, then?"

"I was to tell you not to be uneasy about us, because we hadn't got drowned."

"Oh, Tom, don't lie—don't do it. It only makes things a hundred times worse."

"It isn't a lie, auntie, it's the truth. I wanted to keep you from feeling sad—that was all that made me come."

"I'd give the whole world to believe that. But it

这种事的男孩将来会怎样。想到你让我跑到瑟瑞妮·哈普那儿，又让我出了大丑，而你却一句话不说，我真得难过极了。"

汤姆刚才还觉得早晨开的那个玩笑挺有趣，挺聪明呢，现在看来就只剩下卑鄙了。他低下了头，不知该说什么。过了一会儿他张口了：

"姨妈，我真不该那样做。"

"噢，孩子，你能想到晚上一路从杰克逊岛跑回来，幸灾乐祸地看着我们为你难过；你能想到骗我那是个梦；可你却从未想到可怜我们，把我们从悲痛中拯救出来。"

"姨妈，我那天晚上过来不是笑话你的。"

"那你来干什么？"

"我是要告诉你别为我们不安，我们没有淹死。"

"汤姆，别撒谎了——别这样。这只会使得事情变得更糟。"

"我没有撒谎，姨妈，我说的是真的。我想要让你别难过——我就是为这个回来的。"

"就是把整个世界都给我，我也无法相信你。

isn't reasonable; because, why didn't you tell me, child?"

"Why, you see, when you got to talking about the funeral, I just got all of the idea of our coming and hiding in the church, and I couldn't somehow bear to ruin it. So I just put the wood back in my pocket and kept silent."

"What wood?"

"The wood I had written on to tell you we'd gone pirating. I wish now, you'd woken up when I kissed you—I do, honest."

"The hard lines in his aunt's face relaxed and a sudden tenderness appeared in her eyes.

"Did you kiss me, Tom?"

"Why, yes, I did."

"Are you sure you did, Tom?"

"Why, yes, I did, auntie—certain sure."

"What did you kiss me for, Tom?"

"Because I loved you so, and you laid there moaning and I was so sorry."

The words sounded like truth. The old lady could not hide a trembling in her voice when she said:

"Kiss me again, Tom! —and be off with you to school, now, and don't bother me anymore."

The moment he was gone, she ran to a closet and

你说的一点儿都没道理，既然你回来了，为什么不告诉我呢？"

"嗯，因为听到你说举行葬礼的事儿时，我满脑子想的就是葬礼当天回来，藏在教堂里。我不忍破坏自己的这个计划，所以我把那个木头片又放回兜里，没跟你说一句话。"

"什么木头片？"

"就是我在上面写了'我们去当海盗了'，然后打算给你留下的那个东西。我现在真希望，我亲你的时候你能醒来——实话实说，我真希望是这样。"

汤姆姨妈脸上绷紧的皱纹舒展了，眼中突然露出了温柔的目光。

"你亲我了吗，汤姆？"

"对，我亲了。"

"你肯定你亲了吗，汤姆？"

"是，我肯定，姨妈——我当然肯定。"

"你为什么亲我呢，汤姆？"

"因为我爱你，你躺在那里呻吟着，我很难过。"

"这话听着像是真的。"老太太再说话时声音不禁有些颤抖。

"再亲亲我，汤姆！——然后立刻去上学，别再烦我了。"

汤姆一走，她就跑到衣橱前，取出了那件汤

got out the ruin of a jacket which Tom had gone pirating in. Then she stopped, and said to herself:

"No, I don't care. Poor boy, I think he's lied about it—but it's a blessed, blessed lie, there's such a comfort coming from it. I hope God—I know God will forgive him, because it was such goodheartedness in him to tell it. But I don't want to find out it's a lie. I won't look."

She put the jacket away, and stood by thinking a minute. Twice she put out her hand to take the jacket again, and twice she controlled herself. Once more she ventured, and this time she defended herself with the thought: "It's a good lie—it's a good lie—I won't let it make me feel sad." So she looked in the jacket pocket. A moment later she was reading Tom's piece of wood through flowing tears and saying: "I could forgive the boy, now, if he'd made a million sins!"

Chapter 20
Tom Takes Becky's Punishment

Aunt Polly's kissing Tom swept away his low spirits and made him lighthearted and happy again. He started for school and had the luck of meeting Becky Thatcher at the head of Meadow Lane. His mood always determined

姆当海盗时穿的，如今已成为破烂的夹克衫。她停下来，对自己说：

"不，我不敢看。可怜的孩子，我想他又在撒谎——可那是善意的谎言，听着让人真觉得舒服。我希望上帝——我知道上帝会原谅他的，因为他是好心说出来的，可我还是不想知道他是在撒谎，我不看了。"

她把夹克衫放在了一边，站在那儿想了一会儿。两次她伸出手去拿那件夹克衫，两次她都克制住了自己。她又一次鼓起勇气，并为自己打气说："这是个善意的谎言——这是个善意的谎言——我不会难过的。"她朝夹克衫的兜里看去。一会儿她已经泪流满面地在读汤姆写的那个木头片了，还自言自语地说："我会原谅这个孩子的，哪怕他罪行累累！"

第二十章　汤姆代贝琪受过

波莉姨妈亲了汤姆，这使他低落的情绪一扫而光，又变得轻松、快乐了。他出发去学校，很幸运地在麦德巷口见到了贝琪·撒切尔。汤姆此时

his manner. Without a moment's hesitation he ran to her and said:

"I acted very mean today, Becky, and I'm so sorry. I won't ever, ever do that way again, as long as ever I live—please don't be angry, won't you?"

The girl stopped and looked at him scornfully:

"I'll thank you if you don't speak to me, Mr. Thomas Sawyer. I'll never speak to you again."

She turned her head and passed on. Tom was so astonished that he said nothing. But he was angry. He went sadly into the school-yard wishing she were a boy, and imagining how he would beat her if she were. It seemed to Becky that she could hardly wait to see Tom beaten for the ruined spelling book.

Now, as Becky was passing by the teacher's desk, which stood near the door, she noticed that the key was in the lock! It was a precious moment. She could not resist her curiosity to see what book Mr. Dobbins was always reading. She glanced around, found herself alone, and the next instant she had the book in her hands. The title page carried no information to her mind, so she began to turn the leaves. At that moment a shadow fell on the page and Tom Sawyer stepped in at the door, and caught a glance of the book. Becky closed the book hurriedly and had the bad luck to tear the page down the

的情绪决定了他的态度，他毫不犹豫地奔向贝琪，说：

"我今天做得很卑鄙，贝琪，我非常抱歉。我这一辈子再也不会那样了——请你别生气，好吗？"

女孩停下了，轻蔑地看着他说：

"如果你不跟我说话，我会感激你的，托马斯·索耶先生，我再也不会跟你说话了。"

她转过头去，继续走着。汤姆惊得一句话也说不出来。他非常生气，满脸沮丧地走进了校园，想着她要是个男孩就好了！汤姆想象着如果她是男孩，他会怎么揍她，而贝琪似乎已经等不及想要看汤姆会怎样因为那本被弄污的拼写书而挨揍了。

这时，正当贝琪路过摆在门口的老师的办公桌时，她注意到钥匙就在锁上！这可是个难得的机会。她无法抑制自己的好奇心，想看看道宾斯先生一直在读什么书。她向周围瞄了一眼，发现这儿只有自己，她马上把书拿在了手里。可从印有标题的那一页没看出什么名堂，就开始向后翻。这时，一个影子落在了纸上，她抬头看到汤姆·索耶进了门，还瞥了一眼书。贝琪立刻把书合上，可倒霉的是她把刚看的那一页从中间一下撕破了。

middle. She pushed it into the desk, turned the key, and burst out crying with shame and anger.

"Tom Sawyer, you are just as mean as you can be, to sneak up and look at what a person's looking at."

"How could I know you were looking at anything?"

"You ought to be ashamed of yourself, Tom Sawyer; you know you're going to tell on me, and oh, what shall I do, what shall I do! I'll be beaten, and I never was beaten in school."

Then she stamped her little foot and said:

"Be so mean if you want to! I know something that's going to happen. You just wait and you'll see! Hateful, hateful, hateful!"—and she ran out of the house with a new explosion of crying.

Tom stood still, rather confused by this violent attack. Presently he said to himself:

"What a curious kind of a fool a girl is. Never been beaten in school! That's just like a girl—they're so thin - skinned and chickenhearted. Well, of course I am not going to tell Old Dobbins on this little fool, because there're other ways of revenging on her that isn't so mean; but what of it? Old Dobbins will ask who it was tore his book. Nobody'll answer. Then he'll do just the way he always does—ask first one and then another, and when he comes to the right girl he'll know it, without

她把书推进了办公桌，拧了钥匙，越想越觉得羞耻、生气，不由得哭了起来。

"汤姆·索耶，你真是个卑鄙小人，偷偷地跑来看别人。"

"我怎么知道你在看什么？"

"你应该为自己感到耻辱，汤姆·索耶；你知道你这么做会对我有什么影响。噢，我该怎么办，我该怎么办？我要挨打了，我从未在学校挨过打。"

她跺着脚说：

"汤姆，你要多卑鄙就有多卑鄙！我知道你也要有麻烦，你就等着吧！讨厌，讨厌，讨厌！"——她又痛哭着跑出教室。

汤姆一动不动地站着，被这猛烈的攻击搞得莫名其妙。他自言自语道：

"女孩子真是奇怪的傻瓜，居然在学校没挨过揍。她们都这样——脸皮薄，胆子小。嗯，我当然不会向老道宾斯告这个小傻瓜的状，卑鄙小人才这干。报复她我有的是办法。但这件事会怎么样呢？老道宾斯会问是谁撕了他的书。没人会回答。然后他会按照一惯的做法——一个挨一个地问，等他正好来到贝琪前，不用问就知道了。

any telling. Girls' faces always tell on them. She will be beaten."

Presently the spelling book discovery was made, and Tom's mind was entirely full of his own matters for a while. She did not expect that Tom could get out of his trouble by denying that he spilt the ink on the book himself; and she was right. The denial only seemed to make the thing worse for Tom. Becky supposed she would be glad of that. But when the worst time came, she had an impulse to get up and tell on Alfred Temple, but she made an effort and forced herself to keep quiet—because, "he'll tell about me tearing the picture book sure. I wouldn't say a word, not to save his life!"

Tom took his beating and went back to seat not at all brokenhearted, for he thought it was possible that he had unknowingly spilled on the spelling book himself.

A whole hour passed by, the master sat nodding in his chair. By and by, Mr. Dobbins unlocked his desk, and reached for his book. He took it out and settled himself in his chair to read! Tom shot a glance at Becky. He had seen a hunted and helpless rabbit look as she did, with a gun aimed at its head. Instantly he forgot his quarrel with her. Quick—something must be done! done in a flash, too! Good! —he had an idea! He would run and seize the book, jump through the door and fly. But

女孩子的那张脸总是会泄密的，她会挨揍的。"

这时，他发现自己的拼写书弄污了，满脑子马上被自己的事占据了。贝琪想汤姆不会否认自己把墨水泼到了书上，从而逃避麻烦；她想的没错，否认只会让汤姆的境况更糟。贝琪觉得她会很高兴看到这么一个后果。可当那最糟糕的一幕到来时，她真有种冲动，想站起来，告发艾弗瑞德·泰普。但她还是努力使自己保持沉默——因为，她对自己说："他肯定会告状，说我撕的画册。我什么也不说，我才不会救他呢！"

汤姆挨了打，回到座位上，并没感到心肠俱碎，因为他想有可能是自己不经意把拼写书弄脏的。

整整一个小时过去了，老师坐在他的椅子上，不住地点头。一会儿，道宾斯先生打开了他的办公桌，伸手去拿书。他取了出来，坐在椅子上开始看！汤姆飞快地瞥了一眼贝琪。他看到此时她的神情就像一只枪顶着头的兔子，一副被捕获后绝望的样子。他马上忘记了她和他有过的争吵。快点——得做点儿什么事！马上就干！好！——他想出了一个主意！他要跑过去把书抓过来，然后夺门而出，飞奔离去。可是紧接着老师就看着

it was the next moment the master faced the school. Every eye sank under his gaze. Then he said angrily:

"Who tore this book?"

There was not a sound. One could have heard a pin drop. The silence continued; the master searched face after face for signs of doing wrong.

"Benjamin Rogers, did you tear this book?"

He denied. Another pause.

"Joseph Harper, did you?"

Another denial. Tom's uneasiness grew stronger and stronger. The master glanced at the boys—considered a while, then turned to the girls:

"Amy Lawrence?"

A shake of the head.

"Gracie Miller?"

The same sign.

"Susan Harper, did you do this?"

Another no. The next girl was Becky Thatcher.

Tom was trembling from head to foot with excitement and a sense of the hopelessness of the situation.

"Rebecca Thatcher (Tom glanced at her face—it was white with terror)—did you tear—no, look me in the face—did you tear this book?"

A thought shot like lightening through Tom's brain. He sprang to his feet and shouted, "I did it!"

全班了。在他的注视下所有的眼睛都低下了。他生气地说：

"谁撕我的书了？"

没有声音。教室静得甚至可以听到针掉地的声音。这种沉默持续着；老师一张脸一张脸地看过去，试图寻找做错事以后的迹象。

"本杰明·罗杰斯，你撕书了吗？"

他否认了，接着是一阵沉默。

"约瑟夫·哈普，你呢？"

又一个否认了。汤姆变得愈来愈不安了。老师扫过这些男孩子——想了一会儿，转向女孩：

"艾米·劳伦斯？"

一阵摇头。

"格瑞瑟·米勒？"

同样的反应。

"苏珊·哈普，你撕了吗？"

回答的是"没有"。下一个女孩就是贝琪·撒切尔了。

面对这样的局面，汤姆觉得心潮澎湃，却又似乎无可奈何，他从头到脚都在发抖。

"丽贝卡·撒切尔！（汤姆瞥了一眼她的脸——已经吓得惨白了）——你撕了——不，看着我的脸——你撕了这本书吗？"

一个想法"腾"地闪现在汤姆脑子里。他跳起来，喊道："我撕的！"

The school stared in puzzlement at this unbelievable fool. Tom stepped forward to go to his punishment while the surprise, the thankfulness, the adoration that shone upon him out of poor Becky's eyes seemed pay enough for a hundred beatings.

Tom went to bed that night planning how to revenge on Alfred Temple; for with shame and regret Becky had told him all, and he fell asleep at last, with Becky's last words staying dreamily in his ear—

"Tom, how could you be so noble!"

Chapter 21 Eloquence
—and the Master's Gilded Dome

Vacation was coming. The schoolmaster, always strict, grew more and more strict and exacting than ever, for he wanted the school to make a good showing on Examination Day. His rod was seldom idle now—at least among the smaller pupils. Only did the biggest boys and young ladies of eighteen and twenty escape beating. Mr. Dobbins' beatings were very strong ones, too; for although he carried, under his wig, a perfectly bald and shiny head, he had only reached middle age and there was no sign of weakness in his muscle. As the great day came, he seemed to take a pleasure in punishing the

所有的同学都带着不解的眼光看着这个难以置信的傻瓜。汤姆走上前去，接受惩罚。可就是老师打他一百鞭，贝琪眼中闪出的惊讶、感激与爱慕也足以弥补了。

那天晚上，汤姆躺在床上，计划着如何报复艾弗瑞德·泰普，因为贝琪怀着羞耻与悔恨的心情把那件事全告诉了他。汤姆最后睡着了，梦中耳边还响着最后她向他说的话——

"汤姆，你真伟大！"

第二十一章 展现口才的考试
——老师的镀金秃头

假期就要到来了，一向严厉的老师变得比以往更严格，更苛求了，因为他想让学校同学们在考试那天表现得更好。他的教鞭现在很少闲着了——至少在年龄小一些的学生中。只有那些最大的男孩和十八到二十岁的年轻姑娘才可以免于挨打。尽管假发下面道宾斯先生的头已经完全秃了，亮闪闪的，可他才人到中年，肌肉没有任何衰老的痕迹，所以打人特别狠。随着那重要一天的到来，他似乎变得特别吹毛求疵，而且乐此不疲。

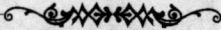

least shortcomings. The result was the smaller boys spent their days in terror and suffering and their nights in planning revenge. They threw away no chance to do the master a mischief, which he could always avoid. At last they made a plan that could have shining victory. They told the plan to the sign painter's boy and asked help. He had his own reasons for being happy, for the master took meals and lived in his father's family and the boy hated him a lot. The master always prepared himself for great occasions by getting very drunk, and the sign painter's boy said he would "manage the thing."

At last the interesting occasion arrived. At eight in the evening the schoolhouse was brilliantly lighted, and beautifully decorated. The master sat in his great chair, with his blackboard behind him. He was looking happy. Three rows of benches on each side and six rows in front of him were occupied by the important people of the town and by the parents of the pupils. To his left, back of the rows of citizens, was a large platform upon which were seated the scholars who were to take part in the exercises of the evening; rows of small boys, washed and dressed to in intolerable state of discomfort; a row of clumsy big boys; rows of girls and young ladies beautifully dressed. All the rest of the house was filled with scholars sitting here to listen.

结果就是那些小一点儿的男孩白天在恐慌中度过，而夜晚满脑子想的就是如何报仇。他们抓住一切机会，向老师搞恶作剧，然而他总是能幸免于难。最后孩子们制订了一个可以取得辉煌胜利的计划，并把这个计划告诉了刷标语那人的儿子，请求帮忙。那孩子很高兴，原因是老师在他们家吃住，而他非常讨厌这个老师。这个老师在重大场合到来之前总是喝得醉醺醺的，刷标语那人的儿子说这事由他"搞掂"。

有趣的一幕终于到来了。那天晚上八点，教室已是灯火辉煌，装饰美丽。老师坐在他的大椅子上。后面是黑板。他看上去很兴奋。教室两边的两三排凳子和老师前面的六排凳子上都坐着镇上重要人物和学生家长。老师的左边，镇上那些人的后面是一个大讲台，上面坐着将参与晚上考试练习的学者们，还有几排坐着小男孩，他们收拾得整整齐齐，干干净净，一个个都觉得别别扭扭的快受不了了；大一些的男生坐了一排，再就是打扮得漂漂亮亮的小女孩和年轻的姑娘们坐了几排。教室其他地方则坐着列席的学者们。

The exercises began. A very little boy stood up and shyly recited, "You'd scarcely expect one of my age to speak in public on the stage," etc. But he finished safely, though cruelly frightened, and got a fine round of applause when he made his bow and left the platform.

A little shy girl recited "Mary had a little lamb," etc., performed a sympathy – inspiring bow, got her applause, and sat down happily.

Tom Sawyer stepped forward with strong confidence and started the exciting "Give me liberty or give me death" speech, with violent body movement and broke down in the middle of it. A terrible stage fright seized him, his legs trembled under him, and he was like to choke. True, he had the obvious sympathy of the house—but he had the house' silence, too. The master frowned, and this completed the disaster. Tom struggld for a while and then left the platform, defeated. There was a weak applause, but it died early.

"The Boy Stood on the Burning Deck" followed; also "The Assyrian Came Down," and others. Then there were reading exercises and a spelling contest. The most important part of the evening was coming now—"original compositions" by the young ladies. Each in her turn stepped forward to the edge of the platform, cleared her throat, held up her paper (tied with beautiful ribbon),

练习开始了。一个特别小的男孩站了起来，害羞地背诵了"你很难料到我们这年龄的孩子能够登台当众讲话"等等。背完了，孩子紧张得要命，可好还没出一点儿错。这令人觉得有些残酷。小孩鞠了躬，离开了讲台。赢得了好一阵掌声。

另一个害羞的小女孩背了"玛丽有个小羊羔"。然后向大家行了一个颇能引起同情的礼，赢得了掌声，高高兴兴地回去坐下了。

汤姆·索耶信心十足地走上前去，开始背"不自由，毋宁死"，说话时手挥动得很厉害；然而背到中间却突然卡壳了。一种可怕的舞台恐惧感向他袭来，他的腿开始发抖，人都好像喘不上气了。没错，他显然赢得了整个教室人们的同情——可他也面对的是整个教室的沉默。老师皱了皱眉，这也就结束了他的灾难。汤姆费劲儿地想了一会儿，就垂头丧气地走下了讲台。下面响起了零零落落的掌声，很快也就消失了。

下一个演讲的题目是"男孩站在燃烧的平台上"，紧接着是"亚述人打败仗了"，还有其他的。接下来的考试内容是阅读练习和拼写竞赛。然后是整个晚上最重要的一项——年轻姑娘朗读她们的"新颖佳作"。一个个轮流着走到讲台边，清清

and read, with attention to "expression" and punctuation. The great topics were the same. As their mothers before them, their grandmothers, and doubtless all their ancestors in the female line had done upon similar occasions, "Friendship" was one, followed by "Dream Land"; 'The Advantages of Culture"; "Forms of Political Government Compared and Contrasted"; "Melancholy"; "Filial Love"; "Heart Longings," etc., etc.

A prevalent feature in these compositions was a careful and lively sadness; another was a wasteful and large flow of "fine language"; another was a tendency to use prized words and phrases; and always ended with a sermon. No matter what the subject might be, much effort was made to offer the moral and religious instructions through the compositions. Then these compositions received satisfactions with whispers like "How sweet!" "How eloquent!" "So true!" etc. and warm applause.

Now the master, happy almost to the verge of kindness, put his chair aside, turned his back to the audience, and began to draw a map of America on the blackboard, to exercise the geography class upon. But he did poorly with his unsteady hand, and laughter spread over the house. He knew what the matter was and set himself to right it, but in vain. He threw his entire attention upon his work, now. He felt that all eyes were fastened up-

嗓子，手捧作文本①，开始朗读，很注意自己的"措辞"与"发音"。题目都是一样的大，就像她们的妈妈、祖母以及家中所有女性前辈在类似场合下选的一样，有"友谊"、"梦乡"、"文化优势"、"政府形式比较"、"忧郁"、"来自儿女的爱"、"心的渴望"等等，等等。

这种作文普遍存在的一个特点就是字里行间流露出的一种忧郁调子，另外就是词藻华丽，再有就是堆砌那些她们偏爱的词语，并且总是以一段经文结束。无论题目是什么，这些姑娘总是努力使她们的文章从道德上、宗教上给人们以指导。这样的文章总能获得大家的满意，人们会低声说："多么优美的文章！""多么雄辩的口才！""多么真实！"等等，同时还会报以掌声。

这会儿，老师高兴得都快变得和蔼起来了，他把椅子放在一边，背向观众，开始在黑板上画美国地图。为地理练习做准备。可是他的手却一点儿也握不稳，所以画得很糟，笑声传遍了整个教室。他知道问题出在哪儿，就开始纠正自己的画，可却没用。他现在把所有的注意力都投向这

①　都用漂亮丝带扎着。

on him. There was a room above, now with some noise over his head and down through this came a cat, hanged around the leg by a string; she had a rag tied about her head and jaws to keep from mewing; as she was put down slowly, she clawed at the air. The laughter rose higher and higher—the cat was within six inches of the attentive teacher's head—down, down, a little lower, and she grabbed his wig with her claws and was seized up into the room in an instant with her award still in her claws! And how the light did shine from the master's bald head—for the sign painter's boy had gilded it! That broke up the meeting. The boys were happy. Vacation had come.

Chapter 22
Huck Finn Quotes Scripture

Tom joined the new order of Cadets of Temperance, [①] because it offered him chance to show off. He promised to give up smoking, chewing, and using a dirty language as long as he remained a member. Now he found out a new thing—namely, that to promise not to do a thing is the surest way in the world to make a body

---

① cadets of Temperance:少年自律团体。

份工作，感到所有的眼睛都在盯着他看。道宾斯先生的头顶上方有一个阁楼，这时传出一些声音，有一只猫从上面吊下来了，它的后腿用一根绳子绑着，头和下巴用一块破布绑着，以防它喵喵乱叫；它在向下吊时，爪子在空中乱抓。人们的笑声越来越大——猫离聚精会神的老师头顶只有六英寸了——下来了，下来了，又下来一点，它用爪子抓下了他的假发，又立刻被吊回房间，爪子还握着它的战利品——老师的秃头金光闪闪，光彩夺目——因为刷标语那人的儿子已经给它镀了层金漆！考试就这么结束了，孩子们很高兴。假期到来了。

第二十二章　哈克贝历·芬恩
引用《圣经》

汤姆加入了少年自律团，这可是显示自己的好机会。他许诺只要自己是这一团之员，就不再吸烟、嚼口香糖、说脏话。现在他发现了一个新的规律——即就是，如果让一个人许诺不要做什

want to go and do that very thing. Tom soon found himself suffer from a desire to drink and curse. Fourth of July was coming, but he soon gave that up because he had fixed his hopes upon old Judge Frazer, justice of the peace, who was apparently on his deathbed and would have a big funeral, since he was so high an official. During three days Tom was deeply concerned about the judge's condition and hungry for news of it. Sometimes his hopes ran high—so high that he would venture to put on his robe and practice before the looking glass. But the judge always discouraged him with the ups and downs of health condition. At last he was pronounced to recover. Tom was upset and felt hurt too. He asked to give up this job— and that night the judge died. Tom decided that he would never trust a man like that again.

Tom presently wondered to find that the vacation he had longed for was not that interesting.

He tried a diary—but nothing happened during three days, and so he gave that up.

There were some boys-and-girls' parties, but they were so few and so happy that they only made the other time harder and more painful.

Becky Thatcher was gone to her Constantinople home to stay with her parents during vacation—so there was no bright side to life anywhere.

么，他肯定是偏偏想干那件事。不久汤姆就发现自己特别想喝酒，想骂人，想得都难受。七月四日很快就到来了，可他马上就放弃了那一天的活动，因为他将希望都投向了老法官弗莱则，他是镇上的治安官，这会儿已经奄奄一息了。因为他的地位颇高，为他举行的葬礼将会非常盛大。在那三天里汤姆密切关注着法官的身体状况，渴望得到任何有关这方面的消息。有时汤姆的希望大增——大到他敢冒险戴上绶带，在镜前操练一番。可是法官的状况却是时好时坏，令他十分沮丧。最后，医生宣布他身体状况好转，现处于恢复阶段。汤姆很难过，还有一种受伤的感觉。他请求放弃这份工作——那天晚上法官死了。汤姆认为他以后再不能信任这样的人了。

汤姆奇怪地发现他盼望已久的假期并不是那么有趣。

他试着写日记——然而接下来的两三天当中什么也没发生，因而他放弃了。

镇上一些男孩、女孩还举办了舞会，可这样的活动太少了，却又令他们那么地欣喜若狂，使得接下来的时间更难熬，更痛苦。

贝琪·撒切尔去她在君士坦丁堡镇的家了，在那里和她爸妈一起度假——因而汤姆的生活中再没有什么灿烂的东西了。

The terrible secret of the murder was a long misery and pain.

Then came the measles.

During two long weeks Tom lay a prisoner, without knowing any happenings in the world. He was very ill and he was interested in nothing. When he got upon his feet at last and moved weakly downtown, a sad change had come over everything and every creature. Everybody had "got religion," not only the adults, but even the boys and girls. Tom went about, hoping against hope for the sight of one happy face, but disappointment upset him everywhere. He found Joe Harper studying a Testament, and turned sadly away from the depressing scene. He looked for Ben Rogers, and found him spreading the religious teachings to the poor. Every boy he met added another ton to his depression; and when, in great disappointment, he flew for help to his bosom friend Huckleberry Finn and was received with a Scriptural quotation, his heart broke and he crept home and to bed realizing that only he in this town was lost, forever and forever.

And that night there came a terrible storm, with heavy rain, horrible noises of thunder, and blinding sheets of lightening. He covered his head with the bedclothes and waited in a horror for his doom.

The next day the doctors were back; Tom had been

保守关于那个谋杀案的秘密真是太可怕了，令汤姆长久处于痛苦之中。

然后汤姆就得上了麻疹。

在接下来的漫长的两个星期，汤姆只好躺在床上，有如一个囚犯，对外面世界发生了什么丝毫不知。他病得很厉害，对什么事都提不起兴趣。最后他终于能站起来了，拖着虚弱的身子朝镇中心走去。他发现镇上的人与物都发生了令人沮丧的变化。每个人都"信教"了，不光大人，甚至还有孩子们。汤姆在镇上游荡着，希望看到一张快乐的脸孔，然而希望却总是破灭，他处处感到失望，难过。他找到乔·哈普，发现他正在攻读《圣经》，只好难过地离开了这令他悲伤的一幕。他去找本·罗杰斯，发现他正在给穷人们布道。汤姆见到的每一个男孩都给他增加了足有一吨重的沮丧，带着巨大的失望，他飞奔到他的知心朋友哈克贝历·芬恩那儿，渴望得到帮助。然而哈克贝历·芬恩迎接他时却读了一段《圣经》。汤姆的心都碎了，他一声不吭地回到了家，上了床，意识到这个镇上只有他迷失了方向，永远，永远。

那天晚上一场暴风雨袭来，雨下得很大，中间夹杂着可怕的雷鸣声与令人目眩的闪电。他用睡衣蒙着头，在恐惧中等待厄运的到来。

第二天医生又来了，汤姆又病了。这回他在

ill again. The three weeks he spent on his back this time seemed an entire age, with no friends playing with him. When he got better, he found Joe Harper and Huck Finn up a street eating a stolen melon. Poor lads! They—like Tom—had been ill too.

Chapter 23
The Salvation of Muff Potter

At last the sleepy atmosphere was stirred—and strongly: the murder trial came on in the court. It became the exciting topic of village talk immediately. Tom could not get away from it. Every talk to the murder sent a shudder to his heart. He took Huck to a lonely place to have a talk with him. It would be some relaxation to untie his tongue for a little while; to divide his burden of sadness with another sufferer. Moreover, he wanted to make sure that Huck had been silent.

"Huck, have you ever told anybody about—that?"

"About what?"

"You know what."

"Oh—of course I haven't. Never a single word. What makes you ask?"

"Well, I was afraid."

"Why, Tom Sawyer, we wouldn't be alive two

床上躺了三个星期，那仿佛是整整一年，没有朋友来找他玩。汤姆好些后就上街了，发现乔·哈普和哈克贝历·芬恩正吃一个偷来的西瓜呢。可怜的孩子，他们——像汤姆一样——又旧病复发了。

第二十三章　穆夫·波特得救了

这令人昏昏欲睡的气氛最后终于——而且是强有力地——被打破了，那场谋杀案要上庭审判了。这立刻成了全村人激动讨论的话题，汤姆也无法避开。只要谁一说到这场谋杀，他就觉得心头一颤。他把哈克叫到了一个偏僻的地方，要和他谈谈。这会儿，汤姆终于可以让他那紧绷着的舌头放开一会儿，与他的患难兄弟共同承担痛苦了，他感到了轻松。而且他还有一个目的，就是确信哈克没有把这事儿说出去。

"哈克，你跟别人说这事了吗？"

"什么事？"

"你知道什么事。"

"噢——当然没，一个字也没。你问这干吗？"

"嗯，我担心。"

"汤姆·索耶，你要知道，如果咱们的秘密泄

days if that was discovered. You know that."

Tom felt more comfortable. After a pause:

"Huck, anybody couldn't get you to tell, could they?"

"Get me to tell? Why, if I wanted that devil to drown me they could get me to tell."

"Well, that's all right, then. I think we're safe as long as we keep silent. But let's swear again, anyway."

"I agree."

So they swore again with great seriousness.

"What is the talk around, Huck? I've heard a power of it."

"Talk? Well, it's just Muff Potter, Muff Potter, Muff Potter all the time. It keeps me in a sweat, always, so I want to hide somewhere."

"That's just the same way they go on round me. Don't you feel sorry for him, sometimes?"

"Most always—most always. He hasn't ever done anything to hurt anybody. Just get drunk; but, God, we all do that—at least most of us. But he's kind of good—he gave me half a fish, once; and lots of times he had supported me when I was out of luck."

"Well, he'd mended kites for me, Huck, and put hooks onto my fishing line. I wish we could get him out of there."

露了，咱们准保活不过两天。"

汤姆感到更欣慰一些了。他停了一会儿，说：

"哈克，谁也不会让你张口的，是吗？"

"让我张口？哼！如果我想让那个魔鬼淹死我的话，他们会让我张口的。"

"那就好。我想只要咱们不吭声，就没事的。无论如何，咱们再发一次誓吧。"

"我同意。"

他们又非常严肃地发了誓。

"周围那些人都说什么来着，哈克？我可听到了不少。"

"说什么？永远都是穆夫·波特、穆夫·波特、穆夫·波特的。听得我总是紧张得一身汗。我真想藏到哪儿。"

"我周围也一样。你有的时候是不是也挺为他难过的？"

"大多数的时候——大多数的时候。他根本没有做任何伤害别人的事，只是醉了。可是上帝呀，人们都会喝醉的——至少我们当中的大多数人。可他挺好的——有一次他给了我半条鱼；还有好多次我运气不好的时候，他总站在我一边。"

"他还给我修过风筝，哈克，还给我的钓鱼绳上加鱼钩。我真希望咱们能把他救出来。"

"My! We couldn't get him out, Tom. And besides, it wouldn't do any good; they'd catch him again."

The boys had a long talk, but it brought them little comfort. As the evening came, they found themselves wandering around the little jail.

The boys did as they had often done before—went to the jail and gave Potter some tobacco and matches. He was on the ground floor and there were no guards.

His thankfulness for their gifts had always upset them, especially when Potter said:

"You've been very good to me, boys—better than anybody else in this town. And I can't forget it. Often I say to myself, says I, 'I used to mend all the boys' kites and things, and show them where the good fishing places were, and befriended them what I could, and now they've all forgot old Muff when he's in trouble; but Tom doesn't, and Huck doesn't—they don't forget him,' says I, 'and I don't forget them.' Well, boys, I did a bad thing—drunk and crazy at the time. But what I want to say is, don't you ever get drunk—then you won't ever get here."

Tom went home miserable, and his dreams that night were full of horrors. The next day and the day after, he stayed around the courtroom, drawn by an almost

"天哪！我们救不出来他的，汤姆。而且，这么做不会给他带来任何好处；他们还会把他抓回去的。"

两个孩子聊了很久，可也没怎么给他们带来什么安慰。已是傍晚了，他们发现自己正在小监狱周围徘徊。

像以往一样——孩子们去了监狱，给波特带去了一些烟和火柴。他正呆在一层，周围没有看守。

波特每回都会感谢他们带来了礼物。可这却让他们听着难过，尤其是当他说：

"你们对我真好，孩子们——比这镇上任何人对我都好。我不会忘记的。我经常对自己说，'我过去经常给村里所有的孩子们补风筝，还有其他东西。还告诉他们哪是钓鱼的好去处，努力和他们交朋友，可我这一有麻烦，他们就都把我这个老穆夫忘了；可汤姆没忘，哈克也没忘——他们没忘了我；我对自己说，'我也不会忘了他们的。'孩子们，我做了一件很糟糕的事情——总是喝醉酒，耍酒疯。我要对你们说的是，永远不要喝醉酒——那你就永远不会到这儿来了。"

汤姆悲伤地回了家。那天晚上他做了一晚上的恶梦。第二天、第三天他都在法庭外呆着，总

irresistible impulse to go in, but forcing himself to stay out. Huck was having the same experience. At the end of the second day, they learned what punishment Potter would certainly get.

Tom was out late that night, and came to bed through the window. He was very excited. It was hours before he got to sleep. All the village went to the court-house the next morning, for this was to be the great day. After a long wait the jury went in and took their places; shortly afterward, Potter, pale and tired, timid and hopeless, was brought in, with chains upon him, and seated where all the curious eyes could stare at him; the same noticeable was Injun Joe, cold as ever. There was another pause, and then the judge arrived and the sheriff announced the opening of the court.

Now a witness was called who proved that he found Muff Potter washing in the stream, at an early hour of the morning when the murder was discovered, and that he immediately escaped.

The prisoner raised his eyes for a moment, but dropped them again when his own counsel said:

"I have no questions to ask him."

The next witness proved the finding of the knife near the dead body.

"I have no questions to ask him," Potter's lawyer

是几乎难以抗拒地想冲进去，但又控制住了自己。哈克也遭受着一样的经历。第二天快结束时，他们知道了波特必定会遭受什么样的惩罚。

汤姆那天晚上很晚时出去了，过了很久又从窗户爬了进来，上了床。他心情异常激动，过了好几个小时才睡着。第二天全村人都来到了法庭。等了很久之后，陪审团进来就座了；很快，波特也被带了进来，一副苍白、疲惫、胆小无助的样子。他的手脚都被链子缚着，众目睽睽之中坐下了；同样引人注目的还有印第安人乔，像以往一样冷冰冰的。又是一阵等候，接着法官也到了，治安官宣布开庭。

首先一个证人被传上庭，他证明自己在谋杀案发生的那天一大早看到穆夫·波特在小河边洗澡。看到有人注意他，就立刻跑掉了。

囚犯抬眼看了一会儿，等到他的律师说话时他又低下了眼睛。律师说：

"我没有问题问他。"

第二个证人证明在死者身边发现了那把刀。

"我没有问题问他。"波特的律师说道。

replied.

A third witness swore he had often seen the knife in Potter's pocket.

Counsel for Potter refused to question him. The faces of the audience began to show unhappiness. Did this lawyer intend to throw away Potter's life without an effort?

Then the prosecution said:

"By the oaths of citizens whose simple word is above doubt, since the witnesses' words are doubtless, the prisoner's crime should be certain. We rest our case here."

Poor Potter made a sad cry and put his face in his hands and moved his body to and fro, while a painful silence was in the courtroom. Many men were moved, and many women burst into tears.

"Your honor, we said Potter did this fearful deed, because he was drunk. We have changed our mind. We shall not offer that statement. (Then to the clerk) Call Thomas Sawyer!"

A puzzled astonishment awoke in every face in the house, not even excepting Potter's. The boy stood up and looked very frightened.

"Thomas Sawyer, where were you on the seventeenth of June, about the hour of midnight?"

第三个证人发誓他经常看到波特兜里揣着那把刀。

波特的律师还是没有提问这个证人。听众的脸上露出了不快。这个律师难道打算眼巴巴地看着波特丧命吗？

接着原告说：

"既然证人已经发誓他们的证词毫无疑问，囚犯的罪责应是确信无疑的。我们的案子就到此为止吧。"

可怜的波特难过得哭了起来，还用手遮着脸，前前后后走动着，整个法庭陷入了一片悲痛与沉默之中。许多男人都被感动了，而许多女人则流下了眼泪。

"尊敬的各位，我们曾经说过波特因为酒醉，干了这件可怕的事情。现在我们的观点变了，我们不能这么说。（转向书记员）叫托马斯·索耶！"

法庭里的每个人脸上都显出了迷惑与惊讶。波特也不例外。男孩站了起来，看上去一副非常害怕的样子。

"托马斯·索耶，六月七日大约半夜的时候你在哪儿呢？"

Tom glanced at Injun Joe's iron face and his tongue failed him. The audience listened breathless, but the words refused to come. After a few moments, however, the boy got a little of his strength back, and managed to put enough of it into his voice to make part of the house hear:

"In the graveyard!"

"A little bit louder, please. Don't be afraid. You were—"

"In the graveyard."

A contemptuous smile went across Injun Joe's face.

"Were you anywhere near Horse William's grave?"

"Yes, sir."

"Speak up—just a bit louder. How near were you?"

"Near as I am to you."

"Were you hidden, or not?"

"I was hidden."

"Where?"

"Behind the elms that's on the edge of the grave."

Injun Joe was surprised.

"Anyone with you?"

"Yes, sir. I went there with—"

"Wait—wait a moment. Never mind mentioning your partner's name. We will call him at the proper

汤姆瞥了一眼印第安人乔冷酷的脸，舌头就僵住了。观众们都屏住了呼吸听着，可他却什么也说不出来。过了一会儿，男孩又有了一点力气，他设法将这股力气注入他的声音，使得一部分人能听到他说：

"在墓地！"
"请大点儿声。别害怕，你在——"

"在墓地。"
印第安人乔的脸上闪过轻蔑的笑。
"你距豪斯·威廉姆的墓近吗？"
"是的，先生。"
"大声说——再大一点儿。有多近？"

"就像你我现在这么近。"
"你藏起来了没有？"
"我藏起来了。"
"藏在哪儿了？"
"墓边那棵橡树后面。"
印第安人乔很惊讶。
"有人和你在一起吗？"
"是的，先生。和我一起去的是——"
"等一下——等一下。不要提你伙伴的名字。我们将在适当的时候叫他来。你去墓地时带什么

time. Did you carry anything there with you?"

Tom hesitated and looked confused.

"Speak out, my boy—be brave. The truth is always respectable. What did you take there?"

"Only a—a—dead cat."

There was some laughter, which the court controlled.

"We will find the skeleton of that cat. Now, my boy, tell us everything that happened—tell it in your own way—don't omit anything, and don't be afraid."

Tom began—hesitatingly at first, but then his words flowed more and more easily; in a little while every sound stopped but his own voice; every eye fixed itself upon him with parted lips. Holding their breath, the audience listened and was absorbed in the tale.

"—and as the doctor fetched the stone around and Muff Potter fell, Injun Joe jumped with the knife and—"

Crash! Quick as lightening the devil jumped for a window, tore his way through all opposers, and was gone!

Chapter 24
Splendid Days and Fearsome Nights

Tom was a shining hero once more—the pet of the

东西了吗?"

汤姆犹豫着，看起来有些为难。

"说出来，我的孩子——勇敢点。真话总是令人尊敬的。你带什么去那儿了?"

"只是一只——一只——死猫。"

观众中传出一阵笑声，被法庭制止了。

"我们会去找那只猫的骨架的。现在，我的孩子，告诉我那儿发生的所有事情——用你自己的方式讲出来——什么都不要省略，别害怕。"

汤姆开始说了——刚开始还犹犹豫豫，然后越来越流畅了；不一会儿整个法庭就只剩下他的声音；每一双眼睛都注视着他，每一张嘴也都张着。人们屏住了呼吸听他讲，都被他的故事吸引了。

"——就在医生从身边抓起了那块木牌子，砸昏了波特的时候，印第安人乔拿着那把刀跳了过去——"

"哗"的一声! 那个恶魔有如闪电一般跳向一个窗户，挣脱所有拦着他的人，逃跑了。

第二十四章　辉煌光荣的白日与
　　　　　　胆战心惊的黑夜

汤姆又一次成了了不起的英雄——老人宠爱

old, the envy of the young. His name even went into the village paper. There were some that believed he would be president, yet, if he escaped being killed.

Tom's days were days of splendor and happiness to him, but his nights were seasons of horror. Injun Joe appeared in all his dreams, and always with signs of killing in his eye. Hardly any temptation could persuade the boy to go out after nightfall. Poor Huck was in the same poor terrified state, for Tom had told the whole story to the lawyer the night before the great day of the trial, and Huck was afraid that Injun Joe might also know he was Tom's partner.

Daily Muff Potter's gratitude made Tom glad he had spoken; but nightly he wished he had tied his tongue.

Half the time Tom was afraid Injun Joe would never be seized; the other half he was afraid he would be. He felt sure he never could draw a safe breath again until that man was dead and he had seen the dead body.

Rewards had been offered, the country had been searched, but no Injun Joe was found.

Chapter 25
Seeking the Buried Treasure

There comes a time in every boy's life when he has

的对象，孩子们羡慕的目标。他的名字甚至出现在了村里发行的报纸上。有人相信，汤姆将来能当上总统，如果他能幸免一害的话。

辉煌与兴奋伴随着汤姆走过一个又一个白天，而恐惧则跟随着他度过一个又一个无尽长夜。他做的所有梦里都有印第安人乔出现，而且总是目露凶光。几乎没有什么能再诱惑这个孩子夜幕降临之后出去。可怜的哈克也处于同样惊恐的状态，因为汤姆在审判日前的晚上将所有的事情都告诉了律师，哈克担心印第安人乔可能也知道他就是跟在汤姆旁边的那个人。

白天穆夫·波特对他表露的感激让汤姆很高兴他说出了真相；而夜晚汤姆真希望他当时能绑住自己的舌头。

有一半的时间汤姆担心印第安人乔永远不会被抓住，而另一半时间汤姆又担心他会被抓住。他确信除非那个人死了，而且自己亲眼见到他的尸体了，否则他将永无宁日。

村里为捉拿印第安人乔已经设立了奖赏，可整个乡村都找遍了，却不见他的踪影。

第二十五章 寻找埋藏的财宝

每一个男孩的生活中都有那么一个时期特别

a strong desire to go somewhere and dig for hidden treasure. This desire suddenly came upon Tom one day. He found Huck Finn the Red-Handed, and told him secretly. Huck was willing. Huck was always willing to take a hand in any thing that offered joy and demanded no money, for he had a lot of time but no money. "Where'll we dig?" said Huck.

"Oh, most anywhere."

"Why, is it hidden all around?"

"No, indeed it isn't. It's hidden in strange places, Huck—sometimes on islands, sometimes in rotten boxes under the end of a branch of an old dead tree, just where the shadow falls at midnight; but mostly under the floor in haunted houses."

"Who hides it?"

"Why, robbers, of course."

"Then how are you going to know where you can find one?"

"Go for all of them!"

"Why, Tom, it'll take all summer."

"Well, suppose you find a pot with a hundred dollars in it or a box full of diamonds. How's that?"

Huck's eyes shone.

"That's nice, plenty nice for me. Just you give me the hundred dollars. I don't wan any diamonds."

想去探宝。这种欲望突然有一天占据了汤姆的脑子。他找来了赤手大盗哈克贝历·芬恩，想着哈克会响应他的。汤姆偷偷地告诉了他。果不其然，哈克很乐意。他总是乐意参与任何让他高兴却不需要钱的事情，因为他有的是大把时间，缺的却是钱。"我们挖哪儿呢？"哈克问。

"大多数的地方都行。"

"好多地方都藏着宝物吗？"

"不，事实上不是这样。它一般藏在很奇怪的地方，哈克——有的时候在岛上，有时放在一个破盒子里，再藏到一棵古老的死树的某个枝头下面，就是半夜树影落下的地方；但是大多数宝物都藏在鬼屋里。"

"谁藏的？"

"当然是强盗了。"

"那你怎么知道你在哪个屋子能找到？"

"所有的屋子都挖。"

"汤姆，这得花一整个夏天！"

"嗯，想想如果你挖到一个罐子，里面装了一百美元；或是挖到一个盒子，里面满是钻石，会怎么样？"

哈克的目光中闪现着光彩。

"那好哇，对我来说太好了。你只分给我一百美元就行了，我不要钻石。"

"All right. But I bet you I'm not going to throw off diamonds. Some of them are worth twenty dollars a piece—"

"Oh! Is that so?"

"Certainly—anybody'll tell you so. Haven't you ever seen one, Huck?"

"Not as I remember."

"Oh, kings have plenty of them."

"Well, I don't know kings, Tom."

"I think you don't. But if you were to go to Europe you'd see plenty of them jumping around."

"Do they jump?"

"Jump? No!"

"Well, what did you say they did for?"

"I only meant you'd see them—not jumping, of course—what do they want to jump for? —but I mean you'd just see them—scattered around, you know."

"But I don't want to be a king. Say—where are you going to dig first?"

"Well, I don't know. Suppose we deal with that old dead tree on the hill of the other side of Still-House branch?"

"I agreed."

So they got a poor pick and a shovel, and set out on their three – mile walk. They arrived hot and breath-

"行。可我打赌我不会把钻石扔了的。有些钻石一个就值二十美元——"

　　"噢！是吗？"

　　"当然——谁都会这么跟你讲的。你见过吗，哈克？"

　　"我记得没见过。"

　　"国王都有很多钻石。"

　　"可我不认识国王，汤姆。"

　　"我想你也不认识。可你如果去欧洲的话你就会看到许许多多的国王跳来跳去。"

　　"他们会跳吗？"

　　"跳？不会！"

　　"那你是什么意思？"

　　"我只是说会见到国王的，当然不是跳——他们跳什么呀？——但我意思是你会看到他们的——有很多。"

　　"可我不想当国王。说说——你打算先从哪儿挖？"

　　"我不知道，咱们先去储藏室另一边山上挖那棵古老的树吧？"

　　"我赞成。"

　　他们找了一把破锄头、一把铁锹扛上，就出发开始了他们三英里的路程。到了以后他们觉得

ing hard, and threw themselves down in the shade of an elm to rest and have a smoke.

"I like this," said Tom.

"So do I."

"Say, Huck, if we find a treasure here, what are you going to do with your share?"

"Well, I'll have pie and a glass of soda every day, and I'll go to every circus that comes here. I'll bet I'll have a happy time."

"Well. Aren't you going to save any of it?"

"Save it? What for?"

"Why, so as to have something to live on, by and by."

"Oh, that isn't any use. What are you going to do with yours, Tom?"

"I'm going to buy a new drum, and a real sword, and a red necktie and a small pet, and get married."

"Married!"

"That's it."

"Tom, you—why, are you crazy?"

"Wait—you'll see."

"Well, that's the most foolish thing you could do. Look at my father and mother. Fight! Why, they used to fight all the time. I remember very well."

"The girl I'm going to marry won't fight."

很热，喘气都费劲儿，就一头倒在一棵橡树下乘凉，休息，抽烟。

"我喜欢这样。"汤姆说。

"我也是。"

"说说，哈克，如果我们在这儿找到宝，你打算用你那份干什么？"

"嗯，我要每天吃馅饼，喝一杯苏打水。我要去看来这儿的每个马戏团的演出，我肯定会过得很快活。"

"你打算存钱吗？"

"存钱？存钱干吗？"

"嗯，就是给以后过日子用。"

"噢，没用。你准备怎么办，汤姆？"

"我打算买一架新鼓，一把真正的剑，一个红色的领带，一个小宠物，然后结婚。"

"结婚？"

"对。"

"汤姆，你——你疯了？"

"等着瞧吧——你会明白的。"

"这可再愚蠢不过了。看看我爸、妈，打架！他们过去打个不停，我记得很清楚。"

"我要娶的女孩是不会打架的。"

"All right—that'll do. Only if you get married, I'll be more lonely than ever."

"No, you won't. You'll come and live with me. Now don't think about it any more and we'll go digging."

They worked and sweated for half an hour. No result. They worked another half an hour without result. Huck said:

"Do they always bury it as deep as this?"

"Sometimes—not always. I think we haven't got the right place."

So they chose a new place and began again. They worked in silence for some time. Finally Tom said:

"Oh, I know what the matter is! You got to find out where the shadow of the branch falls at midnight, and that's where you dig! We've got to do it tonight, too, because if somebody sees these holes they'll know in a minute what's here and they'll go for it. Let's hide the tools in the bushes."

The boys were there that night. They sat in the shadow waiting. The boys talked little. By and by they judged that twelve had come; they marked where the shadow fell, and began to dig. Their hopes began to rise. Their interest grew stronger, and they dug harder and harder. The hole deepened and still deepened, but

"好吧——那行。可如果你结婚了，我就更孤独了。"

"不，你不会的。你可以过来和我住。好了，别再想这事了，我们挖宝吧。"

他们挖了有半个小时，汗流浃背，可毫无结果。又干了半个小时，仍一无所获。哈克说：

"他们总是埋得这么深吗？"

"有的时候——并不总是。我想咱们没找对地方。"

他们又挑了一块新的地方，开始挖。两人一声不吭地干了一会儿。最后汤姆说：

"噢，我知道问题出在哪儿了！你得在半夜找出树枝的影子落在哪儿了，那才是该挖的地方。我们必须今晚继续干，因为如果有人看到这些洞了，他们马上就会明白怎么回事，马上就会挖的。咱们把工具藏在树丛里。"

两个男孩那天晚上又来了。他们坐在树影下等着，很少说话。一会儿他们估计到十二点了；就在树影落下的地方做了标记，开始挖。两人的希望开始升起，兴趣越来越大，挖得越来越卖劲儿。洞一点一点地深了，每次当他们听到锄头敲

every time their hearts jumped to hear the pick strike upon something, they only suffered a new disappointment. It was only a stone or a trunk. At last Tom said: "It isn't any use, Huck, we're wrong again."

"Well, but we can't be wrong."

"I know it, but then there's another thing."

"What's that?"

"Why, we only guessed at the time. Possible enough it was too late or too early."

Huck dropped his shovel.

"That's it," said he. "That's the very trouble. We got to give this one up. We can't ever tell the right time, and it's too horrible at this time of night with witches and ghosts around us. I feel as if something's behind me all the time; and I'm frightened to turn around, because maybe there's a another one in front waiting for a chance."

"Well, I've been feeling much the same too, Huck. They always put in a dead man when they bury a treasure under a tree, to look out for it."

"My God!"

"Yes, they do. I've always heard that."

"Tom, I don't like to fool around much where there's dead people."

"I don't like to stir them up, either. Suppose this

击到什么东西时，心都会怦怦乱跳，可回回都令他们失望。每次都不过是块石头或树干。最后汤姆说："没用了，哈克，我们又选错了地方。"

"可我们错不了。"

"我知道，可还有一件事我们没考虑到。"

"什么？"

"我们只是大概猜了猜时间。很有可能我们把时间猜得太早了或太晚了。"

哈克扔下了他的铁锹。

"对！"他说，"是这个问题。这个洞咱们得放弃了。可咱俩根本没办法知道准确时间。而且在晚上这会儿，在这个巫师鬼神出没的地方挖东西太可怕了。我总觉得我身后有什么东西；可又特别害怕，不敢转过身去。因为我怕前面可能又站了一个准备随时袭击我呢。"

"嗯，我也感觉一样，哈克。他们在树下埋宝时总是会放进一个死人，让他看着这些宝。"

"上帝呀！"

"没错，他们就是这样的。我总听人们这么说。"

"汤姆，我不想在有死人的地方干蠢事了。"

"我也不想惹着他们。想想咱们要是把他的头

one here was to stick his skull out and say something!"

"Don't, Tom! It's terrible."

"Well, it just is. Huck, I feel quite uncomfortable."

"Say, Tom, let's give this place up, and try somewhere else."

"All right, I think we'd better."

"What'll it be?"

Tom considered a while, and then said:

"The haunted house. That's it!"

"I don't like haunted houses, Tom. Dead people might talk and when you aren't noticing, they come to look at you and bite their teeth, the way a ghost does. I couldn't stand such a thing as that, Tom, nobody could."

"Yes, but, Huck, ghosts travel around only at night. They won't keep us from digging there in the daytime."

"Well, that's so. But you know very well people don't go about that haunted house in the day nor the night."

"Well, that's mostly because they don't like to go where a man's been murdered, anyway—but nothing's ever been seen around that house except in the night—just some blue lights moving by the windows—

盖骨给挖出来了,然后他张口说点儿什么!"

"别说了,汤姆! 太可怕了!"

"是这样。哈克,我觉得特别不舒服。"

"喂,汤姆,咱们别在这儿挖了,试试别的地方吧。"

"行,我也觉得咱们最好去别的地方。"

"哪儿呢?"

汤姆想了一会儿。说:

"鬼屋,就是那儿!"

"我可不喜欢鬼屋,汤姆,死人或许会说话的。而且当你没注意时,他们会过来看着你,冲你咬牙切齿,就像鬼一样。我可受不了,汤姆,没人能受得了。"

"是的,可,哈克,鬼魂只在晚上出没。白天他们不会影响我们挖东西的。"

"这倒是。可是你知道,无论白天还是晚上,人们都不会到那儿去的。"

"大多数是因为他们不喜欢去杀过人的地方——但除了晚上,人们在那周围什么也没看到——即使晚上也只有一些蓝光在窗户口移动——没有

no ghosts."

"Well, where you see blue lights moving around, Tom, you can be sure there's a ghost quite close behind it."

"Yes, that's so. But anyway they don't come around in the daytime, so what's the use of our being frightened?"

"Well, all right. We'll dig the haunted house if you say so—but I think it's taking chances."

They had walked down the hill by this time. There in the middle of the moonlit valley below them stood the haunted house. Keeping a safe distance from the house, the boys gazed a while, half expecting to see a blue light moving past a window. Then they took their way homeward through the woods.

Chapter 26
Real Robbers Seize the Box of Gold

About noon the next day the boys arrived at the dead tree; they had come for their tools. Tom was impatient to go to the haunted house; Huck was too. Suddenly an idea hit upon them—it was Friday, a day which they believed would bring them bad luck. So they decided to give up digging and play.

鬼的。"

"汤姆，如果你看到有蓝光移动，那准保紧后面就有鬼。"

"对，没错。可不管怎样，鬼白天是不会出现的，所以我们怕什么呢？"

"嗯，好吧。既然你这么说，咱们就去挖吧——可我觉得咱们还是在冒险。"

这会儿他们已经走下山了，那鬼屋就在他们身下洒满月光的山谷中间。他们与鬼屋保持了一段他们认为安全的距离，朝房子盯了一会儿，多么期望看到窗口有蓝光移动。又过了一会儿，他们就穿过树林回家了。

第二十六章　真强盗挖走一箱金币

第二天大约中午时分，两个男孩来到枯树旁；他们是来取他们的工具的。汤姆已经迫不及待地要去鬼屋了，哈克也一样。突然他们想到了一点——今天是星期五，他们认为星期五总给人们带来厄运，因此决定不去挖宝了，去玩。

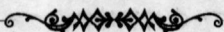

Tom asked:

"Do you know Robin Hood, Huck?"

"No. Who's Robin Hood?"

"Why, he was one of the greatest men that was ever in England—and the best. He was a robber."

"Great, I wish I was. Who did he rob?"

"Only sheriffs and bishops and rich people and kings, and suchlike. But he never bothered the poor. He loved them. He always helped the poor."

"Well, he must be a generous man."

"I bet you he was, Huck. Oh, he was the noblest man that ever was. There aren't any such men now, I can tell you. He could beat any man in England, with one hand tied behind him; and he could take his yew bow[①] and hit a ten-cent coin every time from a mile and a half far."

"What's a yew bow?"

"I don't know. It's some kind of a bow, of course. And if he hit that coin only on the edge he would sit down and cry—and curse. But we'll play Robin Hood—it's funny. I'll teach you."

"I agree."

So they played Robin Hood all the afternoon, now

---

① bow:弯弓。

汤姆问：

"你知道鲁宾汉吗，哈克？"

"不知道。鲁宾汉是谁呀？"

"他是英国历史上最伟大的人——也是最棒的，他是个强盗。"

"太好了，我希望我也是，他都抢谁？"

"只抢治安官，主教，还有富人，还有国王等等。可他从来不骚扰穷人，他热爱他们，他总是帮助穷人。"

"他一定是个慷慨大方的人。"

"我担保他是。哈克，他最高尚了，可以告诉你，现在再也没有这样的人了。他可以一只手绑在身后，用另一只手就能打遍全英国无敌手；他可以从一英里以外的地方拿起他的弯弓，射十分硬币，百射百中。"

"弯弓是什么？"

"我不清楚，当然是一种弓了。如果哪一次他射到的只是硬币的边，他会坐那儿痛哭一场——边哭边骂。不管怎样，现在咱们扮鲁宾汉玩吧——很好玩的，我教你。"

"行啊！"

一整个下午他们都在扮鲁宾汉玩，还不时急

and then looking eagerly at the haunted house and talking about any possibilities there.

On Saturday, shortly after noon, the boys were at the dead tree again. They had a smoke and a chat in the shade, and then dug a little in their last hole, not with great hope, but only because Tom said there were so many cases where people had given up a treasure after getting down within six inches of it, and then somebody else had come along, and turned it up with a single push of a shovel. The thing failed this time, however, so the boys shouldered their tools and went away.

When they reached the haunted house, they felt it was a so strange, silent and horrible place that they were afraid, for a moment, to venture in. Then they crept to the door and took a trembling look first. They saw a weed-grown, floorless room, and everywhere hung ragged cobwebs. Then they entered, softly, with quickened pulses, talking in whispers, ears alert to catch the slightest sound, and muscles tense and ready for instant escape.

In a little while they felt less frightened with the growing familiarity with the house, and they gave the place a critical and interested examination, rather admiring their own bravery, and wondering at it too. Next they wanted to look upstairs. This was something like

切地向鬼屋望去，谈论着可能会挖到什么。

星期六中午刚过，孩子们就又来到那棵枯树旁。他们在树阴下抽了根烟，聊了一会儿。又没抱多大希望地在他们最后挖的那个洞里挖了一会儿，只是因为汤姆说经常有些人挖得离宝不剩六英寸就放弃了，然后别人铲了一铲子就把宝挖出来了。可他们还是没有收获。因而扛上工具就走了。

来到鬼屋前，他们觉得这儿很奇怪而且寂静可怕，因而有那么一会儿害怕进去。他们蹑手蹑脚地来到门前，浑身颤抖着向里面先望了望。屋子没有地板，长得都是野草，到处挂着破蜘蛛网。他们轻轻地走了进去，脉搏也加快了。俩人小声嘀咕着，竖起耳朵听着哪怕是一丁点儿声音，肌肉也紧张起来，随时准备着逃跑。

渐渐地他们对这个屋子有所熟悉，也不那么害怕了。俩人饶有兴趣地对这个屋子进行了一番批判性的检查，对自己的勇气赞叹不已。接着他们想上楼看一看，这意味着他们断掉了自己的逃

cutting off escape, but they got to challenge each other, and of course there could be but one result—they threw their tools into a corner and went upstairs. Up there in one corner they found a closet—there was nothing in it. They were about to go down and begin work when—

"Sh!" said Tom.

"What is it?" whispered Huck, becoming pale with fright.

"Sh! ... There! ... Hear it?"

"Yes! ... Oh, my! Let's run!"

"Keep quiet! Don't move. They're coming right toward the door."

The boys lay waiting in a misery of fear.

"They've stopped ... No—coming ... Here they are. Don't whisper another word, Huck. My goodness, I wish I was out of this!"

Two men entered. As soon as they began to talk, the voice made the boys draw a deep breath and tremble. It was Injun Joe's! There was silence for a time. Then Joe said:

"I wanted to leave this place. I wanted to yesterday, only it wasn't any use trying to have trouble with those bad boys playing over there on the hill. They Could see us clearly if we had gone out yesterday."

"These bad boys" trembled again at these words,

路。相互激励了一番之后，他们就把工具扔到一个角落里，上楼了。在楼上的一个墙角他们看到了一个柜橱——里面什么都没有。他们正准备下楼挖宝，这时——

"嘘！"汤姆嘘了一声。

"那是什么声？"哈克小声问道，脸都吓白了。

"嘘！……在那儿！……听到了？"

"嗯！……天哪！快跑！"

"安静！别动。他们正往门这儿来呢。"

两个孩子在恐惧与痛苦中躺在那儿等待着。

"他们停下来了……不……来了……他们来了，别再说话了，哈克，我的天哪！我要是没在这儿呆着多好！"

有两个人进来了。他们一张口说话，那声音就让两个孩子深吸了一口气，浑身发抖。那是印第安人乔的声音。接着是一阵沉默。然后乔说话了。

"我要离开这儿。我昨天就要走，只是不想被在山那边玩的那些坏小子撞上，惹麻烦。如果咱们昨天出去了的话，他们可把咱看清楚了。"

"这些坏小子"听了这些话又打了个寒战，暗

and thought how lucky it was that they had remembered it was Friday and concluded to wait a day. They wished in their hearts they had waited a year.

The two men got out some food and made a lunch. After a long and thoughtful silence, Injun Joe said:

"Look here, you go back up the river where you belong. Wait there till you hear from me. I'll take the chances of going into this town just once more, for a look. We'll do that dangerous job after I've spied around a little and think things look well for it. Then for Texas! We'll leave together!"

This was satisfactory. Both men presently fell to yawning, and Injun Joe said: "I'm dead for sleep! It's your turn to watch."

He lay down in the weeds and soon began to snore. Presently the watcher began to nod; his head hanged lower and lower, both men began to snore now.

The boys drew a long, thankful breath. Tom whispered:

"Now's our chance—come!"

Huck said:

"I can't—I'd die if they were to wake."

Tom urged—Huck held back. At last Tom rose slowly and softly, and started alone. But the first step he made caused such a terrible noise from the crazy floor

自庆幸他们昨天还记得是星期五，而且决定了推迟一天挖。他们心里恨不得能再推迟一年呢。

两个人取出一些食物，吃了一顿午饭。印第安人乔沉思着，很长时间一声不吭，然后说：

"你先到你一直住着的那条河边等我消息，我会瞅准时机再到这个镇上来一趟看看。等我侦察好了，认为一切妥当了，我们就去冒那个险，然后去得克萨斯！一起走！"

他们对此计划很满意，不一会儿两个人就倒在那儿打开呵欠了。印第安人乔说："我都困死了，该轮你放哨了。"

他躺倒在草丛中，很快就打起呼噜了。不一会儿放哨的那人也开始点头了，他的头悬得越来越低，两个人开始一块儿打鼾。

孩子们终于长出了一口气，很是欣慰。汤姆低声说：

"我们的机会到了——来！"

哈克说：

"我不行——如果他们醒了我非得死不可。"

汤姆催促着——哈克却一再退缩。最后汤姆慢慢地轻轻地站了起来，决定自己走。可他刚迈出第一步，那破地板就发出可怕的声音，他一屁

that he sank down almost dead with fright. He never made a second try. The boys lay there counting the boring moments till it seemed to them that time must be done; and then they were thankful to notice that the sun was setting.

Now one of the robbers stopped snoring. Injun Joe sat up, stared around—smiled upon his comrade, whose head was hanging upon his knees—woke him up with his foot and said:

"Here! You're a watchman, aren't you! All right, though—nothing's happened."

"My! Have I been asleep?"

"Oh, partly, partly. What'll we do with the stolen goods we've got left?"

"I don't know—leave it here as we've always done, I think. No use to take it away till we start south. Six hundred and fifty in silvery is too heavy to carry."

"Yes; we'll just bury it—and bury it deep."

"Good idea," said the comrade, who walked across the room, knelt down, raised one of the stones and took out a bag. He took from it twenty or thirty dollars for himself and as much for Injun Joe and passed the bag to the latter, who was on his knees in the corner, now, digging with his knife.

The boys forgot all their fears, all their miseries in

股坐下来，都要吓死了。汤姆再也没试第二回，两个孩子躺在那儿，计算着无聊的时间，直到觉得时间都要走到尽头了。他们注意到太阳正在落山，这让他们感到欣慰。

这时一个人的呼噜声停住了。印第安人乔坐了起来，向周围盯了一圈。——冲他伙计笑了笑。此时那位的头已经垂到膝盖上了——乔用脚把他踢醒了，说：

"嘿！你是放哨的，不是吗？还好——什么也没发生。"

"天哪！我睡着了吗？"

"噢，没完全，没完全。咱们走后这些偷来的东西怎么办？"

"我不知道——我想像往常一样留到这儿。咱们离开去南方前扛走它也没用。六百五十块银币扛起来太重了。"

"对，我们还是把它埋在这儿——埋深点儿。"

"好主意，"伙计说着走到房间另一头，蹲下来，搬起了一块石头，取出一个包。他从里面给自己和乔都取了二三十美元，然后把包递给了乔。此时，他正在一个角落里跪着用刀挖土呢。

两个男孩马上忘掉了他们所有的恐惧和痛苦。

a minute. With happy eyes they watched every movement. Luck! —the splendor of it was beyond all imagination! Six hundred dollars was money enough to make half a dozen boys rich! Here was treasure—there would not be any bothersome uncertainty as to where to dig. They nudged each other every moment which is easily understood, for they simply meant—"Oh, but aren't you glad now we're here!"

Joe's knife struck upon something.

"Hello!" said he.

"What is it?" said his comrade.

"Half-rotten trunk—no, it's a box, I believe. Here—we'll see what it's here for. Never mind, I've broken a hole."

He reached his hand in and drew it out—

"Man, it's money!"

The two men examined the handful of coins. They were gold. The boys above were as excited as themselves, and as happy.

Joe's comrade said:

"We'll dig it out quickly. There's a pick among the grass in the corner—I saw it a minute ago."

He ran and brought the boys pick and shovel. Injun Joe took the pick, looked at it over carefully, shook his head, said something to himself, and then began to use

他们喜悦地看着他的每一个动作，太幸运了！——这份绝妙的运气简直无法想象！六百美元足够把半打男孩变成富翁的！宝物就在眼前——再也不必为了确定到哪儿挖宝而心烦了。他们不停地用肘碰碰对方，意思很明确——"噢，不高兴我们来这了吗？"

乔的刀子碰到了什么东西。

"喂！"他喊。

"什么？"他伙计问。

"烂了一半的箱子——不，是个盒子，我觉着在这儿呢——咱们看看这儿放个盒子干吗，别急，我已经打开了一个缝。"

他把手伸了进去，又取了出来——

"啊，是钱！"

两个人打量着这满手的硬币，是金的。上面的孩子们也和他们一样激动、兴奋。

乔的伙计说：

"我们快点儿挖出来吧。角落草丛里面有一把锄头——我刚看到的。"

他跑去拿了孩子们的锄头和铁锹。印第安人乔拿过锄头，仔仔细细地打量了一番，摇了摇头，对自己说了些什么，就开始用它挖了，盒子很快

it. The box was soon dug out. It was not very large, but strong. The men looked at the treasure for a while in happy silence.

"Oh, there's thousands of dollars here," said Injun Joe.

"Now you won't need to do that job."

Joe frowned. He said:

"You don't know me. At least you don't know all about that thing. It isn't robbery at all—it's revenge!" and a wicked light shone in his eyes.

"I'll need your help in it. When it's finished— then Texas. Go home to your Nance and your kids, and stay there till you hear from me."

"Well—if you say so. What'll we do with this— bury it again?"

"Yes. (Great happiness overhead.) No! No! (deep sadness overhead.) I'd nearly forgot. That pick had fresh soil on it! (The boys were sick with terror in a moment.) What business has a pick and a shovel here? What business with fresh soil on them? Who brought them here—and where are they gone? Have you heard anybody—seen anybody? What! Bury it again and leave them to come and see the ground dug? Not exactly—not exactly. We'll take it to my house."

"Why, of course! I might have thought of that be-

挖出来了。不大，却很结实，两个人一声没吭，却又兴奋不已地看了一会儿宝物。

"噢，这里有成千上万的美元吧，"印第安人乔说。

"你现在不用再去干那件事了。"

乔皱了皱眉，说：

"你不了解我，至少你对那件事不完全了解，这根本不是为了抢劫——是复仇！"他的眼神中露出邪光。

"我需要你的帮助，等结束了——就去得克萨斯。你先回家和南希，还有孩子呆在一起等我的消息。"

"嗯——如果你这么说，这笔钱怎么办——再埋起来。"

"行。（头顶上的孩子们欣喜若狂）不！不！（头顶上的俩人又陷入了极大的失望）我都差点儿忘了。那把锄头上可有新土！（孩子们一下都吓晕了）这儿放个锄头、铁锹干吗？上面怎么又能有新土！谁带来的——人又哪儿去了？你听到这儿有人吗——看到谁了吗？什么！把它再埋起来，等别人来看到地被挖过？绝对不行——绝对不行。我们把它带到我那儿。"

"对！在这之前我也应该想到这一点。你指的是

fore. You mean Number One?"

"No—Number Two—under the cross. The other place is bad—too common."

"All right. It's nearly dark enough to start."

Injun Joe got up and went about from window to window cautiously looking out. Presently he said:

"Who could have brought those tools here? Do you think they can be upstairs?"

The boys trembled. Injun Joe put his hand on his knife, stopped a moment, undecided, and then turned toward the stairway. The boys thought of the closet, but their strength was gone. The steps came up stairs—the intolerable distress of the situation made the boys come to a decision—they were about to jump for the closet, when the stairs were broken and Joe fell to the ground. He cursed and his comrade said:

"Now what's the use of all that? If it's anybody, and they're up there, let them stay there—who cares? If they want to jump down, now, and get into trouble, who'll be against? It will be dark in fifteen minutes—and then let them follow us if they want to. I'm willing. I'll bet anybody will run away when they see us since they will take us for ghosts or devils."

Joe agreed with his friend that they should leave here soon. Shortly afterward they slipped out of the

一号地?"

"不——二号地——十字架下的那个地方。一号地不好——太普通了。"

"行。咱们走吧，天已经差不多黑了。"

印第安人乔站了起来，从一个窗口走到另一个窗口，谨慎地向外望去。然后他说：

"谁会把这些工具带到这儿来呢？你觉得他们会在楼上吗？"

孩子们战栗起来。印第安人乔用手握住他的刀，停了一会儿，踌躇不决，然后朝楼梯走去。孩子们想到了柜橱，可他们已经吓得一点儿劲都没了。脚步声渐渐逼近楼梯——这局面令孩子们痛苦得无法忍受了。他们作出了决定——要跳到柜橱那儿。就在这时楼梯塌了，乔摔到了一楼地上。他大骂着，伙计说：

"你这么做有什么用？如果有人在楼上，就让他们呆着好了——谁在乎呢？如果他们现在要跳下来惹麻烦，谁又反对呢？十五分钟后天就黑了——如果他们要跟着咱，就让他们跟着好啦。我没意见，我担保只要有人看到咱们都会跑掉了，因为他们肯定把咱们当鬼魂或恶魔了。"

乔觉得他的朋友说得对，他们是该马上离开这里。很快两个人在渐深的暮色中溜出了这个屋子，

house in the deepening twilight, and moved toward the river with their precious box.

Tom and Huck rose up, weak but greatly relaxed. Follow? Not they. They were satisfied to reach ground again without broken necks, and take the townward walk over the hill. They did not talk much. They were too much absorbed in hating themselves—hating the ill luck that made them take the spade and the pick there. Without that, Injun Joe never would have doubted. He would have hidden the silver with the gold to wait there till his "revenge" was satisfied, and then he would have had the bad luck to find that money was lost. Bitter, bitter luck that the tools were ever brought there!

They decided to keep a notice of Joe when he should come to town spying out for chances to do his revengeful job, and follow him to "Number Two," wherever that might be. Then a terrible thought occurred to Tom:

"Revenge? What if he means us, Huck!"

"Oh, don't!" said Huck, nearly fainting.

They talked it all over, and as they entered town they agreed to believe that he might possibly mean somebody else—at least that he might at least mean nobody but Tom, since only Tom had given the evidence.

Tom felt very very uncomfortable to be alone in

抱着宝盒沿河边走去。

汤姆和哈克站了起来，虽然有些无力，但却非常轻松。跟着他们？他们不会的。他们对自己能再次双脚着地而脖子没断已经感到很满足了，于是沿着山间小路朝镇上走去。两人都不太吱声，光在那儿恨自己了——恨自己运气太差，居然把铁锹、锄头留在那儿了，否则的话，印第安人乔一定不会起疑心的，他会把那堆金币、银币藏在那儿，直到他报了仇，回来才发现自己是如何地倒霉，居然把钱丢了。真倒霉，倒霉——工具给放那儿去了！

他们决定等乔回镇上伺机报仇时注意观察他，跟他到"二号地"去，不管那地方在哪儿。这时一个可怕的念头突然闪过，汤姆说：

"报仇？如果他指的是我们怎么办，哈克！"

"噢，别！"哈克说着都要晕倒了。

俩人把这件事整个讨论了一遍，回到镇上时，已经一致认为他可能指的是别人——至少他指的只能是汤姆，因为只有汤姆作了证。

汤姆想到自己独自处于危险之中，非常不舒

danger! It would be obviously better if he had a partner.

Chapter 27
Trembling on the Trail

The adventure of the day greatly tortured Tom's dreams that night. Four times he had his hands on that rich treasure and four times it was lost in his figures as sleep escaped him and wakefulness brought back the hard reality of his bad luck. As he lay in the early morning recalling the incidents of his great adventure, he felt as if they had happened in another world or in a time long gone by. Then it occurred to him that the great adventure itself must be a dream! He was almost persuaded by this idea since the amount of coin he had seen was too great to be real. He had never seen as much as fifty dollars one time before, and he was like all boys of his age and situation, in that he imagined that all words of "hundreds" and "thousands" were only words in speeches, and that no such sums really existed in the world. The uncertainty must be swept away. He went hurriedly to find Huck.

Huck was sitting on the side of a boat, hanging his feet in the water and looking very sad. Tom concluded to

服。很显然，在这种局面下有个伴会好一些。

第二十七章　战战兢兢的追踪

　　白天的那场冒险经历可让汤姆在晚上的睡梦中备受煎熬，有四次他梦到自己的手都放在了宝物上，可四次宝物都从他手上溜走了。因为每当这时他都会醒来，清醒的他不得不面对倒霉而又残酷的现实。一大清早汤姆就躺在床上回忆他那场非凡的冒险经历，他觉得这事似乎发生在另一个世界里，或是很久很久以前，然后又觉着这一定是场梦。他几乎已经相信了这种感觉，因为他见到的那钱币数目太大了，大得让他都觉得不可能是真的。他以前一次连五十美元都没见过。就像这个年龄和阶层的所有男孩，他认为什么像"成千上万"之类的词只可能出现在演说中罢了，现实生活当中根本就不存在。汤姆一定要搞清楚这到底是真的还是梦。他急急忙忙地去找哈克了。

　　哈克正坐在船沿上，脚吊到水里，一副悲伤

let Huck lead up to the subject. If he did not do it, then the adventure would be proved to have been only a dream.

"Hello, Huck!"

"Hello!"

Silence for a minute.

"Tom, if we had left the tools at the dead tree, we would have got the money. Oh, it's too bad!"

"It isn't a dream, then. It isn't a dream! Somehow I most wish it was."

"Dream! If the stairs had not broken down you'd have seen how much dream it was! I've had dreams enough all night—with that Spanish devil going for me all the time!"

"No! Find him! Track the money!"

"Tom, we'll never find him. I'd feel like trembling if I was to see him, anyway."

"Well, so'd I; but I'd like to see him, anyway and track him out to his Number Two."

"Number Two—yes, that's it. I have been thinking about that. But I can understand nothing about that. What do you think it is?"

"I don't know. It's too deep. Say, Huck—maybe it's the number of a house!"

"Good! ... No, Tom, that isn't it. If it is, it

的样子。汤姆决定让哈克先提起这个话题，如果他没提到这个话题，就证明那事只是一场梦而已。

"喂，哈克！"

"喂！"

两人沉默了片刻。

"汤姆，如果咱们不把工具留在那棵枯树旁，钱就是咱们的了。唉，太糟糕了！"

"那这不是梦了，不是梦！我真希望这是个梦。"

"梦！如果楼梯没塌，你就知道那该是如何一场梦了！我整晚上都在做梦，都梦够了——总是梦到那西班牙恶魔来抓我！"

"不行！咱们要找到他！找到那笔钱！"

"汤姆，我们永远也找不到他。我见到他，就会全身发抖。"

"我也一样。可无论如何，我还是想找到他，跟踪他到那个二号地。"

"二号地——嗯，是这个地方。我一直在琢磨，可还是摸不着头脑，你觉得这会是哪儿呢？"

"我不知道，太难了。哈克——这可能是哪个房间。"

"对！……不会，汤姆，不会，如果是的话，

isn't in this small town. There is no number here."

"Well, that's so. Let me think a minute. Here—it's the number of a room—in a tavern, you know!"

"Oh, that's the trick! There are only two taverns. We can find out quickly."

"You stay here, Huck, till I come."

Tom was off at once. He did not care to have Huck stay with him in public places. He was gone half an hour. He found that in the best tavern, No. 2 had long been occupied by a young lawyer, and was still so occupied. In the less splendid house No. 2 was a misery. The tavern-keeper's young son said it was kept locked all the time, and he never saw anybody go into it or come out of it except at night; he did not know any particular reason. He had noticed that there was a light in there the night before.

"That's what I've found out, Huck. I think that's the very Number Two we're after."

"I think it is, Tom. Now what are you going to do?"

"Let me think."

Tom thought a long time. Then he said:

"I'll tell you. The back door of that Number Two is the door that comes out into that little road between the tavern and the brick store. Now you get hold of all the

不会在这个小镇。这儿的房间没有。"

"嗯，是这样，让我想一想，这是房间号——在酒馆里!"

"噢，这想法没错! 镇上有两家酒馆，咱们很快就能查出来的。"

"你在这儿呆着，哈克，等我回来。"

汤姆很快走了，他不喜欢在公共场合与哈克呆在一起。半个小时后，他查出镇上最好的那家酒馆的二号房间长期由一个年轻的律师住着，现在也是这样，而那个差一点的酒馆的二号房间是个谜。酒馆老板年轻的儿子说那房间一直锁着呢，除非是晚上，他从未见过有人进来，他不知道具体原因，但注意到昨晚房间灯亮着。

"这就是我查出来的。哈克，我想那正是我们要跟踪的二号地。"

"我想也是，汤姆，你现在准备怎么办?"

"让我想想。"

汤姆想了很长时间。然后说:

"我告诉你，那个二号地的后门通向酒馆和砖店之间的小路。你现在去找你能找到的所有钥匙。

door keys you can find, and I'll get all of my auntie's, and the first dark night we'll go there and try them. And mind you, keep a notice of Injun Joe, because he said he was going to go to town and spy around once more for a chance to get his revenge. If you see him, you just follow him; and if he doesn't go to that Number Two, that's the place."

"God, I don't want to follow him by myself!"

"Why, it'll be night, sure. He might not ever see you—and if he did, maybe he'd never think anything."

"Well, if it's pretty dark I think I'll track him. I'll try."

"Now you're talking! Don't you ever weaken, Huck, and I won't."

Chapter 28
In the Lair of Injun Joe

That night Tom and Huck were ready for their adventure. They had been wandering around the tavern until after nine for several nights, but faced ill luck.

But Thursday night promised better. Tom slipped out with his aunt's old lantern, and a large towel to cover eyes with. He lit his lantern, wrapped it closely in the

我去拿我姨妈的。等哪天晚上没有月亮，咱们就去试这些钥匙。注意，你要留心印第安人乔，因为他还要回镇上侦察一番，伺机报仇，如果你见到他了，就跟着他；如果他去的不是那个二号地，我们就知道地方了。"

"天哪！我不想就我一人跟着他。"

"你跟他的时候一定是晚上，他可能看不见你——即便他看见你了，或许他也不会多想的。"

"嗯，如果是特别黑的话，我想我就跟着他。我试试吧。"

"这就对了，你永远都不会软弱的。哈克，我也不会。"

第二十八章　印第安人乔的老窝

那天晚上，汤姆和哈克已经为再次冒险做好了准备。他们已经连续几个晚上在酒馆处晃悠到九点了，可运气都不好。

星期四晚上情况却有望好转。汤姆拿着她姨妈的旧灯笼，还有一条蒙眼睛的大毛巾溜了出来。他点着了灯笼，用毛巾紧紧地裹着，两个冒险者在

towel, and the two adventurers crept in the dark toward the tavern. Huck stood watching and Tom felt his way into the road. Then there was a season of waiting anxiety that weighed upon Huck's spirits like a mountain. He began to wish he could see a flash from the lantern—it would frighten him, but it would at least tell him that Tom was alive yet. It seemed hours since Tom had disappeared. Surely he must have fainted; maybe he was dead; maybe his heart had burst under terror and excitement. In his uneasiness Huck found himself drawing closer and closer to the road; fearing all sorts of dreadful things, and for some time expecting some terrible thing to happen that would take away his breath. His heart would soon wear itself out, the way it was beating. Suddenly there was a flash of light and Tom ran to him:

"Run!" said he; "run for your life!"

He needn't have repeated it; once was enough; Huck was making thirty or forty miles an hour before the repetition was made. The boys never stopped till they reached an empty room at the lower end of the village. As soon as Tom got his breath he said:

"Huck, it was terrible! I tried two of the keys, just as soft as I could. But they wouldn't turn in the lock. Well, without noticing what I was doing, I took hold of the knob, and open comes the door! It wasn't locked! I

黑暗中蹑手蹑脚地朝酒馆走去。哈克站在酒馆旁放哨。汤姆则摸黑走到小路上。这焦急的等待对哈克来说实在太长了，有如一座大山一直压着他。他开始希望能看到灯笼的闪现——这会让他惊恐，但至少表明了汤姆还活着。汤姆消失了似乎好几个小时，他肯定是晕倒了；或许是死了，或者他害怕。激动得心都迸开了。在这不安中哈克发现自己离小路越来越近，他一会儿担忧会不会发生各种可怕事情，一会儿又期望真的有什么恐怖的事情发生，好吓得他喘不上气来，因为他的心跳得都累了。突然前面灯闪了一下，汤姆跑向他说：

"快跑！快逃命！"

他不需重复，说一遍就够了；哈克在他说第二遍之前就已经以每小时三十或四十英里的速度逃跑了，两个孩子一直跑到村子下面那头的一个空屋子才停下来。汤姆呼吸稍一平缓就说：

"哈克，太可怕了。我尽可能轻轻地试了两把钥匙，可都打不开锁，然后不知怎么，我糊里糊涂地抓住了门柄，把门打开了。门没锁，我跳了

jumped in, and shook off the towel, and, God!"

"What—what'd you see, Tom?"

"Huck, I nearly stepped onto Injun Joe's hand!"

"No!"

"Yes! He was lying there, sound asleep on the floor, with his arms spread out."

"God, what did you do? Did he wake up?"

"No, never moved. Drunk, I think. I just seized that towel and started!"

"I'd have never thought of the towel, I bet!"

"Well, I would. My aunt would make me quite sick if I lost it."

"Say, Tom, did you see that box?"

"Huck, I didn't wait to look around,"

There was a pause for thinking, and then Tom said:

"Look here, Huck, let us not try that thing any more till we know Joe's not here. It's too frightening. If we watch every night, we'll be certain to see him go out, sometime or other, and then we'll seize that box as quickly as lightening."

"Well, I agree. I'll watch the whole night long, and I'll do it every night, too, if you'll do the other part of the job."

"All right, I will. Now, Huck, I'll go home. It'll

进去，晃掉了毛巾。上帝！"

"什么——你看到了什么，汤姆？"

"哈克，我差点踩到印第安人乔的手上！"

"不可能！"

"没错。他躺在地板上睡得正酣呢，双手还平伸着。"

"上帝，然后你怎么办了？他醒了吗？"

"没，一动没动，醉了，我想。我就抓起那条毛巾跑了！"

"我打赌要是我，根本就想不到毛巾了！"

"嗯，我能。如果把毛巾丢了，我姨妈非把我唠叨得烦死不可。"

"说说，汤姆，你见到那个盒子了吗？"

"哈克，我根本就没停下来看。"

沉默了片刻，汤姆说：

"哈克，等咱们知道印第安人乔不在那儿了再这么干吧，这样太可怕了，如果咱们每天晚上都这么盯着，肯定会看到什么时候他出来，然后咱们闪电一样抓住那个盒子就跑。"

"我同意。我以后整晚都盯着。如果你把其他事干了，我就负责以后每天盯着看。"

"行，其他的我干，现在，哈克，我要回家。

begin to be daylight in a couple of hours. You go back and watch that long, will you?"

"I said I would, Tom, and I will. I'll watch that tavern every night for a year! I'll sleep all day and I'll stand watch all night."

"That's all right. Well, if I don't want you in the daytime, I'll let you sleep. I won't come bothering around. Any time you see something's up, in the night, just come around and meow."

Chapter 29
Huck Saves the Widow

The first thing Tom heard on Friday morning was a glad piece of news—Judge Thatcher's family had come back to town the night before. Both Injun Joe and the treasure sank into secondary importance for a moment, and Becky took the main place in the boy's interest. He saw her, and they had played together for a long time together with their schoolmates. What was more satisfactory was that Becky's mother agreed Becky could hold her long-promised and long-delayed picnic, and she agreed. The invitations were sent out before sunset, and immediately the young children of the village were thrown into a

再过两三个小时天就亮了，你再盯两三个小时，行吗?"

"我说到做到。汤姆，我要每晚都盯着那酒馆，盯它一年! 我以后白天都睡觉，然后整晚上都站在那儿盯着。"

"那行。嗯，如果我白天不需要你，我就让你睡觉，不来打扰你了。晚上任何时候只要你看到有情况，就过来冲我家喵喵叫。"

第二十九章　哈克救了寡妇一命

汤姆星期五早晨听到的第一件事就是个好消息——撒切尔法官一家前一天晚上已经回到镇上了。印第安人乔和宝物都立刻退居次要位置了。贝琪把这个男孩的主要注意力都吸引了过去。汤姆去看她，他们和同学们一起玩了很长时间。更令人满意的是，贝琪的妈妈同意她举行她早已许诺却推迟了很久的野餐。邀请在傍晚前就发出了，村里的孩子们立刻投入了准备工作，沉浸在幸福

fever of preparation and happy expectation. Tom's excitement enabled him to keep awake until quite a late hour, and he had good hopes of hearing Huck's "meow", and of having his treasure to astonish Becky and the picnickers with next day; but he was disappointed. No signal came that night.

Morning came, at last, and by ten or eleven o'clock the noisy happy children were gathered at Judge Thatcher's, and everything was ready for a start. The last thing Mrs. Thatcher said to Becky was:

"You'll not get back till late, Perhaps you'd better stay all night with some of the girls that live near the ferry landing, child."

"Then I'll stay with Susy Harper, mamma."

"Very well. And mind and behave yourself and don't be any trouble."

Presently, as they tripped along, Tom said to Becky:

"Say—I'll tell you what we'll do. Instead of going to Joe Harper's we'll climb right up the hill and stop at Widow Douglas's. She'll have ice cream! She has it almost every day. She'll be very glad to have us."

"Oh, that will be fun!"

Then Becky thought a moment and said:

"But what will mamma say?"

的期盼中。汤姆兴奋得直到很晚才睡着。他非常希望能听到哈克的喵叫声，这样他第二天就可以让贝琪和其他参加野餐的人大吃一惊。可他很失望，那晚没什么信号。

早晨终于来到了。十点，或许是十一点的时候，兴奋的孩子们叽叽喳喳地聚集在撒切尔法官家。一切都准备好了，就等待出发。最后撒切尔夫人对贝琪说：

"你会回来得很晚，或许你最好呆在那些住在摆渡旁的女孩子家里，孩子。"

"那我就呆在苏珊·哈普家，妈妈。"

"很好。说话做事情都规矩点儿，别惹麻烦。"

不一会儿，孩子们就出发了，汤姆对贝琪说：

"喂——我告诉你咱们怎么办，你不要去苏珊·哈普家了，咱们爬山去道格拉斯寡妇家呆着。她家有冰淇淋，几乎天天都有，她会很高兴见到咱们的。"

"噢，那太好了！"

随后，贝琪想了一会儿，说：

"可妈妈会怎么说？"

"How'll she ever know?"

The girl turned the idea over in her mind, and said unwillingly:

"I think it's wrong—but—"

"Your mother won't know, and so what's the harm? All she wants is that you'll be safe; and I bet you she'd have told you to go there if she had thought of it. I know she would!"

Becky was persuaded. Presently it occurred to Tom that maybe Huck might come this very night and give the signal. The thought upset him a bit. Still he could not bear to give up the fun at Widow Douglas's. And why should he give it up, he thought—the signal did not come the night before, so why should it be any more likely to come tonight? The sure fun of the evening was more important than the uncertain treasure; and boylike, he determined to do the thing he was more interested in and not allow himself to think of the box of money another time that day.

After getting on shore, the children enjoyed themselves here and there. Then they had a feast. By and by somebody shouted:

"Who's ready for the cave?"

Everybody was. Bundles of candles were obtained. The mouth of McDougal's Cave was up the hillside. It

"她怎么能知道呢?"

女孩在脑子里琢磨了一会儿,挺不情愿地说:

"我想这样做不好——可是——"

"你妈不会知道的。这样的话你能有什么损失?只要她知道你平安无事就好,我担保如果她想到了道格拉斯寡妇,她会让你去那儿的,我知道她会的!"

贝琪被说服了。这时汤姆想到或许哈克今晚会来他家叫他。一想到这儿,他有点儿烦乱,可又不忍不去道格拉斯寡妇家度过那快乐的时光。为什么不去呢,他在想——哈克昨晚没叫他,那为什么今晚就可能会? 今晚注定将会非常愉快。比那没把握的宝物可重要。他颇具男孩子气概地决定干他更感兴趣的事,不再允许自己那天再想关于那盒子钱的事了。

上岸之后,孩子们到处愉快地玩。他们举行了一场盛宴,过了一会儿有人喊道:

"谁准备好了钻洞?"

所有的人都准备好了。他们收集了一捆捆的蜡烛。麦克道格尔山洞的洞口就在山上,那是一

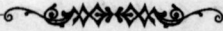

was a large labyrinth of crooked ways that ran into each other and out again and led nowhere. It was said that one might wander days and nights together through its complex breaks and openings and never find the end of the cave; and that he might go down and down, and still down, into the earth, and it was just the same—labyrinth under labyrinth, and no end to any of them. No man "knew" the cave. That was an impossible thing. Most of the young men knew a part of it, and it was not usual to venture much beyond the known part. Tom Sawyer knew as much of the cave as anyone.

Children moved along the main road for a while. Then groups and couples began to slip aside into branch ways in order to meet someone unexpectedly somewhere. But no one moved beyond the "known" ground.

By and by, one group after another came back to the mouth of the cave, breathing hard and happy with the success of the day. Then they were astonished to find that they had been taking no note of time and that night was about at hand. Then they took the ferryboat home.

When eleven o'clock came, and the tavern lights were put out; darkness everywhere, now. Huck had waited here what seemed a boring long time, but nothing happened. His faith was weakening. Was there any use? Was there really any use? Why not give it up?

个由弯弯曲曲的道组成的一个大迷宫。这些道相互交错，没有尽头，据说一个人即便在那些错综复杂的道道里转来转去走上许多个日日夜夜，也找不到头：他可以一直向前走。向下就是到了地面以下，也是一样——迷宫下面还是迷宫，根本没有尽头。没有人熟悉这个洞，那根本不可能。大多数的年轻人知道洞的一部分，如果冒险走出已掌握的那一部分，就算是异乎寻常之举了。和任何人一样，汤姆·索耶对这个洞的了解也多不到哪儿去。

孩子们沿着干道走了一会儿，接着三三两两溜到旁边的支道，为的是能在哪儿与别人不期而遇，可是没人走出"已掌握的"地域。

一会儿，一组一组的孩子们回到了洞口。虽然累得喘着粗气，可却为今天的圆满欢乐不已。他们很吃惊地发现时间怎么过得那么快，夜晚就要降临，于是大伙儿乘着渡船回家了。

十一点的时候，酒馆的灯熄了，到处漆黑一片。哈克已经在这儿等了在他看来又漫长又无聊的一段时间了，可什么都没发生。他的信心在一点点地减退，这样守着有用吗？真有用吗？为什么不放弃呢？

A noise fell upon his ear. He was all attention in an instant. The door closed softly. He sprang to the corner of the brick store. The next moment two men brushed by him, and one seemed to have something under his arm. It must be that box! So they were going to take away the treasure. Why call Tom now? Then the men could get away with the box and never be found again. No, he would follow them; he would believe he was safe from discovery in the dark. So Huck stepped out and moved along behind the men, catlike, with bare feet, allowing them to keep just far enough ahead not to be invisible.

They took the way up Cardiff Hill. They passed by the old Welshman's house, and still climbed upward. They reached the top and went into the narrow path between the tall bushes, and were at once hidden in the dark. Huck closed up and shortened his distance, now, for they would never be able to see him. Then he stopped completely; listened; no sound; none, except that he seemed to hear the beating of his own heart. The hooting of an owl came from over the hill—ominous sound! But no footsteps. Heavens, was everything lost? He was about to jump, when a man cleared his throat not four feet from him! Huck's heart shot into his throat, but he swallowed it again; and then he stood there shiv-

这时他听到了什么声音，立刻全神贯注起来。酒馆门轻轻关上了，他跳到砖店的墙角躲起来，紧接着两个人擦他而过，一个人似乎胳膊底下还夹着什么，一定是那个盒子！他们准备取走宝物，现在去叫汤姆？那这两个人就会带着那个盒子走掉，再也找不到了。不，他不叫汤姆了，他跟着他们；他相信他很安全，在黑暗中谁也看不到他。因而哈克迈出步子，光着脚跟在这两个人后面，像猫似的。他与他们保持了足够远的距离，但仍能看到他们。

他们朝卡迪夫山走去，路过了威尔士曼家，仍向上爬，他们到了山顶，钻进高高的草丛，沿着中间的小路继续向下走，很快就消失在了黑暗之中。哈克紧紧地跟上，缩短了与他们的距离，因为他们现在根本就看不到他。他完全停下来了；听着，没有声音；没有，只有他自己的心跳声。山上传来了猫头鹰叫——不祥之兆！还是没有听到脚步声。天哪，一切都失去了吗？他正准备跳起来，这时离他不到四英尺的地方一个男人清了清嗓子！哈克的心一下跳到嗓子眼，可他又咽了

ering, and so weak that he thought he must surely fall to the ground. He knew where he was. He knew he was quite near Widow Douglas's house. Very well, he thought, let them bury it there; it won't be hard to find.

Now there was a voice—a very low voice—Injun Joe's:

"Damn her, maybe someone's in her house—there're lights, although it's so late."

"I can't see any."

This was that stranger's voice—the stranger of the haunted house. A horrible chill went to Huck's heart—this, then, was the "revenge" job! His thought was, to fly. Then he remembered that the Widow Douglas had been kind to him more than once, and maybe these men were going to murder her. He wished he dared venture to warn her; but he knew he didn't dare—they might come and catch him. He thought all this and heard Injun Joe say:

"I'll never give it up before leaving this country. Her husband was rough on me—many times. He took advantage of me and died. But I'll revenge on her. I'll ruin her looks. I'll tear her nostrils and cut her ears. I'll tie her to bed. If she bleeds to death, is that my fault?"

回去，站在那儿浑身发抖，全身发软。他觉得自己一定会倒在地上。他清楚自己的处境，也知道自己离道格拉斯寡妇家很近。很好，他想，让他们把宝埋在那儿吧！这不难找。

这时——有人说话了——声音压得很低——是印第安人乔：

"该死，她家可能有人——这么晚了，灯还亮着呢。"

"我看不见任何人。"

这是那个陌生人的声音——鬼屋的那个陌生人，他的心一阵可怕的战栗——这，那么，就是他的"报复"行动了，他第一个念头就是跑，可马上他记起了道格拉斯寡妇不止一次地对他非常友善，或许这些人要杀她，他真希望自己敢于冒险去警告她；可他知道他不敢——他们或许会来抓住他。他把这件事整个想了想，听到印第安人乔说：

"在离开这个村子前我是不会放弃的。她丈夫曾经对我很粗暴——他经常捉弄我。他死了，可我要对她报复，我要破她的相，我要撕破她的鼻孔，割掉她的耳朵，我要把她绑在床上。如果她血流过多死了，那是我的错吗？"

"Well, if it's got to be done, let's get at it. The quicker the better—I'm all in a shiver."

"No—we'll wait till the lights are out—there's no hurry."

Huck felt that a silence was going to follow—a thing still more terrible than any amount of talk about murder; so he held his breath and stepped carefully back. There was no sound—the quietness was perfect. His thankfulness was measureless. Now he turned in his tracks, between the walls of bushes—turned himself as carefully as if he were a ship—and then stepped quickly but cautiously along. When he felt safe, he began to fly away. Down, down he ran, till he reached the Welshman's. He banged at the door, and presently the heads of the old man and his two strong sons appeared at the windows.

"Please don't ever tell I told you" were Huck's first words when he got in. "Please don't—I'd be killed, sure—but the widow's been good friend to me sometimes, and I want to tell—I will tell if you'll promise you won't ever say it was me."

"My God, he has got something to tell, or he wouldn't act so!" said the old man. "Say it and nobody here'll ever tell, boy."

Three minutes later the old man and his sons, well

"嗯，如果非要这么做的话，那就开始干吧，越快越好——我浑身发抖。"

"不——我们要等到灯熄了——不急。"

哈克感觉到再下来一定是沉寂——这比谈论杀人还可怕。因此他屏住呼吸，小心地向后退，没闹出什么声音——非常安静，他心中无限感激。这时他踏上了来时走过的路，就在草丛中——他尽可能小心地转过身，就像一艘船一样——然后快步却谨慎地朝前走去。等走到他觉得安全的地方，哈克就开始狂奔，他朝下跑啊跑，跑到了威尔士曼家，砰砰地敲着门。不一会儿老人和他的两位儿子的头就出现在了窗户上。

哈克进屋后说的第一句话就是"别告诉别人是我告诉你们的"。"别——要不我肯定会被杀了的——可是寡妇有时对我很友好，我要告诉你们——如果你们许诺不说是我说的话，我就告诉你们。"

"我的上帝，他有话要说，否则不会这样！"老头说，"说吧，这儿谁也不会告诉别人的，孩子。"

三分钟后，老人和他的儿子们已经全副武装

armed, were up the hill, and just entering the path between bushes on tiptoe, their weapons in their hands. Huck went with them no farther. He hid behind a great stone and fell listening. There was an anxious silence, and then all of a sudden there was an explosion of fire-arms and a cry.

Huck waited for no details. He jumped away and ran down the hill as fast as his legs could carry him.

Chapter 30
Tom and Becky in the Cave

On the early Sunday morning, Huck came cautiously up the hill and knocked gently at the old Welshman's door. The men were asleep, but it was a sleep that was set on a hair trigger, on account of the exciting event of the night. A call came from a window:

"Who's there?"

Huck's frightened voice answered in a low tone:

"Please let me in! It's only Huck Finn!"

"It's a name that can open this door night or day, lad! —and welcome!"

These were strange words to the idle boy's ears, and the pleasantest he had ever heard. The door was quickly opened, and he entered. Huck was given a seat

上山了，手拿着武器，踮着脚走在草丛中的小道上。哈克没有跟他们走多远。他躲在一个大石头后面躺倒了听着呢，周围静得让人着急，突然传出了开枪声与人的大叫声。

哈克没等着知道具体怎么样，就连蹦带跳地离开了，朝山下奔去，快得腿都要跟不上他了。

第三十章　汤姆和贝琪岩洞迷路

星期天一大早，哈克就小心翼翼地上了山，轻轻地敲了老威尔士曼家的门。他们还在睡觉，可由于昨晚发生的那件惊心动魄的事，他们睡得非常轻。拨动一根头发他们都能醒。窗内传来喊声：

"谁？"

哈克惊恐地低声回答道：

"请让我进来！是哈克贝历·芬恩！"

"这个名字无论白天还是晚上都能叫开这个门，小伙子！——欢迎！"

这些话对于这个游手好闲的男孩听来太陌生了，也是他听到的最悦耳的话。门很快开了，他进来了，他们请哈克坐了下来。老头和他两个高大

and the old man and his tall sons quickly dressed themselves.

"Now, my boy, I hope you're good and hungry, because breakfast will be ready as soon as the sun's up, easy about that! I and the boys hoped you'd appear and stop here last night."

"I was much frightened," said Huck, "and I ran. I took out when the guns went off, and I didn't stop for three miles. I've come now because I wanted to know about it, you know; and I come before daylight because I didn't want to run across those devils, even if they were dead."

"Well, poor boy, you do look as if you'd had a hard night of it—but there's a bed for you when you've had your breakfast. No' they're not dead, lad—we are sorry enough for that. You see we knew where to seize them, by your description; so we crept along on tiptoe till we got within fifteen feet of them—just then I found I was going to sneeze. It was the worst kind of luck! I tried to keep it back, but no use—it was certain to come, and it did come! Then those devils ran away and missed our shooting. As soon as we lost the sound of their feet we stopped chasing, and went down and called police. They went off to guard the riverbank, and as soon as it is light the sheriff and a gang are going to beat

的儿子很快就穿好了。

"我的孩子，我希望你一切很好。饿了吧，等太阳一出来早饭就准备好了，别急！我和孩子们还想着你昨晚能来，在这呆一宿呢。"

"我吓坏了，"哈克说，"枪一响我就跑了，一口气跑了三英里，我现在来就是想知道事情怎么样了，之所以天还没亮就来是不想撞上那俩恶魔，哪怕他们已经死了。"

"嗯，可怜的孩子，看起来昨晚你的确过得不怎么样——等会儿吃了早饭你就在这张床上睡会儿。他们没死，小伙子——我们为此很抱歉。当时按照你的描述我们知道在哪儿抓他们；然后就悄没声息地走到离他们不足十五英尺的地方——就在那时我觉得特想打喷嚏。简直太倒霉了，我使劲忍着，可没用——这非得打不可，然后就真打了！那两个恶魔立刻就逃跑了，我们的枪也没打中。然后赶紧去追，可一会儿就听不到他们的声音了。又赶快下山去叫了警察，他们出发去把守河岸。天一亮治安官带一帮人就会在树林里

up the woods. My boys will be with them presently. I wish we had some sort of description of those devils—it would help a good deal. But you couldn't see what they were like, in the dark, lad, I suppose?"

"Oh, yes, I saw them downtown and followed them."

"Splendid! Describe them—describe them, my boy!"

"One's the old deaf-and-dumb Spanish that's been around here once or twice, and the other's a mean-looking, ragged—"

"That's enough, lad, we know the men! I happened to meet them in the woods back of the widow's one day, and they ran away. Off with you, boys, and tell the sheriff—get your breakfast tomorrow morning!"

The Welshman's sons left at once. As they were leaving the room Huck sprang up and said:

"Oh, please don't tell anybody it was me that said anything on them! Oh, please!"

The old man promised to keep secret, and said:

"How did you come to follow these fellows, lad? Were they looking doubtful?"

Huck was silent while he made a suitable cautious reply. Then he said:

"Last night, I couldn't sleep, and so I came along

砍砍敲敲，找那两个人，我儿子马上就去和他们会合。我希望你还能向我描述一下那两个恶魔长什么样——这会有很大帮助的，不过当时漆黑一片，你也看不清他们吧？"

"能，我在镇上就看到他们了，一直跟着呢。"

"太好了！说说他们什么样——说说，我的孩子。"

"一个是又聋又哑的西班牙老头，他曾经在这儿出现过一两回。另一个看着挺卑贱的，一身破破烂烂——"

"这就够了，小伙子，我知道这两个人！有一天我在寡妇家后面的小林子正好碰到过他们，他们当时见人就溜了。快走吧，孩子们，把这个告诉治安官——明天再吃早饭吧！"

威尔士曼家的儿子立即走了。就在他们离开房子时，哈克跳起来说：

"噢，请不要告诉别人是我告的！噢，拜托！"

老人许诺一定为他保守秘密，然后问道：

"你为什么跟着那两个家伙，小伙子？他们是不是看起来很可疑？"

哈克没吱声，脑子里小心地盘算着怎么回答合适。然后他说：

"昨晚我睡不着，半夜时就沿着大街走着。待

up street about midnight, and when I got up street about midnight, and when I got to that old brick store by the Temperance Tavern, I backed up against the wall to have some thinking. Well, just then along came these two men slipping along close by me, with something under their arm and I thought they'd stolen it. One was smoking, and the other one wanted a light; so they stopped right before me and the cigars lit up their faces and I saw that the big one was the deaf-and-dumb Spanish and the other was a ragged – looking devil."

"Could you see the rags by the light of the cigars?"

This astonished Huck for a moment. Then he said:

"Well, I don't know—somehow it seems as if I did."

"Then they went on, and you—"

"Follow them—yes. That was it. I wanted to see what was up. They stood in the dark and I heard the Spanish man swear he'd destroy her looks just as I told you and your two—"

"What! The deaf-and-dumb man said all that!"

Huck had made another terrible mistake! He was trying his best to keep the old man from getting any hint of who the Spanish might be, and yet his tongue seemed determined to get him into trouble in spite of all he could do. He made several efforts to creep out of his awkward

我走到泰普南思酒馆旁的那个老砖店时，我靠着墙琢磨起事来了。这时这两个人紧贴着我身边溜过，胳膊下还夹着什么东西，我估摸肯定是偷的。一个人正抽烟，另一个要火，他们就在我前面停下了。烟火照亮了他们的脸。我看到个儿大的是个又聋又哑的西班牙人，另一个是个穿得破破烂烂的恶魔。"

"你能凭着烟火看到他穿得破破烂烂？"

这让哈克好是吃惊了一会儿，然后说：

"嗯，我不知道——好像我看清了。"

"然后他们继续走了，你——"

"跟上他们了——对，就这样。我要看看会出什么事。他们在黑暗中站着，我听那个西班牙人诅咒说，我要毁她的容，就像我说给你和你的两个——"

"什么！聋哑人居然说了那些话！"

哈克又犯了一个可怕的错误。他尽量不想让老人知道那西班牙人是谁，可无论他费了多少心机，舌头似乎注定要给他惹麻烦。他几番努力想

situation, but the old man's eye was upon him and he made mistake after mistake. Presently the Welshman said:

"My boy, don't be afraid of me. I wouldn't hurt a hair of your head for all the world. No—I'd protect you—I'd protect you. This Spanish man is not deaf and dumb; you've let that slip without intending it; you can't cover that up now. You know something about that Spanish man that you want to keep unknown. Now trust me—tell me what it is, and trust me—I won't betray you."

Huck looked into the old man's honest eyes a moment, then bent over and whispered into his ear:

"It isn't a Spanish—it's Injun Joe!"

The Welshman almost jumped out of his chair. In a moment he said:

"It's all clear enough, now. When you talked about tearing ears and cutting noses I judged that you made it up, because white men don't talk that sort of revenge. But an Injun! That's a different matter completely."

During the breakfast the talk went on, and in the course of it the old man said that the last thing which he and his sons had done, before going to bed, was to get a lantern and examine the place for marks of blood. They

要摆脱这尴尬的局面，可老人的眼睛一直盯着他，害得他犯了一个又一个的错误。这时，威尔士曼说：

"我的孩子，别怕我。无论怎样，我连你的头发丝都不会伤到的，不会——我会保护你——我会保护你的。这个西班牙人既不聋也不哑，你无意之中透露了这一点，现在是无法遮掩了。你了解那个西班牙人的有些事情，可你不想让别人知道，相信我——告诉我是怎么回事，相信我——我不会泄密的。"

哈克注视了一会儿老人那坦诚的眼睛，然后弯下身，在他耳边低声说道：

"他不是西班牙人——他是印第安人乔！"

听到这话威尔士曼都要从椅子上跳起来了。一会儿他说：

"现在很清楚了。你刚才说到撕耳朵、割鼻子时我曾想你是编的，因为白人不会这么报复别人，但是印第安人那就完全不同了。"

吃早饭时，他们继续聊着。老头说他和儿子们昨晚临睡觉前还找了个灯笼，去树丛中看有没

found none, but seized—

"What?"

His eyes were staring wide, now, and his breath stopped—waiting for the answer.

The Welshman started—stared in return—three seconds—five seconds—ten—then replied:

"Thief's tools. Why, what's the matter with you?"

Huck sank back, breathing gently, but deeply, feeling thankful. The Welshman eyed him seriously, curiously—and presently said:

"Yes, thief's tools. That appears to relax you a good deal. But what did you take that for? What were you expecting we'd found?"

There was no time to weigh it, so at a venture Huck said it weakly:

"Sunday-school books, maybe."

Poor Huck was too distressed to smile, but the old man laughed loud and joyously, and ended by saying that such a laugh was money in a man's pocket, because it cut down the doctor's bills like everything. Then he added:

"Poor fellow, you're white – you aren't well a bit. But you'll come out of it. Rest and sleep will make you all right, I hope."

有血迹。血迹没发现，倒是找到了——

"什么?"

他的眼睛瞪得大大的，呼吸也止住了——等待着老人的回答。

威尔士曼盯着他——转过来盯着他——三秒钟——五秒钟——十秒——然后回答说:

"小偷的工具，你怎么啦?"

哈克一屁股坐了回去，深深地吸了口气，平静下来了，感到莫大的欣慰。威尔士曼奇怪而又严肃地看着他——说:

"对，小偷的工具。这回答好像让你轻松了一大截。你认为这怎么啦?你想我们会找到什么呢?"

没有时间琢磨了，哈克冒险低声说:

"主日学校的书。"

可怜的哈克太沮丧，根本笑不出来。可老人却被逗得哈哈大笑，末了说笑可以给人省钱，不用人去医院了，他接着说:

"可怜的小伙子，你脸色苍白——身体一定不舒服吧，我想休息休息，睡睡觉就好了。"

Huck was angry to think he had been such a stupid goose and betrayed so much, for he had shown that the parcel brought from the tavern was the treasure. But on the whole he felt glad, for now he knew certainly that the tool was not the treasure, and so his mind was at rest and very comfortable. Now, the treasure must be still in No.2, the men would be seized and jailed that day, and he and Tom could seize the gold that night without any trouble or any fear of interruption.

Just as breakfast was completed there was a knock at the door. Huck jumped for a hiding place, for he did not want to be connected with the event of last night at all. Several ladies and gentlemen entered, among them the Widow Douglas, and groups of citizens were climbing up the hill—to stare at the place where the event took place. So the news had spread.

The Welshman had to tell the story of the night to the visitors. The widow's thankfulness for being protected was directly expressed.

"Don't say a word about it, madam. There's another one whom you're more thankful to. But he doesn't allow me to tell his name. We wouldn't have been there without him."

This excited stronger curiosity among visitors, but the Welshman refused to tell the secret.

哈克为自己刚才说了那两个人从酒馆拿出的包袱是个宝而生气。他觉得自己是个大蠢蛋，吐露了那么多秘密。不过总的来说，他还是挺高兴的。因为现在他确信丢在那儿的是工具，不是宝，所以心情比较平静，欣慰。那么现在宝物一定还在二号地，今天那两个人肯定会被捉进监狱，那他和汤姆今晚就可以不费吹灰之力，不怕任何干扰地拿到盒子了。

就在早饭吃完时，有人敲门。哈克跳起来，找个地方藏身，因为他可不想把自己和昨晚的事连起来。几位先生女士走了进来，其中有道格拉斯寡妇，还有一群一群的村民正在上山——去看出事的地方。这样消息就传开了。

威尔士曼不得不把昨晚的事讲给那些来访者。寡妇感谢了那些保护她的人。

"你在我面前别提什么感谢话，夫人，你更应该感谢另一个人。可他不允许我说出他的名字，没有他我们是去不了的。"

这话可引起了来人的好奇心，然而威尔士曼却对他的秘密缄口不言。

More visitors came, and the story had to be told and retold for a couple of hours more.

Everybody was early at church. When the sermon was finished, Judge Thatcher's wife met Mrs. Harper as she moved down the passage with the crowd and said:

"Is my Becky going to sleep all day? I just expected she would be tired to death."

"Your Becky?"

"Yes," with astonished look; "didn't she stay with you last night?"

"Why, no."

Mrs. Thatcher turned pale, and sank into a seat, just as Aunt Polly, talking happily with a friend, passed by. Aunt Polly said:

"Good morning, Mrs. Thatcher. Good morning, Mrs. Harper. I've got a boy that's turned up missing. I think my Tom stayed at your house last night—one of yours. And now he's afraid to come to church. I've got to punish him."

Mrs. Thatcher shook her head weakly and turned paler than ever.

"He didn't stay with us," said Mrs. Harper, beginning to look uneasy. An obvious anxiety came into Aunt Polly's face.

"Joe Harper, have you seen my Tom this morn-

更多的人来了，昨晚的事不得不在接下来的几个小时一遍一遍地讲给他们听。

所有的人一大早就来到了教堂，布道结束后，撒切尔法官的妻子正随人群沿着过道走时，碰到了哈普夫人。她说：

"我家贝琪是不是准备睡一天呀？我想她可能都累死了。"

"你家贝琪？"

"对呀。"撒切尔夫人露出了惊讶的神情，"她昨晚没有和你们呆在一起吗？"

"没有。"

撒切尔夫人的脸色变得苍白，一屁股坐到了一个位子上。这时，波莉姨妈正和一个朋友高兴地说着什么，走了过来，她说：

"早上好，撒切尔夫人。早上好，哈普夫人。我们家一个小孩现在不见了。我想我们汤姆昨天躲在你们谁家了——你们两家中的一个。他现在可怕到教堂来了，我得惩罚他。"

撒切尔夫人费力地摇了摇头，脸色更苍白了。

"他没和我们呆在一起，"哈普夫人说，开始显出一副不安的样子。波莉姨妈的脸上也明显地露出焦虑的神情。

"乔·哈普，你今天早晨看到我们家汤姆了

ing?"

"No, Madam."

"When did you see him last?"

Joe tried to remember, but was not sure he could say. The people had stopped moving out of church. Whispers passed along, and every person felt uneasy. Children were anxiously questioned, and young teachers. They all said they had not noticed whether Tom and Becky were on board the ferryboat on the homeward trip; it was dark; no one thought of asking if anyone was missing. One young man finally expressed his fear that they were still in the cave! Mrs. Thatcher fainted away. Aunt Polly fell to crying.

The alarm swept from lip to lip, from group to group, from street to street, and within five minutes the bells were wildly clanging and the whole town was up! The Cardiff Hill event sank into instant insignificance, the devils were forgotten, the ferryboat ordered out, and before the horror was half an hour old two hundred men were pouring down highroad and river toward the cave.

All the long afternoon the village seemed empty and dead. Many women visited Aunt Polly and Mrs. Thatcher and tried to comfort them. They cried with them, too, and that was still better than words. All the slow night the town waited for news; but when the morning dawned

吗?"

"没有,夫人。"

"你最后一次见他是什么时候?"

乔努力回忆着,不敢肯定自己说的话对不对。人们不再往教堂外走了,大家互相低语着,每个人都显得很担忧。人们焦急地问了其他孩子和年轻老师,他们都说没注意到汤姆和贝琪是否登上了回家的渡船;那会儿很黑了,没人想到问问是否有人不见了。一个年轻老师最后忧心忡忡地说:孩子们可能还在山洞里。撒切尔夫人一听立刻晕了过去,波莉姨妈则坐在地上痛哭起来。

这可怕的消息从一个人传到另一个人,从一群人传到另一群人,从一条街传到另一条街。不到五分钟,钟声就猛烈地响了起来,整个镇子都沸腾了!卡迪夫山上发生的事立刻变得不重要了,恶魔也被抛在脑后了。人们叫了渡船,在得知这可怕的消息还没有半个小时,两百名男人已经涌向通往山洞的公路和大河了。

整个漫长的下午村子似乎都空了,一片死气沉沉,许多女人都去看波莉姨妈和撒切尔夫人,都试着安慰她们。她们也陪着一同掉眼泪,这效果要比任何言语强。整个晚上镇子的人们都在等待消息。时间显得过得很慢;最后当天空破晓时,

at last, all the words that came were, "Send more candle—and send food." Mrs. Thatcher was almost crazy;
and Aunt Polly also. Judge Thatcher sent messages of
hope and encouraging words from the cave, but they carried no real cheer.

The old Welshman came home toward daylight. He
found Huck still in the bed and troubled with fever. The
physicians were all at the cave, so the Widow Douglas
came and took care of the patient. She said she would do
her best to him, because, whether he was good, bad, or
cold, he was the Lord's and nothing that was the Lord's
was a thing to be neglected.

Three dreadful days and nights passed, and the village sank into a hopeless situation. No one had heart for
anything. Huck weakly asked—dimly dreading the
worst—if anything had been discovered at the Temperance Tavern since he had been ill.

"Yes," said the widow.

Huck started up in bed, wild-eyed:

"What! What was it?"

"Liquor! —and the place has been shut up. Lie
down, child—what a shock you did give me!"

"Only tell me just one thing—please! Was it Tom
Sawyer that found it?"

The widow burst into tears. "Oh, child! I've told

他们得到的所有的话都是："再拿些蜡烛来——拿些吃的来。"撒切尔夫人几乎都疯了，波莉姨妈也一样。撒切尔法官从洞那边捎来了充满希望的消息，还有安慰人心的话，可她们一点儿也没高兴起来。

老威尔士曼快天亮时回了家。他看到哈克正难受地躺在床上，他发烧了。医生全在洞里，因而叫来了道格拉斯寡妇照看病人。她说她会尽其所能地照顾他，因为无论他是好孩子还是坏孩子，他都是属于上帝的，上帝的一切都不该忽视。

可怕的三天三夜过去了，整个村庄都处于绝望之中，没人有心思干任何事。哈克虚弱地问起——因为他隐隐约约地害怕会有什么最坏的事情发生——自从他病了之后在泰普南思酒馆有没有发现什么？

"有，"寡妇回答。

哈克一下从床上坐起来，眼睛瞪得大大的。

"什么！发现什么了？"

"白酒！——那地方已经关上了，躺下，孩子——你真把我吓着了！"

"只再告诉我一件事——拜托了！是不是汤姆·索耶发现的？"

寡妇哭起来，"噢，孩子！我刚才都告诉你

you before, you must not talk. You are very, very sick!"

Then nothing but liquor had been found; there would have been a great talk if it had been the gold. So the treasure was gone forever—gone forever! But what could she be crying about? Huck felt curious that she should cry.

These thoughts worked their dim way through Huck's mind, and under the tiredness they gave him he fell asleep. The widow said to herself:

"There—he's asleep, poor boy. Tom Sawyer found it! Pity but somebody could find Tom Sawyer! Ah, there aren't many people now who got enough hope and strength to go on searching for Tom."

Chapter 31
Found and Lost Again

Now to return to Tom and Becky's share in the picnic. They walked along the dark passages with the rest of the children, visiting the familiar wonders of the cave. Presently the hide-and-seek game began, and Tom and Becky engaged in it with passion until they felt tired; then they wandered down a winding way holding their candles high and reading the names, dates, post-office

了，你一定不要再说话，你现在病得非常非常重。"

那么除了酒，什么也没有发现。如果是金子的话，她准会滔滔不绝地说个不停，所以宝物永远都没了。——永远都没了！可她哭什么呢？哈克对此感到很奇怪。

哈克在脑子里模模糊糊地琢磨着这些想法，想着想着觉得累了，就又睡着了。寡妇自言自语道：

"他睡着了，可怜的孩子，汤姆·索耶发现的！真可怜，也不知谁能找到汤姆·索耶！啊，现在已经没多少人还心存足够希望，还有足够的劲儿去继续找汤姆了。"

第三十一章　找见了，又丢了

现在再回到去参加野餐的汤姆和贝琪。他们与剩下的孩子在山洞里沿着黑漆漆的道走着，观看那些熟悉的奇迹。一会儿这些孩子玩起了藏猫猫游戏。汤姆和贝琪玩得忘乎所以，直到他们都觉得累了，他们高高举起蜡烛，沿着弯道边走边读用蜡烛烟熏写在岩石壁上的那些人名，日期，

addresses, and mottoes written on the rock walls by candle smoke. Still drifting along and talking, they hardly noticed that they were now in a part of the cave whose walls were not written. They smoked their own names on it and moved on. Presently they came to a place where a little stream of water had formed a waterfall. Tom found that behind it there was a sort of steep natural stairway which was enclosed between narrow walls, and at once the ambition to be a discoverer seized him. Becky responded to his call, and they made a smoke mark for future guidance, and started upon their venture. They wound this way and that, far down into the secret depths of the cave, made another mark, and turned into small passages in search of new things to tell the others. Then they came to a large cave in which there was a spring. Under the roof of the cave many bats had packed themselves together; the lights disturbed the creatures, and they came down by hundreds at the candles. Tom knew their ways and the danger of this sort of conduct. He seized Becky's hand and hurried her into the first corridor that offered; and none too soon, for a bat struck Becky's light out with its wing while she was passing out of the cave. The bats ran after the children a long way; but the children escaped into every new passage that offered, and at last got rid of the dangerous things. Tom

邮局地址，座右铭等。走着，说着，他们几乎没意识到他们已走到一块墙上什么都没写的地方了。俩人用蜡烟熏写了自己的名字，又继续朝前走。一会儿他们来到一个地方，这儿有小溪形成的瀑布。汤姆发现在瀑布后面两个墙中间有一段又窄又陡的天然阶梯。汤姆那想当探索者的野心立刻被唤起了。贝琪响应了他的要求，他们又在墙上熏了一下为以后做标记，然后就开始了探险。俩人在洞里弯弯曲曲地绕来绕去，朝洞的深处那不为人知的地方走了很深，又做了一个标记，然后转到一些小道上探寻新东西，以便告诉别人。他们来到了一个大洞，那儿有一眼泉。洞顶下倒挂着许多只蝙蝠；烛光惊动了他们，那些蝙蝠成百上千地冲蜡烛撞过来。汤姆了解蝙蝠的习性，清楚这样很危险。他抓起贝琪的手，见到通道就急忙进；可是已经晚了，贝琪向洞外跑时一只蝙蝠用翅膀扑灭了她的蜡烛。蝙蝠跟了孩子们很久；他们见道就逃，终于摆脱了那些危险的家伙。很

found a lake, shortly. He wanted to find its borders, but concluded that it would be best to sit down and rest for a while, first. Now, for the first time, the deep quietness of the place disturbed the children. Becky said:

"Why, I didn't notice, but it seems ever so long since I heard any of the others."

"Come to think, Becky, we are away down below them—and I don't know how far away north, or south, or east, or which ever it is. We couldn't hear them here."

Becky grew frightened.

"I wonder how long we've been down here, Tom. We'd better start back."

"Yes, I think we'd better. Perhaps we'd better."

"Can you find the way, Tom? I feel confused."

"I think I could find it—but then the bats. If they put both our candles out it will be terrible. Let's try some other way, so as not to go through there."

"Well. But I hope we won't get lost. It would be so horrible!" and the girl trembled at the thought of the dreadful possibilities.

They started through a corridor, and passed it in silence a long way, glancing at each new opening to see if there was anything familiar about the look of it; but they were all strange. Every time Tom made an examination,

快汤姆看到了一个湖。他想瞧瞧它有多大，可又觉得最好还是先坐下休息一会儿。这时，洞中深深的宁静第一次令孩子们感到不安。贝琪说：

"我没留心，但觉得好像很久没听到别人的声音了。"

"我来想想，贝琪，咱们现在应该在他们下面——我不知道离他们有多远，是在他们北边，南边，东边，还是什么。在这儿听不到。"

贝琪越来越感到害怕。

"我在想咱们下来多久了。汤姆，咱们最好回吧。"

"好，我也觉得最好回去。或许我们最好回去。"

"你能找到路吗，汤姆？我弄不清了。"

"我想我能——可那蝙蝠。如果它们把咱俩的蜡烛都扑灭的话。那就太可怕了。咱们试试别的路吧，避开那儿。"

"好吧。可我希望咱们别迷路，那就太恐怖了！"女孩一想到可能会发生的可怕事情，浑身颤抖。

他们首先穿过了一条通道，不吱一声地走了很长时间，朝遇到的每一个新的通口望去，想看一看有没有什么熟悉的东西；可一切都是陌生的。汤姆每次仔细观察通道情况时，贝琪都在看着他

Becky would watch his face for an encouraging sign, and he would say cheerily:

"Oh, it's all right. This isn't the one, but we'll come to it right away!" But he felt less and less hopeful with each failure, and presently began to turn into any passage at random, in desperate hope of finding the one that was wanted. He still said it was "all right," but there was such a heavy dread at his heart that the words had sounded just as if he had said, "All is lost!" Becky stayed close to him in a pain of fear, and tried hard to keep back the tears, but they would come. At last she said:

"Oh, Tom, never mind the bats, let's go back that way! We seem to get worse and worse off all the time."

Tom stopped.

"Listen!" said he.

Deep silence; silence so deep that even their breathings were easily heard. Tom shouted. The call went echoing down the empty passages and died out in the distance in a faint sound that was like a ripple of mocking laughter.

"Oh, don't do it again, Tom, it is too horrible," said Becky.

"It is horrible, but I'd better, Becky; they might hear us, you know," and he shouted again.

的脸，渴望有什么鼓舞人心的表情。这时汤姆会轻松地说：

"没关系。这个不是，但我们很快会找到的！"可随着一次又一次的失败，他觉得越来越没有希望了，就开始随意拐入任何一条通道，强烈地希望能找到他们要找的那条路。他仍然说着"没关系"，可心里却难过而且沉重，所以说出来的话倒听着像"我们彻底迷路了！"贝琪在痛苦与恐惧中紧贴着他，使劲不让眼泪流出来，可还是不行。最后她说：

"噢，汤姆，别管那些蝙蝠了，咱们还是从那条路回去吧！我们越走越不对了。"

汤姆停了下来。

"听！"

深深的沉寂；静得他们的呼吸声都很容易听到。汤姆大喊了一声。声音在空荡荡的通道里回旋，最后在远处模模糊糊地消失了。就像一连串揶揄的笑声。

"噢，再别这样了，汤姆，太吓人了，"贝琪说。

"是挺吓人的，可我最好还是喊一喊，贝琪；你知道，他们可能会听到咱们的。"他又喊了起来。

The children stood quiet and listened; but there was no result. Tom turned upon the back track at once, and hurried his steps. Immediately he realized another fearful fact—he could not find his way back!

"Oh, Tom, you don't make any marks!"

"Becky, I was such a fool! Such a fool! I never thought we might want to come back! No! —I can't find the way. It's all mixed up."

"Tom, Tom, we're lost! We're lost! We never can get out of this terrible place! Oh, why did we ever leave the others!"

She sank to the ground and burst into such a mad crying that Tom was shocked with the idea that she might die, or lose her reason. He sat down by her and put his arms around her; she buried her face in his chest, she clung to him, she poured out her terrors and her regrets. Tom begged her to pick up hope again, and she said she could not. He fell to scolding himself for getting her into this miserable situation; this had a better effect. She said she would try to hope again, she would get up and follow wherever he might lead if only he would not talk like that. For he was no more to scold than she, she said.

So they moved on again—aimlessly—simply at random—all they could was to move, keep moving.

孩子们静静地站在那儿，听着；可还是没有结果。汤姆马上就返回到了原来的那条路上，加快了步伐。他很快就意识到了另一个可怕的事实——他找不到回去的路了！

"噢，汤姆，你一个标记都没有留！"

"贝琪，我太蠢了，我太蠢了！我从没想我们还要回来的！没有！——我找不到回去的路了，一切都乱了。"

"汤姆，汤姆，我们走丢了！我们走丢了！我们再也走不出这可怕的地方了！噢，我们为什么要离开其他人呢！"

她一屁股坐在地上，痛哭起来。汤姆惊呆了，他觉得她都可能哭死，或是哭疯。他坐在她旁边，胳膊搂着她；她将脸埋在他的胸前，紧紧地抱着他，她一股脑儿倒出了自己的恐惧与后悔。汤姆求她一定要振作起来，她说她做不到。他跪在地上责怪自己把她带进了这样痛苦的处境；这么一说倒挺管用。她让他别这么说，她会试着重新拾起希望，无论领她到哪儿，她都会站起来跟着走。因为，她说，他们俩一样有错。

他们又继续走下去——漫无目的地——只是随便走着——俩人所能做到的只有走，不停地走。

By and by Tom took Becky's candle and blew it out. This saving meant so much! Words were not needed. Becky understood, and her hope died again. She knew that Tom had a whole candle and three or four pieces in his pockets—yet he must save the candle.

By and by, they felt tired; the children tried to pay no attention, for it was dreadful to think of sitting down when time had grown to be so precious; moving, in some direction, in any direction, was at least progress and might bear fruit; but to sit down was to invite death.

At last Becky's weak legs refused to carry her farther. She sat down. Tom rested with her, and they talked of home, and friends there, and the comfortable beds and, above all, the light! Becky cried, and Tom tried to think of some way of comforting her, but all his encouragements were not effective. Becky was so tired that she fell asleep. Tom was thankful. He sat looking into her face and saw it grow smooth and natural under the influence of pleasant dreams; and by and by a smile appeared and rested there. The peaceful face offered peace to his spirit. While he was deep in thinking, Becky woke up and began to cry again.

"Oh, how could I sleep! I wish I never, never had woken! No! No, I don't, Tom! Don't look so! I won't say it again."

一会儿，汤姆拿过贝琪的蜡烛，把它吹灭了。这种节省意味深长，无需什么言语来解释。贝琪明白，她的希望又破灭了。她知道汤姆手里拿着一整根蜡烛，兜里还揣着三四根——可是他还必须要节省蜡烛。

不久，俩人感到累了；孩子们试着不去注意这种感觉，因为浪费时间太可怕了，他们想时间那么宝贵，而自己只是单单地坐着；走，朝某个方向走，朝任何方向走，至少都是在前进，或许就会有收获；可坐在那儿就意味着等死。

最后贝琪觉得腿实在没劲儿了，走不动了，她坐了下来。汤姆与她一起休息，他们谈到了家，还有那儿的朋友，舒适的床，尤其是灯光！贝琪哭了，汤姆试着想办法安慰她，可一切的安慰都没用。贝琪太累了，她睡着了。汤姆很欣慰，他坐在那儿看着她的脸，睡着了的她可能做了什么美梦，脸儿也变得平静而且自然了；一会儿，笑容出现了，停驻在她的脸上。看着她那平静的脸孔，汤姆觉得自己的精神也有了片刻的宁静。当他正沉思时，贝琪醒了，又哭了起来。

"噢，我怎么睡觉了！我希望我永远，永远都不要醒来！不！不，我不这么说了。汤姆！别这么一副表情！我再不这么说了。"

"I'm glad you've slept, Becky; you'll feel rested, now, and we'll find the way out."

"We can try, Tom; but I've seen such a beautiful country in my dream. I think we are going there."

"Maybe not, maybe not. Cheer up, Becky, and let's go on trying."

They rose up and wandered along, hand in hand and hopeless. They tried to estimate how long they had been in the cave, but all they knew was that it seemed days and weeks, and yet it was clear this could not be, for their candles were not used up yet. A long time after this—they could not tell how long—Tom said they must go softly and listen for dripping water—they must find a spring. They found one presently, and Tom said it was time to rest again. Both were cruelly tired, yet Becky said she thought she could go on a little farther. She was surprised to hear Tom disagree. She could not understand it. They sat down, and Tom fastened his candle to the wall in front of them with some clay. Nothing was said for some time; then Becky spoke:

"Tom, I am so hungry!"

Tom took something out of his pocket.

"Do you remember this?" said he.

Becky almost smiled.

"It's our wedding cake, Tom."

"我很高兴你睡了一觉，贝琪；现在你会觉得平静一些的，我们会找到出洞的路的。"

"我们可以试试，汤姆；我做梦梦到了那么美丽的一个国家。我想咱们是要去那儿了。"

"或许不是，或许不是。振作起来。贝琪，咱们继续试试吧。"

他们站起来，手拉手沮丧地向前走着。俩人试图估摸自己在洞里呆了多久，感觉好像都已经很多天，甚至很多个星期了。然而很明显，那不可能，因为他们的蜡还没有用完。过了很长时间——他们也弄不清有多久——汤姆说他们必须轻轻走，留心听水滴声——他们必须找到泉水。不久俩人找到了一个，汤姆建议又该休息。这会儿俩人累得都有些吃不消了。可贝琪还坚持说觉得自己还能再走一会儿。听到汤姆不同意，她很吃惊，不明白为什么。俩人坐了下来，汤姆用湿泥把蜡烛固定在了他们前面的墙上。片刻的沉默之后，贝琪张口了：

"汤姆，我特别饿！"

汤姆从口袋里取出了什么东西。

"你还记得这个吗？"他说。

贝琪都快要哭了。

"这是我们的结婚蛋糕，汤姆。"

"Yes—I wish it was as big as a barrel, for it's all we've got."

"I saved it from the picnic for us to dream on, Tom, the way grown-up people do with wedding cake— but it'll be our—"

She dropped the sentence where it was. Tom divided the cake and Becky ate with good appetite, while he ate only a little at one time. There was plenty of cold water to finish the dinner with. By and by Becky suggested that they move on again. Tom was silent a moment. Then he said:

"Becky, can you bear it if I tell you something?"

Becky's face paled, but she thought she could.

"Well, then, Becky, we must stay here, where there's water to drink. That little piece is our last candle!"

Becky burst into tears and cried. Tom did what he could to comfort her, but with little effect. At last Becky said:

"Tom!"

"Well, Becky?"

"They'll miss us and look for us!"

"Yes, they will! Certainly they will!"

"Maybe they're hunting for us now, Tom."

"Why, I think maybe they are. I hope they are."

"是的——我真希望它能跟桶一样大，因为我们只有这个东西了。"

"我是吃野餐时给咱俩留的，为的是再看到它，可以有很多的美梦，就像大人对待他们的结婚蛋糕一样——可这却成了我们的——"

她没有再说下去。汤姆把蛋糕分开成两半。贝琪胃口大开，吃得很香，而汤姆自己只吃了一点儿。水他们倒是喝了个够。过了一会儿，贝琪建议继续走下去。汤姆沉默了一会儿，说：

"贝琪，如果我告诉你一件事，你能承受得了吗？"

贝琪的脸白了，但她觉得她能承受。

"贝琪，我们必须在这儿呆着，这儿有水喝。那一小段蜡烛是我们最后一点儿了！"

贝琪的眼泪又涌了出来，她又哭了。汤姆尽量地安慰她，可没多大用处。最后贝琪说：

"汤姆！"

"嗯，贝琪。"

"他们会想我们的，会来找我们的！"

"对，他们会的！他们一定会的！"

"或许他们现在正找我们呢，汤姆！"

"嗯，我想或许是吧。我希望他们正在找我们。"

"When would they miss us, Tom?"

"When they get back to the boat, I think."

"Tom, it might be dark then—would they notice we hadn't come?"

"I don't know. But anyway, your mother would miss you as soon as they got home."

A frightened look in Becky's face brought Tom to his senses and he saw that he had made a mistake. Becky was not to have gone home that night! The children became silent and thoughtful. In a moment a new burst of sadness from Becky showed Tom that the thing in his mind had struck hers also—that only on Sunday mornirg could Mrs. Thatcher discover that Becky was not at Mrs. Harper's.

The children fastened their eyes upon their bit of candle and watched it melt slowly and pitilessly away— the horror of complete darkness controlled them!

How long afterward it was that Becky came to a slow consciousness that she was crying in Tom's arms, neither could tell. Tom said they must have been missed long ago, and no doubt the search was going on. He would shout and maybe someone would come. He tried it; but in the darkness the distant echoes sounded so horrible that he tried it no more.

The hours wasted away, and hunger came to torture

"他们什么时候会想到我们呢，汤姆？"

"等他们一回到船上。"

"汤姆，那会儿可能天都黑了——他们会注意到我们没上船吗？"

"我不知道。但不管怎样，他们一回家你妈妈会发觉的。"

贝琪的脸上露出了惊恐的表情。这使汤姆意识到他犯了一个错误。贝琪那天晚上是不回家的！两个孩子一声不吭，琢磨着。一会儿，贝琪又难过起来，这让汤姆明白他们俩正都想着同一件事——只有等到礼拜日上午，撒切尔夫人才会发现贝琪没在哈普太太家。

孩子们盯着那点儿蜡烛，看着它慢慢地无情地融化，烛光消失了——他们现在完全被黑暗的恐怖笼罩着。

谁也说不清过了多久，贝琪才慢慢意识到她正躺在汤姆的胳膊上哭呢。汤姆说村里的人们肯定很久以前就想他们了，毫无疑问正在搜寻他们。他要大声喊，或许有人听到会来的。他试了，可黑暗中远处的回音听着那么可怕，他再也不想试了。

一个小时一个小时被白白地浪费掉了，他们

the children again. A part of Tom's half of the cake was left; they divided and ate it. But they seemed hungrier than before.

By and by Tom said:

"Sh! Did you hear that?"

Both held their breath and listened. There was a sound like the faintest, far-off shout. Instantly Tom answered it, and, leading Becky by the hand, started feeling along the corridor in its direction. Presently he listened again; again the sound was heard, and obviously a little nearer.

"It's them! Said Tom. "They're coming! Come along, Becky—we're all right now!"

The joy of the children was great. Their speed was slow, however, because pitfalls were somewhat common, and had to be guarded against. They shortly came to one and had to stop. It might be three feet deep, it might be a hundred—there was no passing it, at any rate. Tom got down on his breast and reached as far down as he could. No bottom. They must stay there and wait until the searchers came. They listened; obviously the distant shouting was growing more distant; a moment or two more and they had gone completely. The heart-sinking misery of it! Tom shouted until he was hoarse; but it was of no use. He talked hopefully to Becky; but an age of

又开始为饥饿折磨着。汤姆的那半个蛋糕还剩了一块，他们分开吃了。可这使他们觉得比以前更饿了。

一会儿，汤姆说：

"嘘，你听到什么声音了吗？"

俩人都屏住呼吸听着，好像是来自远方的非常模糊的呼喊。汤姆回应了，沿着通道领着贝琪开始朝那个方向摸着走去。过了一会儿他又听了听；又听到了那声音，而且显然声音近了一点儿。

"是他们？"汤姆说，"他们来了！跟上，贝琪——我们现在没事了！"

孩子们欣喜若狂。可是他们走的速度很慢，因为这里面有很多坑，必须要小心谨慎。没一会儿他们就被前面的坑挡住了去路。这坑大约有三英尺深，或许有一百英尺——无论怎样都是过不去的。汤姆趴下身去，尽可能地向下摸，却摸不着底。他们只有在这儿呆着等寻找他们的人来。俩人仔细听着，显然远处的呼喊声越来越远了；一会儿就完全消失了。他们的心又沉了下来，陷入了悲伤之中！汤姆喊啊喊，喊得嗓子都哑了，可是没用。他充满信心地跟贝琪说话；俩人在焦

anxious waiting passed and no sounds came again.

The children felt their way back to the spring. The boring time went on; they slept again. Tom believed it must be Tuesday by this time.

Now an idea struck him. There were some side passages near at hand. It would be better to find some way than wait idly. Then they started to walk. Tom saw, not twenty yards away, a human hand holding a candle appearing from behind a rock! Tom lifted up a happy shout, and instantly that hand was followed by the body it belonged to—Injun Joe's! Tom was frightened; he could not move, he was quite satisfied the next moment to see the devil take to his heels and get himself out of sight. Tom wondered why Joe had not recognized his voice and come over and killed him for testifying in court. But the echoes must have made his voice sound different. Without doubt, that was it, he thought. Tom's fright weakened every muscle in his body. He said to himself that if he had strength enough to get back to the spring he would stay there, and nothing should tempt him to run the risk of meeting Injun Joe again. He was careful to keep from Becky what it was he had seen. He told her he had only shouted "for luck."

But hunger and misery defeated fears at last. Tom believed that it must be Wednesday or Thursday or even

急中等了很久，可再也没有什么声音了。

　　孩子们又摸着路回到了泉边。时间在百无聊赖中一点一点地过去了；他们又睡着了。汤姆估计这会儿一定是星期二了。

　　这时他又萌生了一个想法，周围会有一些小道的。与其无所事事地等待，不如去找路。接着他们就开始走了。汤姆看见不到二十码远的地方。有一只手举着一根蜡烛从大石头后面走了出来，汤姆高兴地喊了一声，很快那只手后面的身体也露了出来——是印第安人乔！汤姆感到恐惧；他一动也不能动，紧接着看到那恶魔走远了，看不见了，他非常欣慰。汤姆不明白乔为什么没有听出他的声音，过来杀掉他，以报汤姆作证之仇。一定是回声使得他的声音听起来不一样了。毫无疑问，肯定是这个原因。汤姆琢磨着。那一阵惊吓使汤姆觉得周身无力。他对自己说，如果他有足够的力气回到喷泉跟前，他就会呆在那儿，什么也别想再让他去冒险碰到印第安人乔了。他小心不让贝琪知道自己看到的一切，称他只是"碰运气"喊喊。

　　可最终饥饿与痛苦还是战胜了恐惧。汤姆想现在一定是周三周四甚至周五周六了。人们不会

Friday or Saturday, now, and that the search had been given over. He proposed to find another passage. He felt willing to risk Injun Joe and all other terrors. But Becky was so weak that she could not be aroused. She said she would wait, now, where she was, and die—it would not be long. She told Tom to go with the kite line and find the way if he chose; but she begged him to come back every little while and speak to her; and she made him promise that when the last moment came, he would stay by her and hold her hand until all was over.

Tom kissed her, with a choking feeling in his throat, and made a show of being confident of finding the searchers or an escape from the cave; then he took the kite line in his hand and went feeling down one of the passages on his hands and knees, sad with hunger and sick with signs of coming death.

Chapter 32
"Turn Out! They're Found!"

It was Tuesday evening. The village of St. Petersburg was still in sadness. The lost children had not been found. Most searchers had given up looking for children, saying that it was clear the children could never be found. Mrs. Thatcher was very ill. People said it was

再来找了。他打算自己再去找一条路，哪怕冒险遭遇到印第安人乔和所有其他恐怖的事情。可是贝琪一点劲儿都没有了，根本鼓动不起来。她说她现在就在这儿等着，然后死去——不会很久了。她告诉汤姆如果愿意的话，找路时带着风筝线；她求他每隔一会儿就能回来跟她说说话；她要他许诺当最后时刻到来时，他会呆在她身旁，握着她的手，直到一切都结束。

汤姆吻了她，嗓子有种哽咽的感觉，却信心十足地表示他会找到寻找他们的人的，或者是找到出洞的路的；之后他就手拿着风筝线，沿着一个通道爬着向前摸索，饥肠辘辘的他想到死亡即将来临，悲伤极了。

第三十二章 "出来！找到他们了！"

这会儿是星期二晚上。圣彼兹堡镇仍沉浸在一片悲痛之中。丢失的孩子还没有找到。大多数去搜寻的人们都已放弃了寻找，说很明显，孩子们永远不可能再找到了。撒切尔夫人病得很重。

heartbreaking to hear her call her child, and raise her head and listen a whole minute at a time, then lay down again with a moan. Aunt Polly had been so sad that her gray hair had grown almost white. The village went to its rest on Tuesday night, sad and hopeless.

Away in the middle of the night a wild ringing burst from the village bells, and in a moment the streets were full of excited people, who shouted, "Turn out! Turn out! They're found! They're found!" Tin pans and horns were added to the noise, the population gathered and moved toward the river, met the children coming in an open carriage.

Nobody went to bed again; it was the greatest night the little town had ever seen. During the first half hour villagers entered Judge Thatcher's house, seized the saved ones and kissed them, pressed Mrs. Thatcher's hand, tried to speak but couldn't—and drifted out raining tears all over the place.

Tom lay upon a sofa and told the story of the wonderful adventure, putting in many striking additions to make the story more absorbing; and closed with a description of how he followed two passages as far as his kite line would reach; how he followed a third to the fullest stretch of the kite line, and was about to turn back when he saw a far-off speck that looked like day-

人们说她不停地呼唤孩子，然后抬起头，听上一分钟，接着又呻吟着倒下，那样子让人看着心都碎了。波莉姨妈伤心得头发都几乎全变白了。星期二晚上，整个村子的人们怀着悲伤绝望的心情都去休息了。

半夜时分村子里的钟声疯狂地响了起来，一会儿街上就满都是激动的人们喊着："找到了！找到了！找到他们了！找到他们了！"金属锅盆和号角也加入了这喧闹之中，人们聚集起来，朝河边涌去，去接坐敞篷马车回来的孩子们。

没有人再去睡觉，这是小镇有史以来最不平凡的一夜了。半个小时内村里的人们就都来到撒切尔法官家，抓住逃生回来的孩子们，亲着他们，还紧握住撒切尔夫人的手，欲说不能——整个房间的人们都是泪如雨下。

汤姆躺在一个沙发上，向人们讲述他那精彩的冒险经历。为了使故事更具吸引力，还添加了许多有趣的细节，最后他描述了他是如何沿着两条通道走下去，一直走到风筝线够不着的地方。然后他又如何沿着第三条通道走下去，也是走到了风筝线的尽头，正准备返回时看到远处有一块亮点，好像太阳光射下的一样；他放下风筝线，

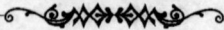

light; dropped the line and felt toward it, pushed his head and shoulders through a small hole and saw the broad Mississippi rolling by! And if it had only happened to be night he would not have seen that speck of daylight and would not have found that passage any more! He told how he went back for Becky and broke the good news and she told him not to upset her with such words, for she was tired, and knew she was going to die, and wanted to. He described how he persuaded her and how she almost died with joy when she had walked to where she actually saw the blue speck of daylight; how he pushed his way out at the hole and then helped her out; how they sat there and cried for gladness; how some men came along in a boat and Tom called them and told them their situation and their great hunger; how the men didn't believe the wild tale at first, "because," said they, "you are five miles down the river below the valley the cave is in"—then took them aboard, rowed to a house, gave them supper, made them rest till two or three hours after dark, and then brought them home.

Tom learned of Huck's sickness and went to see him on Friday, but couldn't be admitted to the bedroom; later, he was allowed, but was warned to keep silent about his adventure and introduce no exciting topic. The Widow Douglas stayed by to see that he obeyed. At

走了过去，将自己的头和肩从上方的小洞探了出去，看到了宽广的密西西比河滚滚向前流去！如果那时恰好是晚上，他就看不到那个亮点了，再也找不到那条通道了！他还讲他是如何回去找贝琪，把这好消息告诉贝琪的，而她却说不想再听那些烦心的话了，她累了，她知道自己要死了，也想死了。汤姆描述着自己怎么说服她，带她走到能看到湛蓝色光点的地方，贝琪一看高兴坏了；之后他又如何把自己和贝琪拽出那个洞的；他们是如何坐在那儿，高兴地大哭起来；然后一些人乘船过来了，汤姆呼喊他们，告诉了他们自己的遭遇，还说他们很饿；那些人刚开始压根儿不相信这离奇的故事，"因为"，他们说，"你们已经在山洞所在峡谷下游的五英里处了！"——不久他们把他俩带上船，划回家，让他们吃了晚饭，一直休息到天黑后两三个小时，然后就把他们俩带回家了。

汤姆知道哈克生病了，就在星期五去看他，可却没被允许进卧室；后来让他进来了，但警告他不许说任何关于自己的冒险经历，不要提任何让人激动的话题。道格拉斯寡妇呆在了床边，监

home Tom learned of the Cardiff Hill event; also that the "ragged man's" body had finally been found in the river near the ferry landing; he had been drowned while trying to escape, perhaps.

Two weeks after Tom's leaving from the cave, he started off to visit Huck, who had grown plenty strong enough, now, to hear exciting talk, and Tom had some that would interest him, he thought. Judge Thatcher's house was on Tom's way, and he stopped to see Becky. The judge and some friends set Tom to talking, and someone joked with him by asking if he thought he wouldn't like to go to the cave again. Tom said he thought he wouldn't mind it. The judge said:

"Well, there are others just like you, Tom. I've not the least doubt. But we have taken care of that. Nobody will get lost in that cave any more."

"Why?"

"Because I had made an iron door at the entrance two weeks ago and locked—I've got the keys."

Tom turned as white as a sheet.

"What's the matter, boy! Here, run, somebody! Fetch a glass of water!"

The water was brought and thrown into Tom's face.

"Ah, now you're all right. What was the matter with you, Tom?"

督他是否遵守警告。回到家汤姆知道了发生在卡迪夫山的事情；还了解到那个衣着破烂的人的尸体在停靠渡轮附近的河里发现了；他可能是试图逃跑时淹死了。

汤姆逃出洞有两个星期了，他又准备去看哈克。哈克此时身体恢复得已很强壮，能听激动的事了，而且觉得汤姆肯定有有趣的事告诉他。汤姆去哈克那儿路过了撒切尔法官家，他停下来去看贝琪。法官与一些朋友见到汤姆就和他聊了起来。有人开玩笑问汤姆是否还愿意去那山洞，汤姆说他再去一趟也没关系。法官说：

"毫无疑问，有你这种想法的人大有人在。可问题我们已经解决了，再没有人会在那洞里迷路了。"

"为什么？"

"因为两个星期前我就在洞口安了铁门，锁上了——我拿着钥匙呢。"

汤姆的脸像纸一样白。

"怎么啦，孩子！快，来人！拿杯水来！"

水拿来了，泼在了汤姆的脸上。

"啊，你现在好了。你怎么啦，汤姆？"

Chapter 33
The Fate of Injun Joe

Within a few minutes the news had spread, and a dozen boats of men were on their way to McDougal's Cave, and the ferryboat, well filled with passengers, soon followed. Tom Sawyer was in the boat with Judge Thatcher.

When the cave door was unlocked, a sorrowful sight presented itself in the dim twilight of the place. Injun Joe lay stretched upon the ground, dead, with his face close to the crack of the door, as if his longing eyes had been fixed, to the latest moment, upon the light and the cheer of the free world outside. Tom was touched, for he knew by his own experience how this man had suffered, but nevertheless he felt greatly relieved and safe now when a weight of dread could be removed which had been lying upon him since he lifted his voice against this de vil. Injun Joe's knife lay close by, its blade broken in two as a result of cutting the firm door open. Yet this effort was useless. Usually some bits of candle would be found in the cave, left there by tourists; but there was none now. The devil had searched them out and eaten

第三十三章　印第安人乔的可悲下场

不到几分钟，消息就传开了。十几艘船载着人们向麦克道格尔山洞驶去，渡轮也满载着人们很快地跟了去。汤姆·索耶与撒切尔法官同乘一艘船。

洞门一打开，可悲的一幕就在这昏暗的暮色中展现在人们的面前。印第安人乔平展着身子躺在那儿，死了。他的脸紧贴着门缝，那双充满渴望的眼睛一直盯着外面那明亮、快乐的自由世界，直到最后一刻。汤姆被感动了，因为他自身的经历使他很清楚这个人曾遭受了什么痛苦，然而他还是感到非常轻松，安全，自从他张口作证揭发这个恶魔以来一直压抑着的他的那种恐惧感终于消除了。印第安人乔的刀丢在了一边，为了砍开那结实的门，刀已经断成了两半。然而他的努力是徒劳的。一般情况下洞里总会有一些游客留下的小块蜡烛，可现在全没了。恶魔已经把它们全

them. He had also caught a few bats, and these, also, he had eaten, leaving only their claws. The poor unfortunate had starved to death.

Injun Joe was buried near the mouth of the cave; all people came here and admitted that they had had almost as satisfactory a time at the funeral as they could have had at the hanging.

The morning after the funeral Tom took Huck to a private place to have an important talk. They had learned each other's adventures. Tom said:

"Huck, that money wasn't ever in Number Two!"

"What!" Huck searched his comrade's face eagerly.

"Tom, have you got on the track of that money again?"

"Huck, it's in the cave!"

Huck's eyes burned.

"Say it again, Tom."

"The money's in the cave!"

"Tom, is it fun or earnest?"

"Earnest, Huck—just as earnest as ever I was in my life. Will you go there with me and help get it out?"

"I bet I will! I will if it's where we can get out and not get lost."

"Huck, we can do that without the least bit of trou-

找来，吃掉了。他还抓了几只蝙蝠吃，只剩下了爪子。这可怜不幸的家伙最终被饿死了。

印第安人乔被埋在了洞口；村里所有的人都来了，说看到他的这场葬礼有如看到他被绞死一样的心满意足。

葬礼之后的第二天早晨，汤姆把哈克带到了一个隐蔽的地方，要和他谈要紧事。他们已经知道了彼此的冒险经历。汤姆说：

"哈克，那钱不在二号地！"

"什么！"哈克急切地在他伙伴的脸上寻找答案。

"汤姆，你又找到那笔钱的线索了？"

"哈克，钱在山洞里！"

哈克的眼睛大放异彩。

"你再说一遍，汤姆。"

"钱在山洞里！"

"汤姆，你是开玩笑，还是当真？"

"当真，哈克——我这辈子什么时候骗过你？你愿意跟我去。帮我取出来吗？"

"我当然愿意！只要我们到那儿后能出来。不会迷路。"

"哈克，这可费不了吹灰之力。"

ble in the world."

"Good as wheat! What makes you think the money's—"

"Huck, you just wait till we get in there. If we don't find it I'll agree to give you my drum and everything I've got in the world. I will."

"All right. When do you say?"

"Right now, if you say it. Are you strong enough?"

"Is it far in the cave? I can't walk more than a mile, Tom—at least I don't think I could."

"It's about five miles into there the way anybody but me would go, Huck, but there's quite a short cut that anybody but me know about. Huck, I'll take you right to it in a boat."

"Let's start right off, Tom."

"All right. We want some bread and meat, and our pipes, and a little bag or two, and two or three kite strings, and some matches. I tell you, many times I wished I had some when I was there before."

A little time past noon the boys borrowed a small boat. When they were several miles below "Cave Hollow," Tom said:

"Do you see that white place where there's been a landslide? Well, that's one of my marks. We'll get ashore, now."

"太好了，你怎么想到钱是在——"

"哈克，等咱们到那儿你就明白了。如果在那儿找不到的话我可以把我的鼓和所有的东西给你。我说到做到。"

"行。你说咱们什么时候出发？"

"既然你这么问，那咱马上就走。你身体行吗？"

"那是在洞里很深的地方吗？我现在走路超过一英里就不行了，汤姆——至少我觉得我不行。"

"任何人——除了我——要是走的话，得走五英里，哈克，但有一条捷径只有我知道。我带你乘船直接去那儿。"

"咱们现在立刻出发吧，汤姆。"

"行。我们还需要带一些面包，肉，咱俩的烟斗，两个小布袋，两三根风筝线，还有一些火柴。我告诉你，我在洞里那会儿就总想着要有这些东西就好了。"

中午刚过，两个孩子就借了一艘小船。他们划到离"爱谷"还有几英里的地方时，汤姆说：

"你看到塌方的那一片有一个白色的地方吗？那就是我的一个记号。咱们现在就登岸吧。"

They landed.

"Now, Huck, where we're standing you could touch that hole I got out of with a fishing pole. See if you can find it."

Huck searched all the place about, and found nothing. Tom proudly marched into a thick clump of bushes and said:

"Here you are! Look at it, Huck; it's the most secret hole in this country. You just keep silent about it. All along I've been wanting to be a robber. We'll let Joe Harper and Ben Rogers in and set up Tom Sawyer's Gang, it sounds splendid, doesn't it, Huck?"

"Well, it just does."

By this time everything was ready and the boys entered the hole, Tom in the lead. They went their way to the farther end of the cave, then made their kite strings fast and moved on. A few steps brought them to the spring, and Tom felt a shudder all through him. He showed Huck a little part of candlewick against the wall, and described how he and Becky had watched the flame struggle and put out.

The boys began to quiet down to whispers, now, for the quietness and darkness of the place oppressed their spirits. They went on, and presently entered and followed Tom's other corridor until they reached the

俩人上岸了。

"现在，哈克，站在这儿就可以用根鱼竿捅到我从里面钻出来的洞。看看你能不能找到。"

哈克把整个地方都找了一遍，可什么也没发现。汤姆自豪地迈进一块稠密的草丛中，说：

"在这儿！看，哈克；这是咱们这一片村子最隐秘的洞了。你不要告诉别人，我一直想当的是强盗。我们让乔·哈普和本·罗杰斯也加入，成立一个汤姆·索耶帮，这主意听着挺了不起的，是吗，哈克？"

"没错。"

这时一切都准备好了，两个孩子进洞了，汤姆走在前。他们朝洞的深处走去，然后系上了风筝线，又继续前行，走了几步就到了那眼泉边。汤姆浑身打了个冷战。他给哈克看固定在墙上的那一小块蜡芯，讲他和贝琪是如何看着火焰挣扎着，然后熄灭的。

孩子们渐渐安静了下来，说话都是低声低语的。因为这儿的寂静与黑暗实在是太压抑了。他们继续朝前走着，进到了汤姆指的另一个通道，

"jumping – off place." Tom whispered:

"Now I'll show you something, Huck."

He held his candle high and said:

"Look as far around the corner as you can. Do you see that? There—on the big rock over there—drawn with candle-smoke."

"Tom, it's a cross!"

"Now where's your Number Two? 'Under the cross' hey? It's in that place that I saw Injun Joe held his candle, Huck!"

Huck stared at the mysterious sign for a while, and then said with a shaky voice:

"Tom, let's get out of here!"

"What! And leave the treasure?"

"Yes—leave it. Injun Joe's ghost is round about there, certain."

"No, it isn't, Huck, no, it isn't. It could haunt the place where he died—away out at the mouth of the cave—five miles from here."

"No, Tom, it wouldn't. It would hang around the money. I know the ways of ghosts, and so do you."

Tom began to fear that Huck was right. Worries gathered in his mind. But presently an idea occurred to him:

"Look here, Huck, what fools we're making of

一直来到了那个"断崖边"。汤姆低声说：

"现在我告诉你地方，哈克。"

他高高地举起蜡烛，说：

"使劲儿朝那个角看，看到了吗？那——在那个大岩石上——用蜡烟熏的。"

"汤姆，那是个十字架！"

"你的二号地在哪儿呀？'在十字架下'，嗯？就在那个地方我看到印第安人乔举着蜡烛，哈克！"

哈克盯了一会儿那神秘的标记，然后用颤抖的声音说：

"汤姆，咱们离开这儿吧！"

"什么？丢下宝物不要了？"

"嗯——不要了。印第安人乔的鬼魂肯定在这儿。"

"不，不会的，哈克。不，不会的。它出没在他死的地方——在那洞那边——离这儿五英里呢。"

"不，汤姆，不会的。它肯定守着这笔钱的，我了解鬼，你也一样。"

汤姆开始担心哈克说的没错。他心里充满了担忧。可这时一个念头闪过他的脑子。

"看这儿，哈克，我们真是自个儿吓自个儿！

ourselves! Injun Joe's ghost isn't going to come around where there's a cross!"

The point was well taken. It had its effect.

"Tom, I didn't think of that. But that's so. It's luck for us, that cross is. I think we'll climb down there and have a hunt for that box."

Tom went first. Huck followed. Four passages opened out of the small cave which the great rock stood in. The boys examined three of them with no result. They found a small recess in the one nearest the base of the rock, with a blanket spread down in it; also an old suspender, some bacon rind, and the well-gnawed bones of two or three fowls. But there was no money box.

"He said under the cross. Well, this comes nearest to being under the cross. It can't be under the rock itself, because that sets firm on the ground."

They searched everywhere once more, and then sat down discouraged. Huck could suggest nothing. By and by Tom said:

"Look here, Huck, there are footprints and some candle grease on the clay about one side of this rock, but not on the other sides. Now, what's that for? I bet you the money is under the rock. I'm going to dig in the clay."

"That isn't a bad idea, Tom!" said Huck with ex-

印第安人乔的鬼魂不可能在这有十字架的地方！"

这么一说特管用。哈克也赞成。

"汤姆，我没想到那点，可确实是这样。十字架给咱带来了好运。咱们爬下去找那盒子吧。"

汤姆先行，哈克跟着。那个大石头所在的小洞里一共延伸出来四条路。孩子们查看了三条，都没发现什么。他们在离石头底基最近的那条通道看到了一个很小的凹室，里面地上铺了个毛毯；还有一个旧背带，一些烤肉皮，啃得干干净净的两三只鸟骨头，可是没有钱盒。

"他说在十字架下，这是十字架下最近的地方，石头这么结实地立在地上，不可能在它底下。"

他们又把周围搜寻一遍之后，垂头丧气地坐下了。哈克这会儿没什么主意。过了一段时间，汤姆说：

"看这儿，哈克。石头这边的湿土上有脚印和蜡泪，可那边没有。这是什么意思？我打赌钱就在石头底下，我要挖这儿的土了。"

"这主意不错，汤姆！"哈克激动地说。

citement.

Tom brought out his knife at once, and he had not dug four inches before he struck wood.

"Hey, Huck! —do you hear that?"

Huck began to dig and scratch now. Some boards were soon uncovered and removed. They had shown a natural opening which led under the rock. Tom got into this and held his candle as far under the rock as he could, but said he could not see to the end of it. He intended to go farther and look. He bent down and passed under; the narrow way went down gradually. He followed its winding way, first to the right, then to the left, Huck at his heels. Tom turned a short turning, by and by, and shouted:

"My goodness, Huck, look here!"

It was the treasure box, sure enough, occupying a secret little cave, along with an empty powder keg, a couple of guns in leather cases, two or three pairs of shoes, a leather belt, and some other rubbish wet by the water-drip.

"Got it at last!" said Huck, putting his hands among the coins. "My, but we're rich, Tom!"

"Huck, I always thought we'd get it. It's just too good to believe, but we have got it, sure! Say—let's not fool around here. Let's get it. Let me see if I can

汤姆立刻取出了他的刀子，还没挖四英尺就碰到了木头。

"嘿，哈克！——你听到了吧？"

哈克立即开始连挖带抓了。很快看到了一些木板，挪走了。木板底下是天然形成的通口。汤姆进去了，把蜡烛尽可能地朝前举着，可却说还是看不到头。他想要再向前走一走，看一看。他弯腰过去了；窄窄的通道弯弯曲曲地向前延伸着。他先向右拐，然后再向左拐，哈克在后面跟着。前面出现了一个拐弯处，汤姆转了过去，一会儿就喊了起来：

"我的天，哈克，在这儿呢！"

就是那个宝盒，没错。放在一个隐秘的小洞里，旁边是一个空火药桶，两三把带皮套的枪，两三双鞋，一条皮带，还有一些其他乱七八糟的东西，被水浸湿了。

"终于找到了！"哈克说着，把手塞进了一堆钱币中，"天哪，我们有钱了，汤姆！"

"哈克，我总想我们会得到的，这简直好得让我无法相信，可咱们还是弄到手了，没错！嘿——咱们别在这儿浪费时间了，拿上走吧。让我

lift the box."

It weighed about fifty pounds. Tom could lift it, but very hard.

"I thought so," he said, "I think I was right to think of fetching the little bags along with us."

The money was soon in the bags and the boys took it up to the cross rock.

"Now let's fetch the guns and things," said Huck.

"No, Huck—leave them there. They're just the tricks to have when we go robbing. We'll keep them there all the time, and we'll hold our party there, too. It's quite a secret place for holding parties of ours."

"What party?"

"I don't know. But robbers always have parties, and of course we've got to have them, too. Come along, Huck; we've been in here a long time. It's getting late, I think. I'm hungry, too. We'll eat and smoke when we get to the boat."

They presently appeared into the clump of bushes, looked carefully out, found the coast clear, and were soon lunching and smoking in the boat. Then they landed shortly after dark.

"Now, Huck," said Tom, "we'll hide the money in the loft of the widow's woodshed, and I'll come up in the morning and we'll count it and divide, and then

看看我是不是抬得动这个盒子。"

盒子大约有五十磅重。汤姆能抬得起来，可很吃力。

"我来前就想到了，"他说，"所以拿来了个小布袋子，看来想得没错。"

钱很快就装到袋子里了，孩子们把它带上了画有十字架的岩石旁。

"咱们再去把枪和其他东西拿上来吧。"哈克建议道。

"不，哈克——把那些东西留这儿吧。这样等我们当强盗时好有把戏玩。我们把这些东西一直放在这儿，然后到这儿来举行聚会。这地方可够隐秘的了。"

"什么聚会？"

"我也说不清。但是强盗总是有聚会的，当然我们也要有的。跟上，哈克，咱们在这儿已经呆了很长时间。我想天都晚了，而且我也饿了。咱们上船吧，在船上吃点儿什么，再抽点儿烟。"

不一会儿他们就出现在了一堆堆的树丛里，小心地向四周望着，看到河岸上没什么人，很快就登上了船吃着，抽着。天黑不久他们就到岸了。

"现在，哈克。"汤姆说，"咱们把钱藏在寡妇家木材屋的阁楼里吧。等我早晨过来，咱们把钱

we'll hunt up a place out in the woods for it where it will be safe. Just you lay quiet here and watch the treasure till I run and steal Benny Taylor's little wagon; I won't be gone a minute."

He disappeared, and presently returned with the wagon, put the two small bags into it, threw some old rags on top of them, and started off. When the boys reached the Welshman's house, they stopped to rest. Just as they were about to move on, the Welshman stepped out and said:

"Hell, who's that?"

"Huck and Tom Sawyer."

"Good! Come along with me, boys; you are keeping everybody waiting. Here—hurry up—I'll pull the wagon for you. Why, it's not as light as it might be. Got bricks in it? —or old metal?"

"Old metal." said Tom.

"I judged so; the boys in this town will take more trouble and time finding old iron and sell only six bits. If they do the regular work, they can make twice the money. But that's human nature—hurry along, hurry along!"

The boys wanted to know what the hurry was about.

"Never mind; you'll see when we get to the Widow Douglas's."

一数，就分了。然后再在林子里找个地方藏起来，那儿挺安全的。现在你就静静地躺在这儿，看着钱，我跑去把本尼·泰勒的小货车偷来，用不了一分钟。"

汤姆走了，一会儿就推着货车回来了，两人把两个小袋子放进去，上面盖了一些破布，就出发了。孩子们走到威尔士曼家时停了下来歇口气。就在准备上路时，威尔士曼走了出来，说：

"喂，谁？"

"哈克和汤姆·索耶。"

"好啊！跟我来，孩子们；大家都在等你们。这儿，快点儿——我给你推车，哇，这车可不轻呀。上面装的砖——还是废铜烂铁？"

"废铜烂铁。"汤姆说。

"我估摸也是；咱们镇上的孩子们都爱找点儿废铜烂铁，卖上七八毛钱，也不愿干点儿省事、省时的正经事，而且赚的钱能多一倍。人啊！"

孩子们想知道让他们快点干什么事。

"你别管，等到了道格拉斯寡妇家你就知道了。"

Huck said with some fear—for he was long used to being falsely scolded:

"Mr. Jones, we haven't been doing anything."

The Welshman laughed.

"Well, I don't know, Huck, my boy. I don't know about that. Aren't you and the widow good friends?"

"Yes. Well, she has been good friend to me, anyway."

"All right, then. What do you want to be afraid for?"

This question was not entirely answered in Huck's slow mind before he found himself pushed, along with Tom, into Mrs. Douglas's drawing room. Mr. Jones left the wagon near the door and followed.

The place was grandly lighted, and everybody that was of any influence in the village was there. The Thatchers were there, the Harpers, the Rogerses, Aunt Polly, Sid, Mary, the minister, the editor, and a great many more, and all dressed in their best. The widow received the boys as heartily as anyone could well receive two such looking beings. They were covered with clay and candle grease. Aunt Polly felt ashamed and her face turned red. She frowned and shook her head at Tom. Nobody suffered half as much as the two boys did, how-

哈克有些害怕，因为他老是无缘无故受到责骂，只听他说道：

　　"琼斯先生，我们什么事也没做呀。"

　　威尔士曼笑了。

　　"嗯，我不知道，哈克，我的孩子，我不清楚。你和寡妇不是好朋友吗？"

　　"是，不管怎样，她对我很友好。"

　　"那就行了。你怕什么？"

　　哈克的脑子转得很慢，还没等他想清这个问题时，就发现自己已和汤姆一起被推进了道格拉斯夫人家的客厅。琼斯先生把货车停在了门口，也跟了进来。

　　屋子里灯火辉煌，镇上凡是有头有脸的人都在那儿。撒切尔一家在那儿，还有哈普一家，罗杰斯一家，波莉姨妈，赛德，玛丽，牧师，编辑，还有许多其他人，都穿着他们最好的衣服。面对浑身是泥巴和蜡油的两个孩子，道格拉斯寡妇对他们的欢迎已经相当热情了。波莉姨妈感到不好意思，脸都红了。她皱了皱眉，对汤姆摇了摇头。可这儿谁再难受，都不及两个孩子的一半。这时，

ever. The widow said:

"Come with me, boys."

She took them to a bedchamber and said:

"Now wash and dress yourselves. Here are two new suits of clothes—shirts, socks, everything complete. They're Huck's—no, no thanks, Huck—Mr. Jones bought one and I the other. But they'll fit both of you. Get into them. We'll wait—come down when you are tidy enough."

Chapter 34 Floods of Gold

Huck said: "Tom, we can escape here, if we can find a rope. The window isn't high from the ground."

"What do you want to escape for?"

"Well, I'm not used to that kind of crowd. I can't stand it. I'm not going down there, Tom."

"Oh, it isn't anything. I don't mind it a bit. I'll take care of you."

Sid appeared.

"Tom," said he, "auntie has been waiting for you all the afternoon. Mary got your Sunday clothes ready, and everybody has been worrying about you. Say— aren't these candle grease and clay on your clothes?"

"Now, Mr. Sid, you just mind your own business.

寡妇说：

"跟我来，孩子们。"

她把他们带到了一个卧室，说：

"现在把你们自己洗干净，换上干净衣服。这儿有两套新衣裳——衬衣，袜子，全套的。这些是哈克的——不，不用谢，哈克——琼斯先生买了一套，我买了一套。这两身你们俩人穿都合适，穿上吧。我们等你——整齐了就下来。"

第三十四章　一大堆金币

哈克说："汤姆，我们如果找到绳子的话，可以从这儿逃走，窗户离地面不高。"

"你为什么要逃走呢？"

"嗯，我不习惯那么多的人，受不了，我不准备下去，汤姆。"

"噢，不要紧。我一点儿也不在乎。我会照顾你的。"

赛德来了。

"汤姆，"他说，"姨妈整个下午都在等你，玛丽把你的礼拜服都准备好了。这儿所有的人都在为你们担心。说说——你们衣服上的不是蜡烛油和泥巴吗？"

"赛德先生，管好你自己的事儿就行了。这个

What's this party about, anyway?"

"It's one of the widow's parties that she's always having. This time it's for the Welshman and his sons, who helped her the other night. And say—I can tell you something, if you want to know."

"Well, what?"

"Why, old Mr. Jones is going to try to say something to the people here tonight, but I overheard him tell auntie today about it, as a secret, but I think it's not much of a secret now. Everybody knows—the widow, too, for all she tries to show she doesn't. Mr. Jones was certain Huck should be here—couldn't tell his secret without Huck, you know!"

"Secret about what, Sid?"

"About Huck tracking the robbers to the widow's. I think Mr. Jones was going to surprise the others with his secret, but I bet you it will not."

Sid laughed in a very satisfied way.

"Sid, was it you that told?"

"Oh, never mind who it was. Somebody told— that's enough."

"Sid, there's only one person in this town mean enough to do that, and that's you. If you had been in Huck's place you'd have escaped down the hill and never told anybody about the robbers. You can't do any

聚会是干什么的?"

"是寡妇经常举办的那一种。这次是为威尔士曼和他儿子们举办的。他们那天晚上救了他。如果你们想知道,我还可以再告诉你们点儿别的事。"

"什么事?"

"老琼斯先生今晚还打算向来这儿的人们说点儿事。他今天中午悄悄地告诉姨妈了,被我偷听到了,现在我想这已不再是什么秘密了。所有的人都知道——寡妇也知道,她只是使劲儿表现出自己不知道的样子。琼斯先生确信哈克会来这儿的——因为没有哈克他无法把他的秘密告诉大家!"

"关于什么的秘密,赛德?"

"关于哈克如何跟踪强盗到寡妇家的。琼斯先生还想大家听了他的秘密后会大吃一惊。可我打赌肯定不可能了。"

赛德非常得意地笑着。

"赛德,是你告的密吗?"

"噢,别管是谁。有人说了——这就足够。"

"赛德,这个镇上只有一个人卑鄙得足以干出这种事,那就是你。如果你当时处在哈克那样的情况,你准会一溜烟地逃到山下,谁也不告诉的。

but mean things, and you can't bear to see anybody praised for doing good ones." Tom hit Sid's ears and helped him to the door with several kicks. "Now go and tell auntie if you dare—and tomorrow you'll catch it!"

Some minutes later the widow's guests were at the supper table, and a dozen children were at little side tables in the same room, after the fashion of that country and that time. At the proper time Mr. Jones made his little speech, in which he thanked the widow for the honor she was doing himself and his sons, but said that there was another person who should be thanked. That's Huck who helped quite much in the adventure.

Huck was praised and thanked so much that he almost forgot the nearly intolerable discomfort of his new clothes in the entirely miserable discom fort of being set up as a target for everybody's gaze and praise.

The widow said she meant to give Huck a home under her roof and have him educated; and that when she had enough money she would help him do business, not quite large at first. Tom's chance came. He said:

"Huck doesn't need it. Huck's rich."

People controlled them not to laugh over this plea sant joke for being polite. But the silence was a little awkward. Tom broke it:

"Huck's got money. Maybe you don't believe it,

你除了卑鄙的事情再干不出什么了。你无法忍受看到别人因为做好事而受到表扬。"汤姆打了赛德一耳光,又几脚把他踢了出去,"如果你有胆现在就告诉姨妈去——明天你就有好果子吃了。"

几分钟之后寡妇请来的客人都坐在了饭桌旁,而十几个孩子则按照当时那片村子的习俗,坐在了同一间屋子放在一边的小桌子上。琼斯先生找了个恰当的时候发表了他那简短的讲话。感谢寡妇款待他和他的儿子们,并说其实还有一个人需要感谢,那就是哈克,他在那次冒险经历中帮了大忙。

哈克得到了如此多的感谢与表扬。众目睽睽之下的他觉得特别不自在,都几乎忘却了新衣服的别扭。

寡妇说她打算让哈克住在这里,把这儿当成家,还让他受教育;等她有足够的钱了,她会帮他做生意,从小本买卖开始。汤姆的机会来了,他说:

"哈克不需要,哈克有钱。"

听了这个有趣的玩笑话,人们出于礼貌都忍住没笑。可是那种沉寂有点儿让人尴尬。汤姆打破沉寂说:

"哈克有钱了。或许你不相信,可他现在有很

but he's got lots of it. Oh, you needn't smile—I think I can show you. You just wait a minute."

Tom ran out of doors. The people looked at each other with a puzzled interest—and at Huck, who was tongue-tied.

Tom entered, struggling with the weight of his bags. Tom poured yellow coins upon the table and said:

"There—what did I tell you? Half of it's Huck's and half of it's mine!"

The scene took the breath away from people. All gazed, nobody spoke for a moment. Then all called for an explanation. Tom told the long tale. There was hardly an interruption from anyone to break the charm of its flow.

The money was counted. The sum amounted to a little over twelve thousand dollars. It was more than anyone present had ever seen at one time before, though several persons were there whose properties were larger than that.

Chapter 35
Respectable Huck Joins the Gang

The readers may rest satisfied that how Tom and Huck's good luck had excited the poor little village of

多钱。噢，你们别笑——我想我可以给你们看看。你们等一分钟。"

汤姆跑出了门。人们饶有兴趣地互相看着，脸上露出惊愕——还看着哈克，此时他正张口结舌，说不出话来。

汤姆进来了，那两个包很重，压得他走起路很费劲儿。汤姆把黄灿灿的金币倒在了桌子上，说：

"看这儿——我说什么来着？这一半是哈克的，一半是我的！"

看到这么多的钱，人们不禁惊呆了。所有的人都盯着那笔钱，一时没人说话。随后大家纷纷让汤姆作以解释。汤姆滔滔不绝地讲了很长时间，故事太吸引人了，几乎没有任何人打断它。

钱数了，一共是一万两千多美元。尽管在场的几个人的家产的总和要比这多，可谁也没有见过这么多钱。

第三十五章　体面的哈克加入强盗帮

读者现在可以休息了，可以高兴地看到汤姆和哈克的好运是如何令圣彼兹堡这个贫穷的小

St. Petersburg. So large a sum, all in actual cash, seemed almost unbelievable. Every "haunted" house in St. Petersburg and the neighboring villages was examined carefully, and its foundations dug up and searched completely for hidden treasure—and not by boys, but men. Wherever Tom and Huck appeared they were flattered, admired, stared at. The boys were not able to remember that their words had been important before; but now their sayings were treasured and repeated; everything they did seemed somehow to be regarded as remarkable; they had clearly lost the power of doing and saying commonplace things; moreover, their past history was collected and discovered to be obviously creative. The village paper published stories of the boys.

Judge Thatcher had a great opinion of Tom. He said that no commonplace boy would ever have got his daughter out of cave. When Becky told her father secretly how Tom had taken her beating at school, the judge was moved, saying Tom was a great noble boy. Becky thought her father had never looked so tall and so superb as when he said that. She went straight off and told Tom about it.

Judge Thatcher hoped to see Tom a great lawyer or a great soldier someday. He said he meant to help Tom to be admitted to the National Military Academy and af-

村子为之一振的。那么大的一笔钱，全部都是实实在在的金币，简直难以令人置信。为了寻宝，圣彼兹堡以及附近村庄的每一间"鬼"屋都被仔仔细细地检查了一遍，地基挖开了，角角落落地都找了——做这事的不是孩子，而是大人。无论汤姆和哈克在哪儿，都受到人们的奉承、羡慕与注视，两人根本不记得他们以前说过的话受到过什么重视，可现在他们的话被奉为至宝，到处引用；他们做过的每一件事似乎都被认为是非凡的；显然，他们已经没能力说常人的话，做普通的事了。而且，人们把两个孩子过去的经历收集起来，发现很明显地表现出他们不寻常的创造性。乡村报纸还刊登了孩子们的许多故事。

撒切尔法官也很看重汤姆。他说一般的孩子是绝对不可能把他女儿带出洞的。当贝琪偷偷地告诉她爸爸汤姆是如何在学校代她受过，挨老师打时，法官感动了，称汤姆是个了不起的孩子。贝琪觉得她爸爸说这话时比以往什么时候都高大非凡。她直接跑去告诉了汤姆。

撒切尔法官希望看到汤姆有一天能成为一个了不起的律师或伟大的军官。他说他打算帮助汤姆去国家军事学院学习,然后再去全国最好的律

terward trained in the best law school in the country, in order that he might be ready for either job or both.

Huck Finn's wealth and the fact that he was now under the Widow Douglas's protection introduced him into society—no, pulled him into it, and his sufferings were almost more than he could bear. The Widow's servants kept him clean and neat, combed and brushed, and they bedded him nightly in so clean a bed that had not one little spot to be his friend. He had to eat with knife and fork; he had to use napkin, cup, and plate; he had to learn his book, he had to go to church; he had to talk so properly that speech became boring in his month; wherever he turned, he was controlled by rules of civilization.

He bravely bore his miseries three weeks, and then one day turned up missing. For forty-eight hours the widow hunted for him everywhere in great distress. The public were deeply concerned; they searched high and low, they looked in the river for his body. Early the third morning Tom Sawyer wisely went looking among some old empty hogsheads down behind the slaughter-house, and in one of them he found Huck. Huck had slept there; he had just breakfasted upon some stolen food, and was lying off, now, in comfort, with his pipe. He was dirty, untidy, uncombed, and covered by the

师学校接受培训，准备将来做一名律师或军官或两者兼备。

哈克贝历·芬恩有钱了，而且他现在是在道格拉斯寡妇的保护下，这两方面将他引入了上流社会——更合适的说法是把他推进了上流社会。他觉得这样很遭罪，几乎都受不了了。寡妇的仆人们总是把他搞得干干净净，整整齐齐，帮他梳头，让他刷牙，而且他们晚上给他铺的床干净得连个小污点都不留下给他做伴。吃饭时他不得不用刀啊，叉啊，还得用纸巾，茶杯，盘子；他不得不读书，不得不去教堂；说话时不得不得体，搞得他觉得张口说话真没劲；无论他做什么，都被限制在文明人的条条框框之中。

他勇敢地忍受了三个星期这种痛苦的生活，然后有一天就不见了。寡妇非常难过地到处找他，找了整整四十八个小时。人们都非常关切这件事。他们爬高下低地找他，还到河里看有没有他的尸体。第三天早晨汤姆·索耶又作出了一个聪明之举。他来到屠宰场后面的一堆破旧的空啤酒桶那儿，在其中的一个桶里见到了哈克。哈克晚上就在那儿睡觉，此时刚把偷来的东西当做早饭吃了，正舒服地躺在那儿抽着烟，打着瞌睡呢。他浑身又脏又乱，头发没梳，身上盖着破布片子。汤姆

old ruin of rags. Tom woke him up, told him the trouble he had been causing, and urged him to go home. Huck's face lost its peace and took a sad cast. He said:

"Don't talk about it, Tom. I've tried it, and it doesn't work, Tom. It isn't for me; I'm not used to it. The widow's good to me, and friendly; but I can't stand their ways. She makes me get up just at the same time every morning; she makes me wash, they comb me; she won't let me sleep in the woodshed; I have to wear their clothes that just make me unable to breathe, Tom; they're so nice that I can't sit down, nor lay down, nor roll around anywhere; I have to go to church—I hate the sermons! I can't catch a fly there, I can't chaw. I have to wear shoes all Sunday. The widow eats by a bell; she goes to bed by a bell; she gets up by a bell—everything's so regular that a body can't bear it."

"Well, everybody does that way, Huck."

"Tom, I'm not everybody, and I can't stand it. It's so bad to be tied up so. And food comes too easy. I have to ask to go fishing, and I have to ask to go swimming. Well, I have to talk so nice, but it isn't comfortable. The widow doesn't let me smoke; she doesn't let me yell, she doesn't let me gape, nor stretch, nor scratch, before folks. And, she prays all the time! I

把他叫醒了。告诉他惹了什么麻烦，敦促他赶快回家。哈克一听脸上立刻显出一副不安难过的样子。他说：

"别提这事了，汤姆，我已经努力了，可不行。汤姆，这样的生活不属于我；我不习惯。寡妇对我很好，很友善，可我受不了他们的生活方式。她让我每天早晨同一时间起床；她让我洗脸，她们给我梳头；她不让我睡在柴火房；我得穿他们让我穿的衣服，那些衣服简直让人喘不上气。汤姆，那些衣服太好了，我穿着那样的衣服不能坐，不能躺，不能到处打滚；我还得去教堂——我讨厌布道！我不能在那儿抓苍蝇玩，我不能——整个礼拜天我都得穿着鞋。寡妇是铃响吃饭，铃响睡觉，铃响起床——她生活太有规律了，让人受不了。"

"每个人都是这样的，哈克。"

"汤姆，我不是每个人，我受不了。受到如此约束，太糟糕了，而且吃的来得太容易了。另外，我得请求他们允许我去钓鱼，我得请求他们允许我去游泳。嗯，我说话还得有分寸，有礼貌。寡妇不让我抽烟，不允许我喊叫。她还不让我在人前傻看别人，不许我伸懒腰，不许我浑身乱抓乱挠，还有，她整天都在祷告！我真没见过这样的

never see such a woman! And besides, that school's going to open and I'd have to go to it—well, I can't stand it. Tom, I wouldn't ever get into all this trouble if it hadn't been for that money; now you just take my share of it along with you, and give me a ten-cent sometimes— not many times, because I don't feel happy for a thing that comes too easily—and you go and beg off for me with the widow."

"Oh, Huck, you know I can't do that. It isn't fair; and besides, if you'll try this thing just a while longer you'll come to like it."

"Like it! No, Tom, I like the woods, and the river, and hogsheads, and I'll stick to them, too. Blame it all! Just as we had got guns, and a cave, and been prepared to be a robber, this foolish thing came up and ruined it all!"

Tom saw his chance:

"Look here, Huck, being rich isn't going to keep one back from turning robber."

"Are you earnest, Tom?"

"Yes. But, Huck, we can't let you into the gang if you aren't respectable, you know."

Huck's joy was cooled.

"Can't let me in, Tom? Didn't you let me go for a pirate?"

女人！而且，学校马上就要开学了，我又得去上学——我受不了。汤姆，如果不是因为那笔钱我就不会搅到这团麻烦里；你现在就把我那份钱拿走，有时给我个十美分，但别经常给，因为我觉得凡事来得太容易了就没劲——你现在就替我去向寡妇求情，让我离开她吧。"

"噢，哈克，你知道我是不会这么做的，这不公平；而且，你再努力多适应一段时间，你就会喜欢的。"

"喜欢！不，汤姆，我喜欢树林、河流、大啤酒桶，我永远都离不开它们——咱们刚刚有枪，有山洞，准备好了当强盗，出了这么件蠢事，把一切全毁了！"

汤姆看到他的机会来了。

"看，哈克，有钱并不是说就当不了强盗。"

"你说的是真的，汤姆？"

"对。可，哈克，如果你不体面一些的话，我们是不会让你加入我们这一帮的。"

满怀喜悦的哈克被浇了一头冷水。

"不让我加入，汤姆？你不是还让我当海盗了吗？"

"Yes, but that's different. A robber is nobler than what a pirate is—as a general thing. In most countries they're quite high up in the nobility—dukes and such."

"Now, Tom, haven't you always been friendly to me? You wouldn't shut me out, would you, Tom? You wouldn't do that, now, would you, Tom?"

"Huck, I wouldn't want to, and I don't want to— but what would people say? Why, they'd say, 'Mph! Tom Sawyer's Gang! Pretty low characters in it!' They'd mean you, Huck. You wouldn't like that, and I wouldn't."

Huck was silent for some time, engaged in a mental struggle. Finally he said:

"Well, I'll go back to the widow for a month and deal with it and see if I can come to stand it, if you'll let me belong to the gang, Tom."

"All right, Huck, it's great! We'll let the boys together and have the initiation tonight, maybe."

"Have the what?"

"Have the initiation."

"What's that?"

"It's to swear to stand by one another, and never tell the gang's secrets, even if you're cut into pieces, and kill anybody and all his family that hurts one of the gang."

"是,可那不一样。强盗要比海盗高贵——一般来说,大多数的国家的强盗在上流社会中地位相当高——公爵什么的。"

"汤姆,你不是对我一直挺够哥儿们的? 你不会把我排挤出你们这圈子吧,汤姆? 你不会吧,汤姆?"

"哈克,我不愿意那么做,我也不想那么做——可人们会怎么说? 他们会说,'哼,汤姆·索耶那一帮! 都是些什么乌合之众!'他们指的是你,哈克,你不喜欢这样吧,我是不喜欢。"

哈克沉默了一会儿,思想斗争着,最后他说:

"嗯,如果你让我加入你们,汤姆,我会回到寡妇家再适应一个月,看看我是不是受得了。"

"行,哈克。太好了! 或许我们今晚就叫上那帮小子,举行个入帮仪式。"

"举行什么?"

"入帮仪式。"

"什么意思?"

"就是发誓即便被割成片儿,我们也要相互支持,永不泄密,如果有人伤害了我们当中的任何人,那个人以及他的全家就要被杀掉。"

"That's a great fun, Tom, I tell you."

"Well, I bet it is. And all that swearing's got to be done at midnight, in the most lonely, horrible place you can find—a haunted house is the best, but they're all ruined now."

"Well, midnight's good, anyway, Tom."

"Yes, so it is. And you've got to swear on a coffin, and sign it with blood."

"Now, that's something great! Why, it's a million times better than pirating. I'll stick to the widow till I rot, Tom; and if I get to be a great robber, and everybody is talking about it, I think she'll be proud since she helped me to be like that."

Conclusion

That's the end of the story. Since it is a history of a boy, it must stop here; the story could not go much further without becoming the history of a man. When one writes a novel about grown people, he knows exactly where to stop—that is, with a marriage; but when he writes of young boys and girls, he must stop where he best can.

Most of the characters that perform in this book still live, and are successful and happy. Some day it may

"太好玩了，汤姆，我跟你说。"

"这肯定有意思。发誓是要在半夜进行的，地点是能找到的最偏僻、最恐怖的地方。可这些地方现在全毁了。"

"嗯，不管什么地方，半夜就行了，汤姆。"

"行，就这样。你得站在一个棺材上发誓，用血写上你的名字。"

"真棒！这可比当海盗强一百万倍，我要一直呆在寡妇身边，直到我烂掉。汤姆，如果我成为一个了不起的强盗，如众人所说的那样，我想她一定会很自豪的。因为是她帮的我。"

结　尾

故事写到这儿就结束了。因为这一本书写的是一个男孩子的故事，到这儿就必须搁笔了；再写下去，就成了一个男人的故事。写关于成人的小说时，你非常清楚在哪儿结束——那就是写到结婚为止。可写男孩子、女孩子的故事时，必须在恰到好处时收尾。

这本书里的大多数人物都还活着，而且过着成功、幸福的生活，或许有一天我们值得将这些

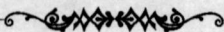

seem worth while to take up the story of the younger ones again and see what sort of men and women they turned out to be; therefore it will be wisest not to show any of that part of their lives at present.

年轻人的故事再写下去，看看那些人都长成了什么样的人。因而现在明智的做法就是不要透露他们生活的任何点点滴滴。